ACKNOWLEDGE

My sincere thanks to all those who contribut[ed] this book, in particular the many people wh[o] and comment on the draft versions, including Hampshire, Karen Verheul (proof-reader), Dave Walkiden and everyone ~~contributed in any way and who I have omitted to mention. Also a special thank you to Jim Watson for the superb cover, illustrations, cartoons and maps.

By the same publisher:

Buying a Home Abroad
Buying a Home in Florida
Buying a Home in France
Buying a Home in Italy
Buying a Home in Portugal
Buying a Home in Spain
Living and Working in America
Living and Working in Australia
Living and Working in Britain
Living and Working in France
Living and Working in New Zealand
Living and Working in Spain
Living and Working in Switzerland

What Readers and Reviewers Have Said About Survival Books

When you buy a model plane for your child, a video recorder, or some new computer gizmo, you get with it a leaflet or booklet pleading 'Read Me First', or bearing large friendly letters or bold type saying 'IMPORTANT – follow the instructions carefully'. This book should be similarly supplied to all those entering France with anything more durable than a 5-day return ticket. It is worth reading even if you are just visiting briefly, or if you have lived here for years and feel totally knowledgeable and secure. But if you need to find out how France works then it is indispensable. Native French people probably have a less thorough understanding of how their country functions. – Where it is most essential, the book is most up to the minute.

Living France

We would like to congratulate you on this work: it is really super! We hand it out to our expatriates and they read it with great interest and pleasure.

ICI (Switzerland) AG

Rarely has a 'survival guide' contained such useful advice This book dispels doubts for first-time travellers, yet is also useful for seasoned globetrotters – In a word, if you're planning to move to the USA or go there for a long-term stay, then buy this book both for general reading and as a ready-reference.

American Citizens Abroad

It is everything you always wanted to ask but didn't for fear of the contemptuous put down – The best English-language guide – Its pages are stuffed with practical information on everyday subjects and are designed to complement the traditional guidebook.

Swiss News

A complete revelation to me – I found it both enlightening and interesting, not to mention amusing.

Carole Clark

Let's say it at once. David Hampshire's *Living and Working in France* is the best handbook ever produced for visitors and foreign residents in this country; indeed, my discussion with locals showed that it has much to teach even those born and bred in *l'Hexagone*. – It is Hampshire's meticulous detail which lifts his work way beyond the range of other books with similar titles. Often you think of a supplementary question and search for the answer in vain. With Hampshire this is rarely the case. – He writes with great clarity (and gives French equivalents of all key terms), a touch of humour and a ready eye for the odd (and often illuminating) fact. – This book is absolutely indispensable.

The Riviera Reporter

The ultimate reference book – Every conceivable subject imaginable is exhaustively explained in simple terms – An excellent introduction to fully enjoy all that this fine country has to offer and save time and money in the process.

American Club of Zurich

BUYING A HOME IN IRELAND

by

Joe Laredo

SURVIVAL BOOKS • LONDON • ENGLAND

First published 1999

Survival Books Limited, Suite C, Third Floor
Standbrook House, 2-5 Old Bond Street
London W1X 3TB, United Kingdom
☎ (44) 171-493 4244, Fax (44) 171-491 0605
E-mail: survivalbooks@computronx.com
Internet: www.computronx.com/survivalbooks

British Library Cataloguing in Publication Data.
A CIP record for this book is available from the British Library.
ISBN 1 901130 10 X

Printed and bound in Great Britain by Page Bros. (Norwich) Ltd., Mile Cross Lane, Norwich, Norfolk NR6 6SA, UK.

What Readers and Reviewers Have Said About Survival Books

What a great work, wealth of useful information, well-balanced wording and accuracy in details. My compliments!

Thomas Müller

This handbook has all the practical information one needs to set up home in the UK – The sheer volume of information is almost daunting – Highly recommended for anyone moving to the UK.

American Citizens Abroad

A very good book which has answered so many questions and even some I hadn't thought of – I would certainly recommend it.

Brian Fairman

A mine of information – I may have avoided some embarrassments and frights if I had read it prior to my first Swiss encounters – Deserves an honoured place on any newcomer's bookshelf.

English Teachers Association, Switzerland

Covers just about all the things you want to know on the subject – In answer to the desert island question about *the one* how-to book on France, this book would be it – Almost 500 pages of solid accurate reading – This book is about enjoyment as much as survival.

The Recorder

It's so funny – I love it and definitely need a copy of my own – Thanks very much for having written such a humorous and helpful book.

Heidi Guiliani

A must for all foreigners coming to Switzerland.

Antoinette O'Donoghue

A comprehensive guide to all things French, written in a highly readable and amusing style, for anyone planning to live, work or retire in France.

The Times

A concise, thorough account of the DO's and DON'Ts for a foreigner in Switzerland – Crammed with useful information and lightened with humorous quips which make the facts more readable.

American Citizens Abroad

Covers every conceivable question that may be asked concerning everyday life – I know of no other book that could take the place of this one.

France in Print

Hats off to Living and Working in Switzerland!

Ronnie Almeida

CONTENTS

4. FINDING YOUR DREAM HOME 131

5. ARRIVAL & SETTLING IN 207

6. APPENDICES 219

INDEX 235

ORDER FORM 240

IMPORTANT NOTE

Readers should note that the laws and regulations regarding buying property in Ireland aren't the same as in other countries and are also liable to change periodically. **I cannot recommend too strongly that you check with an official and reliable source (not always the same) and take expert legal advice before paying any money or signing any legal documents. Don't, however, believe everything you're told or read, even, dare I say it, herein!**

To help you obtain further information and verify data with official sources, useful addresses and references to other sources of information have been included in all chapters and in appendices A and B. Important points have been emphasised throughout the book **in bold print**, some of which it would be expensive or foolish to disregard. **Ignore them at your peril or cost.** Unless specifically stated, the reference to any company, organisation, product or publication in this book *doesn't* constitute an endorsement or recommendation. Any reference to any place or person (living or dead) is purely coincidental.

AUTHOR'S NOTES

- The book covers buying property in the Republic of Ireland (*Poblacht na hÉireann* or simply *Éire*) and doesn't include the counties of the province of Ulster (Antrim, Armagh, Down, Fermanagh, Londonderry and Tyrone), that comprise the region known as Northern Ireland, which remained part of the United Kingdom when the Republic was established in 1921.

- Frequent references are made throughout this book to the European Union (EU), which comprises Austria, Belgium, Denmark, Finland, France, Germany, Greece, Ireland, Italy, Luxembourg, the Netherlands, Portugal, Spain, Sweden and the United Kingdom. The European Economic Area (EEA) includes the EU countries plus Iceland, Liechtenstein and Norway.

- All prices are shown in Irish punts (IR£) unless otherwise noted. Prices quoted should be taken as estimates only, although they were mostly correct when going to print and fortunately don't usually change overnight. Although prices are sometimes quoted exclusive of value added tax (VAT) in Ireland, most prices are quoted inclusive of tax, which is the method used when quoting prices in this book unless otherwise noted.

- His/he/him/man/men (etc.) also mean her/she/her/woman/women (no offence ladies!). This is done simply to make life easier for both the reader and, in particular, the author, and **isn't** intended to be sexist.

- The Irish translation of some phrases and words is shown in brackets in *italics*.

- Warnings and important points are shown in **bold** type.

- Lists of **Useful Addresses** and **Further Reading** are contained in **Appendices A** and **B** respectively.

- A **Map of Ireland** showing the counties is included in **Appendix C** and a map showing the major cities and geographical features is on page 6.

- A list of property, mortgage and other terms used in this book is included in a **Glossary** in **Appendix D**.

- A **Service Directory** containing the names, addresses, telephone and fax numbers of companies and organisations doing business in Ireland is contained in **Appendix E**.

INTRODUCTION

If you're planning to buy a home in Ireland or even just thinking about it — this is THE BOOK for you! Whether you want a mansion, farmhouse, cottage or an apartment, a holiday or a permanent home, this book will help make your dreams come true. The aim of *Buying a Home in Ireland* is to provide you with the information necessary to help you choose the most favourable location and most appropriate home **to satisfy your individual requirements.** Most important of all, it's intended to help you avoid the pitfalls and risks associated with buying a home in Ireland, which for most people is one of the largest financial transactions they will make during their lifetimes.

You may already own a home in your home country; however, buying a home in Ireland (or any foreign country) is a different matter altogether. One of the most common mistakes many people make when buying a home in Ireland is to assume that the laws and purchase procedures are the same as in their home country (which is unlikely to be the case). Buying property in Ireland is, however, generally very safe, particularly when compared with certain other European countries. Nevertheless, if you don't follow the rules provided for your protection, a purchase can result in serious financial loss, as some people have discovered to their cost.

Before buying a home in Ireland you need to ask yourself *exactly* why you want to buy a home there? Is your primary concern a good long-term investment or do you wish to work or retire there? Where and what can you afford to buy? Do you plan to let your home to offset the running costs? What about capital gains and inheritance taxes? *Buying a Home in Ireland* will help you answer these and many other questions. It won't, however, tell you where and what to buy, or whether having made your decision you will be happy – that part is up to you!

For many people, buying a home in Ireland has previously been a case of pot luck. However, with a copy of *Buying a Home in Ireland* to hand you'll have a wealth of priceless information at your fingertips. Information derived from a variety of sources, both official and unofficial, not least the hard won personal experiences of the author, his friends, colleagues and acquaintances. This book doesn't, however, contain all the answers (most of us don't even know the right questions to ask). What it *will* do is reduce the risk of making an expensive mistake that you may regret later and help you make informed decisions and calculated judgements, instead of costly mistakes and uneducated guesses (forewarned is forearmed!). **Most importantly of all, it will help you save money and will repay your investment many times over.**

The world recession in the early '90s caused an upheaval in world property markets, during which many so-called 'gilt-edged' property investments went to the wall. However, property remains one of the best long-term investments (particularly in Ireland) and it's certainly one of the most pleasurable. Buying a home in Ireland is a wonderful way to make new friends, broaden your horizons and revitalise your life – and it provides a welcome bolt-hole to recuperate from the stresses and strains of modern life. I trust this book will help you avoid the pitfalls and smooth your way to many happy years in your new home in Ireland, secure in the knowledge that you have made the right decision.

Good Luck!   **David Hampshire (Editor)**
                                                            November 1998

1.

WHY IRELAND?

If you're seeking a retreat from the noise and stresses of modern life; open spaces and stunning scenery; simple, traditional pleasures and a slower, gentler way of life; and a wide choice of homes at affordable prices, then Ireland could be just what you're looking for. Perhaps you also wish to steer clear of unfamiliar languages, strange customs, exotic food and sweltering climates, and want a place where you'll be readily accepted into the community and can relax and feel at home, in which case you'll find Ireland hard to beat. It's the least densely populated country in Western Europe (outside Scandinavia), with just 51 people per square kilometre compared, for example, with 245 in the UK. There's not only space but time in Ireland (an old Irish saying goes: "When God made time, he made plenty of it.") and it has almost no motorways and bustling cities. What it does have is an abundance of tranquil countryside, rivers and lakes; a rugged beautiful coastline and some of the greenest vegetation in the world.

However, there's more to the Emerald Isle than beautiful scenery. Although the modern state is politically less than 80 years old, Ireland can trace its roots to an ancient civilisation almost undisturbed by history: untouched by the Romans, the Reformation, the Industrial Revolution and two world wars. Ireland nurtures its links with the its past and its people are proud of their cultural heritage, their myths and legends, their writers and music – not forgetting their famous beer! Catholics comprise over 90 per cent of the population and their religion is all pervasive; divorce has only recently been made legal and even schooling is mostly church-controlled. However, the traditional antipathy towards Protestants (a legacy of centuries of British rule) has largely disappeared and most people are tolerant of other religions and beliefs. The capital, Dublin, is a sophisticated cultural centre and Dubliners have a reputation for knowing everything about everything (just as northerners are said to be direct and the people of the south-west poetic), although everywhere in Ireland you'll find those distinctive features of Irishness: friendliness, loquacity and irreverent humour.

Ireland is a virtually classless society and pastoral life survives as almost nowhere else in Western Europe. Ireland's towns, including Dublin, are still essentially country towns and it isn't unusual to find horse-drawn carts in the streets. While it's a place of refuge for those seeking peace and relaxation, it's also a lively country for the young with an abundance of youthful vigour. Ireland has the youngest population in Europe (around 45 per cent are under 25) and the highest birth rate in the European Union (EU). The population is expected to rise by 20 per cent (to 4.5 million) by the year 2006, which would be its highest level since before the famines of the mid-nineteenth century.

Ireland's attractions are many and varied. It's important to bear in mind when buying a property in Ireland that you aren't simply buying a home, but a lifestyle, and therefore you shouldn't be under any illusions as to what you can expect from a home there. The first and most important question you need to ask yourself is exactly why you want to buy a home in Ireland. For example, are you seeking a holiday or a retirement home? If you're seeking a second home, will it be mainly used for long weekends or for lengthier stays? Do you plan to let it to offset the mortgage and running costs? If so, how important is the property income? Are you primarily looking for a sound investment or do you plan to work or start a business in Ireland?

Often buyers have a variety of reasons for buying a home in Ireland, for example many people buy a holiday home, with a view to living there permanently or semi-permanently when they retire. If this is the case, there are many more factors to take into account than when 'simply' buying a holiday home which you plan to occupy for just a few weeks a year (when it's usually wiser not to buy at all!). If, on the other hand, you plan to work or start a business in Ireland, you'll be faced with a whole different set of criteria. Can you really afford to buy a home in Ireland? What of the future? Is your income secure and protected against inflation and currency fluctuations? Buying a home abroad can be a good long-term investment, although in the last decade a lot of people have had their fingers burnt in the volatile property market in many countries (although Ireland suffered less than most in this respect).

Economically, Ireland is currently enjoying a period of greater prosperity than at any time since its creation. It is, in fact, Europe's fastest expanding country, with a growth rate three times the EU average (between 1988 and 1994, GNP grew at an annual average of around 5 per cent, rising to 7 per cent between 1994 and 1997), which has earned it the nickname 'the Celtic Tiger'. Exports totalled IR£33 billion in 1997 and are growing annually by almost 10 per cent. Current predictions are that the economy will continue to grow at an average of 6 per cent a year until around 2007 (barring recessions). Despite this rapid growth, inflation has remained reasonably low, averaging around 2.5 per cent a year between 1990 and 1995 and falling to an all-time low in 1996/97, although it rose to over 3 per cent in 1998 (above the EU average), largely due to a weaker Irish punt. Average income per head is similar to that of Britain, although the cost of living is slightly higher than in the UK (but lower than in some other European countries).

Home ownership in Ireland is an astonishing 80 per cent, which is the highest in Europe (compared with some 65 per cent in the UK and just 35 per cent in Germany) and one of the highest in the world. The country boasts a million homeowners out of a population of 3.5 million and the growth in property investment (by both nationals and foreigners) in the '90s has been phenomenal. With relatively low interest rates and low inflation, there's hardly ever been a better time to buy a home in Ireland. In recent years immigration has reached record levels, with around 45,000 people making Ireland their home in 1996/97. Not surprisingly, Britons make up the largest expatriate community. Ireland has also traditionally been popular with the British for holiday homes, particularly among outdoor sports enthusiasts (e.g. the hunting, shooting and fishing fraternity), but it's becoming increasingly popular with continental European buyers (particularly Germans and the Dutch, but also Swedes, Swiss, French and Italians), plus Japanese and Americans. In the counties of West Meath and Cavan, for example, there's a growing enclave of Italians, while Americans seem to prefer the west coast and the river Shannon area as well as Dublin (where there's a substantial American population).

The demand for property in recent years has exceeded the supply (at one time there were an esṯimated five purchasers for each property coming onto the market), with the result that prices have soared. Since 1994 property values have been increasing at an average of 15 to 20 per cent a year and in some areas – particularly in and around Dublin, but also in Galway, County Kerry and other parts of Munster – annual increases of over 40 per cent have been recorded. This boom has in turn encouraged investors to buy property for letting, to such an extent that by early 1998 one-fifth of all property purchases were for investment. However, radical changes to the taxation laws in April 1998 have 'cooled' the market somewhat, but Irish property is still a good investment in most areas.

Fears of an impending property crash like that which hit the UK in the late '80s and early '90s are considered by most experts to be unfounded for several reasons including Ireland's sound economy, its large owner-occupier base, and the relatively tight controls on mortgage lending by banks and building societies. There's a demographic reason also: the children of the '60s and '70s baby boom are now entering the property market, and it's estimated that over 100,000 people will reach the average house-buying age (28 to 34) between 1999 and 2003. Despite the recent price rises, property remains more 'affordable' for those borrowing from an Irish bank than it was in the early '90s, when interest rates were at a near-record high. Last but not least, the cost of maintaining a property in Ireland is low in comparison with other western European countries.

Therefore, all things considered, it's a good time to buy a home in Ireland, whether for letting or for temporary or permanent residence. You'll find plenty of properties to choose from, whether you're seeking an imposing 'castle' or stately home, a simple cottage or farmhouse, or indeed a modern bungalow or apartment. However, you shouldn't expect to make a fast buck when buying property in Ireland, but should look upon it as a long-term investment in your family's future happiness, rather than merely in financial terms.

As in all countries, there are both advantages and disadvantages to buying a home in Ireland, although for most people the benefits far outweigh any drawbacks. Among the many advantages are good value for money; easy and inexpensive access (at least for most western Europeans); good rental possibilities (in many areas); excellent local tradesmen and services (particularly in the more popular areas); fine food at reasonable prices; a slower, relaxed pace of life; the friendliness and warmth of the Irish people; the dramatic and rugged beauty of Ireland on your doorstep; and, last but not least, a superb quality of life. Among the disadvantages are the relatively high purchase costs associated with buying property; unexpected renovation and restoration costs (if you don't do your homework); the dangers of buying a property with debts and other problems (if you don't take legal advice); overcrowding in popular tourist areas during the peak summer season; and the expense of getting to and from Ireland if you own a holiday home there and don't live in a nearby country (or a country with good air connections).

Unless you know exactly what you're looking for and where, it's advisable to rent a property for a period until you're more familiar with an area. As when making all major financial decisions, it's never a good idea to be too hasty. A number of foreign purchasers buy badly, soon become dissatisfied with their home and resell within a few years. Too many buyers also assume that the buying process is the same in Ireland as in their home country. Some people make expensive errors when buying homes in Ireland, usually because they do insufficient research and are in too much of a hurry, often setting themselves ridiculous deadlines such as buying a home during a long weekend break or a week's holiday. Not surprisingly, most people wouldn't dream of acting so rashly when buying property in their home country. It isn't uncommon for buyers to regret their decision after some time and wish they had purchased a different property in a different region (or even in a different country!).

Before deciding to buy a home in Ireland, it's wise to do extensive research and read a number of books especially written for those planning to buy a home or live there (like this one). It also helps to study the ads. in specialist property magazines such as *World of Property* and *International Property* (see **Appendix A** for a list), and to visit overseas property exhibitions such as those organised by Outbound Publishing in Britain. Bear in mind that the cost of investing in a few books or magazines (and other research) is tiny compared with the expense of making a big mistake. However, don't believe everything you read!

This chapter provides information about permits and visas, retirement, working, starting a business, communications, getting to Ireland and getting around, including the vagaries of Irish driving!

DO YOU NEED A PERMIT OR VISA?

Before making any plans to buy a home in Ireland, you must check whether you'll need a visa or residence permit and ensure that you'll be permitted to use the property when you wish and for whatever purpose you have in mind. If there's a possibility that you or a family member may want to live permanently or work in Ireland, you should enquire whether it will be possible before making any plans to buy a home there. If you were born in a European Union (EU) or European Economic Area (EEA) country (Austria, Belgium, Denmark, Finland, France, Germany, Iceland, Ireland, Italy, Liechtenstein, Luxembourg, Netherlands, Norway, Portugal, Spain, Sweden and the UK) or can show that at least one of your parents or grandparents was born in Ireland, you're free to live in the country without restrictions, providing that you're able to support yourself (and any dependants) without state assistance. However, non-UK nationals must report to the police within three months and, after this time, obtain a residence permit from the Department of Justice, Equality and Law Reform.

Unless you're retired or otherwise financially independent, the duration of a residence permit is governed by the length of your employment or course (in the case of students) up to a maximum of five years. If you're employed in Ireland, the permit must be completed by your employer, who must also submit a letter detailing the nature and period of your employment. If you're a student, retired or financially independent, you must have private health insurance. In addition, anyone applying for a residence permit may be required to undergo a medical examination. You'll need to produce your passport or national identity card, marriage and children's birth certificates (as applicable), and four passport-size photographs. If you intend to stay for less than a year but more than three months, you'll be issued with a temporary residence permit.

Apart from the requirement to obtain a residence permit, the authorities prefer that EU/EEA citizens register with the Aliens Registration Office (ARO) in Dublin (part of the Department of Justice). Although three out of four EU/EEA nationals don't bother, it can be in your own interest to do so (unless you don't want anyone to be able to track you down!). You'll need to go to the ARO in person with your passport.

Non-EU/EEA nationals wishing to stay in Ireland for more than three months must register with the *Garda Síochána* (police) in the area where they intend to stay, e.g. in the Dublin area you must report to the ARO (☎ 01-475 5555). If you're coming to Ireland to work, you'll require a work permit or at least written confirmation from the Department of Enterprise, Trade and Employment (DETE) that a work permit is being processed. Those planning to set up a business must obtain a letter permitting this from the Department of Justice, Equality and Law

Reform. You'll also need your passport, documentation relating to your entry into Ireland and four passport-size photographs. There's no registration fee.

Registration gives you permission to live in Ireland, but the period is determined by the duration of your work permit (or course, if you're attending a school or college). On registration you'll be given a Certificate of Registration (also called an 'Alien's Registration Book' or 'Green Book'), which you must keep up-to-date for the duration of your stay in Ireland. Note that it isn't usually possible to enter Ireland as a tourist and change your status to that of an employee, student or resident, nor indeed to remain in Ireland for any purpose other than that for which your visa and permission to remain were originally granted. If you want to change your residence status, you'll usually need to return to your country of residence and re-apply for a visa.

Once you have been legally resident for ten years, you can apply for a 'residence stamp' allowing you to reside permanently. However, unless you become naturalised, you'll still require relevant visas, work permits, etc. Non-EU nationals can acquire Irish citizenship in two ways. The first is to take up residence for five years with an undertaking to live in Ireland for at least 50 days in the two years following naturalisation. The other is to buy an Irish home and make an investment of at least IR£1M (spread over seven years) in job-creation in Ireland.

Visitors

Visitors from EU/EEA countries (including British dependent territories) *don't* need a visa to visit Ireland, neither do visitors from Andorra, Argentina, Australia, Bahamas, Barbados, Botswana, Brazil, Brunei, Canada, Chile, Costa Rica, Cyprus, the Czech Republic, El Salvador, Estonia, Greece, Grenada, Guatemala, Honduras, Hong Kong, Hungary, Israel, Jamaica, Japan, South Korea, Latvia, Lesotho, Lithuania, Malawi, Malaysia, Malta, Mexico, Monaco, Nauru, New Zealand, Nicaragua, Panama, Paraguay, Poland, San Marino, Singapore, Slovakia, Slovenia, South Africa, Swaziland, Switzerland, Tonga, Trinidad & Tobago, the USA, Uruguay, Venezuela, Western Samoa and Zimbabwe. All other nationalities require at least a 'short-visit' visa (valid for a maximum of 90 days) to visit Ireland. Most visitors require a full passport, although EU/EEA and Swiss nationals can enter Ireland with a national identity card only.

If you require a visa, you should apply to the Irish embassy or consulate in your country of permanent residence and you may be required to attend an interview. If there's no Irish embassy or consulate in your country of residence, you may apply to any Irish embassy or consulate, or direct to the Visa Office in Dublin. You'll need to submit your passport, which must be valid for at least six months after the intended date of departure from Ireland. You'll also need to send three passport-size photographs and documents relevant to your intended visit, e.g. an invitation from an Irish company or conference organiser if you're visiting on business; a letter of registration from a school or college if visiting for educational purposes; or confirmation of a hotel booking or a letter of reference from an Irish resident who's to accommodate you if you're planning a holiday. Children under 16 who are accompanying a parent or guardian don't require a visa to enter Ireland, providing that they have their own passports or are named on those of a parent or guardian.

Note that the granting of a visa doesn't necessarily give you permission to enter the country and that Irish immigration officials have the authority to deny you admission. You should therefore ensure that you take with you the originals or copies of all documents submitted with your visa application. You'll also need a visa each time you enter Ireland, even if you travel to the UK. This also applies if you have permission to reside in Ireland, when you may apply for a re-entry visa at the Visa Office in Dublin (☎ 01-478 0822).

The visa fee varies depending on your country of residence; your local Irish embassy or consulate will inform you. If you're married to an EU citizen, there's no fee. You should allow at least three weeks (five weeks if you apply by post) for your visa application to be processed, although certain applications are decided quickly, e.g. those of government officials, 'well-travelled' business people, and people with residence rights in Ireland or another EU country or with valid visas for other EU states. For an additional fee you can have your application speeded up. There's also an appeals process for those whose visa applications are refused, which is handled by the Department of Justice, Equality and Law Reform (☎ 01-602 8202).

An Irish visa doesn't grant permission to stay in Ireland for any set period. The date of validity shown on the visa indicates only the date by which it must be presented to immigration. The length of stay is decided by immigration officers at the port of entry, who grant 'permission to remain' for up to three months by way of a stamp in your passport. You'll need to produce a valid passport and evidence that you have sufficient funds to support yourself and any dependants. Students need confirmation of registration with a school or college and evidence that the necessary fees have been paid. Employees and the self-employed must present a work permit or confirmation from the DETE that a work permit will be issued. If you're coming from the UK, you won't be subject to immigration control on arrival in Ireland, but you may not stay longer than one month without obtaining permission to remain.

RETIREMENT

Retired and financially independent EU/EEA nationals can obtain a residence permit in the normal way (see above), but all non-employed residents must provide proof that they have an adequate income or financial resources to live in Ireland without becoming a burden on the state. There's no specified minimum income for EU/EEA nationals, but it must be more than you would be paid if you were in receipt of Irish social welfare payments. The minimum income for non-EU/EEA pensioners is under review and details should be sought from the Department of Justice (☎ 01-602 8202).

WORKING

If there's a chance that you or any family members may wish to work in Ireland, you must ensure that this will be possible before buying a home. If you don't qualify to live and work in Ireland by birthright, family relationship or as a national of an EU or EEA country, obtaining a work permit may be difficult or even impossible.

Work permits aren't required by EU nationals or nationals of an EEA country, although they need to apply at their local *Garda* (police) station for a residence permit if they plan to stay longer than three months. To obtain a residence permit to be self-employed in Ireland, non-EU nationals must be able to demonstrate that their business will fulfil a need and that it won't displace an indigenous business. In other words, they will need to have a USP (unique selling point) and find a niche market.

Non-EU nationals who carry out any activity for monetary gain in Ireland require a work permit as well as a residence permit (issued simultaneously for the same duration). Applications for work permits must be made by a prospective employer to the Department of Enterprise, Trade and Employment (DETE) in Dublin. Some companies are under the impression that their employees need to apply for their own permits, therefore they may need reminding that this isn't the case. Indeed, it's important to note that work permits are specific not only to one company, but also to a particular position within that company. If you wish to move to another company or even obtain promotion within a company, you'll need to apply for a new work permit and there's no guarantee that it will be granted. Work permits should be obtained before your arrival in Ireland or at least an application must be submitted, otherwise you may be refused entry. Ideally, applications should be made at least six weeks before employment is due to start or before a current permit expires.

The number of work permit applications has increased considerably in recent years. There were some 6,000 applications in the first nine months of 1998, a rise of 50 per cent over the same period in 1997, and the DETE is finding it hard to cope (so the earlier your prospective employer applies the better). Although work permits are issued for one year at a time only, it's usually a formality to obtain an extension for subsequent years. The fees for a work permit are IR£25 per month for the first four months and IR£125 for the next eight months. Fees are waived in cases where the employee is married to or is the dependent child of an EU national or has an Irish born dependent child, although this isn't a guarantee of obtaining a work permit (it isn't unusual for women to 'arrange' to give birth in Ireland in an attempt to obtain a work permit for themselves or their partners). The spouses of work permit holders are permitted to stay in Ireland, but aren't automatically granted a permit to work and must undergo the same procedure to obtain a work permit as their spouse.

Although in theory it's the DETE that grants or refuses work permits, it's the Department of Justice that decides who may work in Ireland. The basic criterion is that no suitable EU candidate can be found for the job and the onus is on the employer to 'prove' that all reasonable steps have been taken to recruit a suitably qualified EU national. The issue of a work permit to a non-EU national is considered to be a privilege rather than a right and doesn't in itself authorise entry to or residence in Ireland, which are subject to the control of the immigration authorities. A work permit isn't required to buy property, make an investment, start an Irish company or register a foreign company in Ireland, although the person in Ireland who's responsible for a company's activities must have a work permit, as must anyone visiting Ireland in connection with an Irish business.

Before moving to Ireland to work, you should dispassionately examine your motives and credentials. What kind of work can you realistically expect to do in Ireland? What are your qualifications and experience? Are they recognised in Ireland? How good is your English? Unless your English is fluent, you won't be competing on equal terms with the Irish (you won't anyway, but that's a different matter!). Most Irish employers aren't interested in employing anyone without, at the very least, an adequate working knowledge of English. Are there any jobs in your profession or trade in the area where you wish to live? The answers to these and many other questions can be quite disheartening, but it's better to ask them *before* moving to Ireland rather than afterwards.

Unemployment in Ireland has fallen from 17 per cent in 1990 to around 9.5 per cent in late 1998 (similar to the EU average) and is predicted to drop to 7 per cent or less by the end of the century, a level not seen since the '60s. More than half of those out of work are long-term unemployed (a much higher level than in most other European countries), so job-hunting in Ireland is rather easier than in many countries. There are in fact plenty of jobs available and an annual increase of some 40,000 jobs is required to sustain the country's new-found prosperity. Ireland has been particularly successful in attracting overseas investment. Companies supported by the Industrial Development Agency (IDA) are creating more than 1,000 new jobs a month and the IDA (a subsidiary of the DETE which deals with incoming industry) has set a target of 42,000 new first-time jobs between 1998 and the year 2000. The purchasing of Irish-made components and raw materials has increased by 90 per cent over the past six years, and spending on Irish services by over 60 per cent. Some 30 per cent of all US 'greenfield' investment in Europe and 40 per cent of its investment in European electronics now comes to Ireland.

Irish companies have also been successful in expanding the job market: 130,000 new jobs with indigenous companies were created between 1995 and 1997 with 100,000 more expected in 1998 and 1999. The recent IR£1.6 billion plan to transform Dublin's docklands will alone create up to 40,000 new jobs. New businesses have also added significantly to employment figures in recent years and 16,000 new businesses were registered in 1997 alone, creating 50,000 new jobs. These huge increases in the workforce in Ireland have been the result not only of foreigners coming to work there (a net inflow of 18,000 per year), but also an increasing number of women joining the workforce (women accounted for some 80 per cent of the rise in the labour supply in the last five years). The only drawback for foreign job-hunters is that it's often difficult to access vacancies from outside Ireland, although a lot of information is available in Irish newspapers sold abroad and on the Internet (see below).

The recent boom in electronics and software manufacturing, aided by an IR£5 million government capital investment in training and university places, led to job growth of almost 35 per cent in this sector in 1996. In fact, Ireland is now recognised as the European capital of software localisation and production, and five of the world's top ten software companies have major operations in Ireland and some 50 per cent of software sold in Europe is produced there. Exports of electronics' products account for a third of Ireland's total exports and some 6,000 new jobs are expected to be created in the electronics and IT sectors annually. Ireland is also

Europe's prime location for telemarketing, customer support and technical services through call centres. Since 1995 more than 40 major companies have chosen Ireland as the base for their new European call centres. Health care and pharmaceuticals, in which 2,500 new jobs were created in 1996, are forecast as the biggest growth areas for the rest of the decade. Thirteen of the world's top pharmaceutical companies and ten of the world's top fifteen medical products' companies also have operations in Ireland, which has been ear-marked as the top growth area for the remainder of this century. Automotive components and aerospace technology are also important and rapidly growing sectors, as is the financial services sector in which new jobs grew by almost 35 per cent in 1996.

Dublin's International Financial Services Centre (IFSC), established in 1987, is a major world financial centre housing over 400 of the world's leading financial institutions, including most major international banks. The construction industry is also expanding as a result of the recent housing boom and grew by some 50 per cent in the period 1994–96. Other significant industry sectors in Ireland are insurance and aircraft leasing. Dublin is the location of the central ticketing offices of a number of major airlines (e.g. American Airlines and Lufthansa) and car hire companies (such as Hertz). In many of these sectors European languages are particularly sought-after and TEFL (teaching English as a foreign language) is also a good potential source of employment as a large number of people come to Ireland each year to learn English (some 100,000 in 1997).

Irish newspapers available abroad generally have job supplements (e.g. The *Irish Times* on Fridays, the *Irish Independent* on Thursdays, the *Sunday Independent*, the *Sunday Business Post* and *Job News*). The *Irish Times* is also available on the Internet (www.irish-times.com). Other useful Internet sites are *The Appointments Page* (www.tap.gtc.ie/tap) and the *IE Professional* and *Irish Emigrant* (e-mail: iepro@iol.ie). There are also numerous employment agencies in Ireland as well as executive search and recruitment companies such as Merc Partners and John Harty & Associates. FÁS (the Irish Training & Employment Authority) provides a number of services for job seekers, mainly targeted at young people entering the job market and the long-term unemployed, but also including such initiatives as re-integration training for older, experienced workers and women returning to the workforce. You don't need to be an Irish resident to register with FÁS. The EURES (European Employment Services) system established by the European Commission aims to facilitate job mobility throughout the EU and can be accessed via member states' employment services.

Executive salaries in Ireland have been outstripping inflation for the past 30 years and continue to increase at roughly 5 per cent per annum compared with inflation at 3 per cent. Senior managers can expect to earn between IR£30,000 and IR£60,000, and junior managers and other executives between IR£20,000 and IR£30,000. The best paid sector is financial services, followed by the chemical industry, pharmaceuticals, health care and telecommunications. Location seems to make little difference to levels of pay, but sex does. Although Ireland has recently made some progress towards equality of opportunity and pay for women, they still earn up to 20 per cent less than their male counterparts. There's no statutory minimum wage in Ireland, except for a few low-paid jobs such as cleaning.

However, although jobs are plentiful, competition is fierce and standards high. Foreigners looking for work in Ireland will be competing with the many emigrants returning to their native country to share in its new prosperity. Job-seekers therefore need to be well prepared. Although business is often conducted in a cordial, not to say casual atmosphere, smart dress and punctuality are demanded. The Irish may be friendly but they are nevertheless shrewd and Irish companies are increasingly looking for staff with good interpersonal and teamwork skills. *Working and Living in Ireland* (see **Appendix B**) includes a list of the top companies currently recruiting. Some companies cover certain relocation expenses (e.g. the legal fees and stamp duty involved in buying a house and removal costs) if you need to move to Ireland to take up a position, but you should check with the prospective employer whether such payments are taxable and, if so, who pays the tax. In general, employee legislation in Ireland is reasonable and fair to both employers and employees. Trade Union membership is a right guaranteed to all employees under the Irish Constitution, although membership has declined in recent years.

Many people turn to self-employment or start their own business (see below) to make a living, although this path is strewn with pitfalls for the newcomer and most foreigners don't do sufficient homework before moving to Ireland. While hoping for the best, you should plan for the worst, and have a contingency plan and sufficient funds to last until you're established (this also applies to employees).

SELF-EMPLOYMENT

If you're an EU national or a permanent resident with a residence permit, you can work as a self-employed person or as a sole trader in Ireland. If you wish to be self-employed in a profession or trade in Ireland, you must meet certain legal requirements and register with the appropriate organisation, e.g. a professional must become a member of the relevant professional college. Members of some professions and trades must possess professional qualifications and certificates recognised in Ireland and are usually required to sit a written examination. You're subject to any professional codes and limitations in force, e.g. a medical practitioner must have his qualifications accepted by the medical college of the county where he intends to practise and any controlling bodies. You must also show that you're in good standing with the professional authorities in your home country. In certain professions, such as the law, it's unusual to be permitted to practise in Ireland without Irish qualifications. If you're thinking of setting up your own business, whether as a sole trader or a limited company, you should seriously consider obtaining quality certification. Certification is becoming increasingly important in Ireland. In fact in some areas of business, it's essential and ISO 9000 is now a minimum requirement if you want to supply many foreign-owned multi-nationals.

Another recognised scheme in Ireland is the Q-Mark, awarded by the Irish Quality Association (Merrion Hall, Strand Road, Sandymount, Dublin 4, ☎ 01-269 5255), which is important in certain areas. Note that both the Small Firms Association and the Irish Small and Medium Enterprises Association operate group ISO schemes to alleviate the cost of certification. If you set up as a self-employed person, you should inform your local tax office. You won't need to pay any tax until after your first year of trading and two months before the year ends you'll be sent a preliminary tax notice informing you when your first tax payment is due. You must register for VAT if your taxable supplies are likely to exceed certain levels (see below). Unlike many other European countries, Ireland doesn't require new businesses to be registered with the local Chamber of Commerce, although doing so can be useful. The address of your local chamber can be obtained from Chambers of Commerce in Ireland (☎ 01-661 2811).

As a self-employed person you don't have the protection of a limited company should your business fail, although there are certain tax advantages. On the other hand, it may be advantageous to operate as a limited company. Always obtain professional advice before deciding whether to operate as a sole trader or form a company in Ireland, as it has far-reaching social security, tax and other consequences (**see Chapter 3**). All self-employed persons must register for income tax and Pay-Related Social Insurance (PRSI), and in certain cases pay government levies for health, training, employment and apprenticeship training. Anyone with an income in Ireland requires a Revenue and Social Insurance (RSI) number and must register with the Department of Social, Community and Family Affairs (formerly the Department of Social Welfare) using form SE3, available from local Social Welfare Offices or from the Self-Employment Section of the Social Welfare Services Office (☎ 01-874 8444 or 051-874177).

Social Insurance: There's a special social insurance scheme for self-employed workers, most of who are liable for what are called PRSI Class S contributions. In addition to covering social insurance, these include a health contribution and an employment and training levy when your income reaches a certain level. In general, PRSI contributions for the self-employed are lower than for salaried employees, but you receive fewer benefits. Unlike an employee, who's entitled to dental and optical treatment, plus sickness and unemployment benefit, you'll receive little more than an old age pension. Self-employed women are also entitled to maternity benefits, but the wives or partners of self-employed men aren't. Note that if a relative such as your husband, wife, mother, father, brother, sister, son or daughter helps with the business without being an official partner, they're exempt from PRSI contributions. On the other hand, if they're paid a salary they should contact the Scope Section of the Department of Social, Community and Family Affairs for a decision as to their insurability.

Tax Registration: You must register as a self-employed worker or professional with the Taxes Central Registration Office (TCRO). If your turnover is expected to be less than IR£100,000 per year, you should use the Small Traders Registration (STR) form to register for income tax, PAYE/PRSI (if you're an employer) and VAT (see below).

Value Added Tax (VAT): You must register for VAT if your taxable supplies are likely to exceed IR£40,000 (in the case of goods) or IR£20,000 (in the case of services). You aren't obliged to register if your turnover will be below those limits, although you may register voluntarily. It's worth taking advice, however, before doing so. Registration for VAT is done on form TR1 or TR2 and it must be declared and paid every two months, and an annual return of sales and purchases submitted (which can be for any 12-month period you choose). You must keep a record of all sales and purchases for six years. You can pay VAT by direct debit or, in certain cases, annually. The Revenue Commissioners publish a guide to VAT for Small Businesses (IT49), available from the Revenue's Forms and Leaflets Service (☎ 01-878 0100).

STARTING A BUSINESS

Entrepreneurs were once disparaged in Ireland, although this is far from the case today. It's estimated that there are some 160,000 small and medium-sized businesses (called SMEs) in Ireland and that the number is increasing by 10 per cent a year.

Getting started: There's considerable, although fragmented, state support for industry in Ireland, principally for manufacturing and internationally traded services. Other kinds of service industries, with the notable exception of tourism, don't benefit from state support, although this situation may change. Nevertheless, there are many organisations to help people start and develop businesses, some of which are state or state-aided bodies, while others operate on a commercial basis. The following is a summary of the various organisations and their areas of responsibility:

- The Department of Enterprise, Trade and Employment (DETE) has overall responsibility for enterprise. Its provisions are carried out nationally through Forbairt (see below) and regionally through Shannon Development and *Údarás na Gaeltachta*, and locally through the City and County Enterprise Boards and Area Partnership Companies. The DETE publishes a guide entitled *Starting Your Own Business – A How To Guide*, available from the Government Publications Sales Office, Sun Alliance House, Molesworth Street, Dublin 2 (☎ 01-661 3111), price IR£10, and a free leaflet entitled *Look Before You Leap*, available from the County Enterprise Boards (see below). It also has information on starting your own business on the Internet (www.irlgov.ie/entemp/syob);

- IDA Ireland is a subsidiary of the DETE which deals with incoming industry;

- Forbairt exists to facilitate the development of indigenous Irish business, particularly manufacturing and internationally traded services. It provides programmes like the Small Business Programme, Capability Development Programme, Enterprise Preparation Programme and National Linkage Programme, as well as grants for employment, capital, leasing, product and process development, training, management development, a mentor programme, and various technology-related programmes;

- Shannon Development (officially the Shannon Free Airport Development Company) is the Regional Development Agency for the Shannon region (Counties Limerick, Clare, north Tipperary, south-west Offaly and north Kerry) and provides similar grants and assistance to Forbairt within these areas, such as the START Programme and Entrepreneurs' Programme;

- *Údarás na Gaeltachta* provides incentives and support schemes for new businesses in the *Gaeltacht* (Gaelic speaking) regions of Donegal, Mayo, Galway, Kerry, Cork, Waterford and Meath;

- FÁS is the national Training and Employment Authority, offering training and employment programmes and a recruitment service. FÁS runs 'start your own business courses' during which you can receive the equivalent of unemployment benefit and any other benefits you're entitled to plus Enterprise Payments of IR£40 per week (IR£65 if you have dependants) providing that your proposed business meets certain criteria;

- Worker co-operatives can obtain support and grants from the FÁS Co-Operative Development Unit;

- Rural development initiatives can benefit from the EU LEADER II Programme, but until the end of 1999 only;

- The National Advisory Council on Teleworking was set up in 1998 to encourage job creation in remote areas through teleworking;

- The Irish Trade Board (*An Bord Tráchtála*) is a state organisation responsible for promoting and developing exports, and provides advice, services, incentives and a Market Activities Grant of up to 50 per cent to companies planning to export;

- The Irish Tourist Board (*Bord Fáilte*) provides incentives and support for tourism-related projects and administers the European Regional Development Fund, which also provides grants of up to 50 per cent;

- The Irish Business and Employers' Confederation operates a graduate training scheme called the European Orientation Programme to encourage Irish exporting. Grants of up to 50 per cent are available from various state organisations (see above);

- The 35 City and County Enterprise Boards are responsible for developing projects that aren't covered by the state industrial development agencies – specifically industrial projects likely to employ fewer than ten people and service projects requiring grants of less than IR£50,000 and investment of not more than IR£100,000. A booklet entitled *Starting Your Own Business* is available from the Dublin City Enterprise Board or the Dublin Business Innovation Centre;

- Area Partnership Companies operate at local level in accordance with a Local Development Plan to generate jobs with a particular emphasis on employing the long-term unemployed and minority groups;

- The International Fund for Ireland runs various programmes to assist small businesses;

- The Small Firms Association (SFA) represents the interests of small businesses and provides various member discount schemes including insurance, standards, health insurance and debt collection (the Irish Small and Medium Enterprises Association does the same for owner-managed businesses);

- The Chambers of Commerce of Ireland represent the interests of a broad range of businesses, with a particular emphasis on overseas promotion and foreign investment in Ireland;

- Six EU Business Innovation Centres were established in 1988 with EU support to nurture new businesses during their first three to five years;

- The Liffey Trust is a voluntary, non-profit organisation devoted to job creation with private sector funding. To date the Trust has helped nearly 200 businesses in various ways;

- The Project Development Centre helps graduate entrepreneurs set up their own businesses;

- The Bolton Trust, the Business Incubation Centre and SPADE offer cheap office accommodation for start-ups in Dublin.

In addition to the above, there are various organisations dealing with specific industry sectors, including the following:

- *Bord Iascaigh Mhara* is a state agency responsible for the development of the fishing industry and provides grants and training;

- The National Food Centre, a division of TEAGASC (the Agriculture and Food Development Authority) provides help with research, consultancy, training, product and process development to businesses in the food industry (except milk products, which are the responsibility of the National Dairy Products Centre). TEAGASC also provides services and training programmes;

- The National Microelectronics Research Centre in Cork provides technological assistance to all kinds of industrial businesses;

- The National Microelectronics Application Centre in Limerick (owned by Shannon Development) is concerned with developing electronic, software and IT products for Irish industry and can help if you have a worthwhile idea;

- The Food Product Development Centre assists with innovative food concepts.

Additional information and advice can be obtained from the local County Development Officers and the Central Statistics Office.

The City of Dublin Vocational Educational Committee (CDVEC) runs a 'Start Your Own Business' course (they also publish a free *Guide to Courses*), Whitehall Language and Commercial College teaches entrepreneurial skills, and the Revenue Commissioners publish a free *Starting in Business* guide (IT48), available from local tax offices (listed in the green pages of the phone book) or the Revenue's Forms and Leaflets Service (☎ 01-878 0100). More detailed information on the various agencies which provide start-up help can be found in *Working and Living in Ireland*, *Starting a Business in Ireland*, and *Enterprise Ireland* (see **Appendix B**), and a complete list of information and advice sources is obtainable from the Department of Enterprise and Employment in Dublin (☎ 01-661 4444).

At the time of publication the whole area of state support for enterprise was under review and Forbairt, *An Bord Trachtala* and the services to business function of the FÁS were due to be amalgamated into a 'super agency' called Enterprise Ireland (for more information ☎ 01-808 2000). Most of the state-related bodies help through grant-aid, though that also is changing. In order to find out whether your business idea will qualify for aid, you should start by calling the Forbairt's 'Enterprise Link' helpline (☎ 850-353333).

Obtaining grants: Grants for feasibility studies (i.e. market research, financial projections, assessments of manufacturing processes, plant and equipment, raw materials, negotiation of joint-ventures or manufacturing licenses) are offered by City and County Enterprise Boards (for businesses of fewer than ten employees), by Forbairt or Shannon Development (for businesses of more than ten employees), and by *An Bord Tráchtála* (in cases where there's an overseas marketing element). Grants are most likely to be awarded to manufacturing or international service businesses and are usually for 75 per cent of the research cost to a maximum of IR£5,000, providing that the project is deemed viable. If you're applying for a grant, presentation is all-important.

Bear in mind that the authorities are looking for innovative ideas that will fill new market niches and create economic growth for Ireland. They will foster indigenous business which leads to 'import substitution', not projects which are likely to infringe on existing domestic businesses or in sectors already suffering over-capacity. Your project must have the potential for providing long-term jobs and demonstrate likely success. Note that most new businesses don't receive grant-aid for this reason, but the application process can be beneficial in itself, as it will force you to assess the viability of your business idea and also give you access to valuable information, expertise and advice.

Raising finance: Most Irish financiers operate on a 'matching funds' basis, therefore it's important to raise as much as possible yourself. Various sources of finance are listed in *Working and Living in Ireland* (see **Appendix B**), which are summarised below:

Equity is available from the ACT Enterprise Fund (IR£100,000 to IR£750,000 for early stage SMEs); ACT Venture Capital (IR£400,000 to IR£5M); Bank of Ireland Entrepreneurs Fund (IR£100K to IR£500K for early stage technology and food businesses); The Business Innovation Fund (IR£25,000 to IR£75,000 for small start-ups and early stage businesses); Smurfit Venture Investments Ltd. (50 per cent Forbairt funded – IR£125,000 to IR£250,000 for growth-oriented businesses); Shannon Development, which provides Early Stage Finance (IR£100,000 to IR£250,000) and a Tourism Enterprise Fund of up to IR£50,000 for tourism projects. Small Irish resident businesses seeking additional capital can also make use of the Relief for Investment in Corporate Trades (also known as the Business Expansion Scheme). Business Innovation Centres will match businesses seeking funds with individuals or companies looking for investment opportunities, and the *Venture Capital Report* (a UK monthly newsletter) profiles businesses seeking equity finance. The Financial Services Sector of the *Kompass Directory* is also a useful reference for sources of venture-capital.

Seed Capital is available from: Shannon Development (IR£10,000 to IR£100,000); Dublin Business Innovation Centre, which manages the Dublin Seed Capital Fund (50 per cent Forbairt funded – IR£25,000 to IR£100,000); the Forbairt Fund (EU-subsidised and operated by AIB, Bank of Ireland and Ulster Bank); and the Revenue Commissioners, who will repay income tax up to IR£25,000 to people leaving employment to start their own business (their booklet, *The Seed Capital Scheme: Tax Refunds for New Enterprises*, is available from the Revenue's Forms and Leaflets Service (☎ 01-878 0100).

Loans (properly called debt) are of course available from banks. Most major banks have special start-up schemes. AIB Bank, for example, has an Enterprise Loan Scheme and provides discounts to new businesses; the Bank of Ireland will lend between IR£20,000 and IR£150,000 as well as offering incentives and advice; ICC Bank has various services including Flexiloan (loans of up to 20 years) and Supplier Payline (working capital); the National Irish Bank has a New Enterprise Loan Fund (loans of between IR£15,000 and IR£75,000); TSB Bank and Ulster Bank also offer some assistance and incentives; the Irish Trade Union Trust makes low-interest loans for workers' co-operatives; and the Guinness Workers' Employment Fund does likewise (mainly for manufacturing and craft businesses).

If you want to operate a business under a name other than your own, you must register it with the Registrar of Business Names (Parnell House, 14 Parnell Square,

Dublin 1, ☎ 01-804 5200) by completing form RBN1. Registration costs IR£10. The cost of forming a limited company is IR£100, which is payable to the Companies Office, but if you use an accountant or solicitor to do the paperwork it will cost between IR£250 and IR£400. To form a co-operative (which can also be a limited company) you'll need to register with the Registry of Friendly Societies (Parnell House, 14 Parnell Square, Dublin 1, ☎ 01-804 5499), which can cost as little as IR£100.

A single form is used to register a business for the various taxes for which it will be liable: STR (for individuals with an annual turnover of less than IR£100,000); TR1 (for individuals whose annual turnover is in excess of IR£100,000, partnerships and foreign businesses); and TR2 (for limited companies). Your PAYE/PSRI number, VAT number and Corporation Tax number are the same, but a company's Registered Number, issued by the Companies Office, is different.

PAYE Income Tax: All employees earning over IR£6 per week must be registered for PAYE (Pay As You Earn). This is a system of computing individuals' income tax according to the tax rate applicable to them (specified in the government's annual budget) after deducting their tax-free allowance (which varies from individual to individual). All employees are issued with a Tax Deduction Card by the tax office indicating their tax liability. (*An Employer's Guide to PAYE* and a guide to *PAYE/PRSI for Small Employers* are available from the Revenue's Forms and Leaflets Service (☎ 01-878 0100). If you hire employees, you must obtain their P45 or tax-free allowance certificate and notify the tax office that you have employed them. If neither a P45 nor a current year's tax-free allowance certificate is available (e.g. with first-time employees), you'll need to complete form P46 and operate PAYE/PRSI on an 'emergency' basis until a tax-free allowance certificate is received (first-time employees should complete form 12A).

The above obviously applies in reverse if you become an employee in Ireland (i.e. you must provide a P45 or tax-free allowance certificate or you'll be subject to emergency tax). If you plan to live in Ireland, you'll probably receive the full allowance, but if you start work part way through the tax year intending to stay only a few months, you may be restricted to a temporary or emergency tax allowance. Note that if you lose your P45, a copy may not be made and the necessary information must be sent by your employer in a letter to the Revenue Commissioners.

If you're a director of a limited company, you must submit a P45 or P46 to the tax office yourself. As an owner-director you'll make lower PRSI contributions than other employees, but will incur the same rate of PAYE. You'll also need to make a self-assessment of your income. At the end of each tax year, you're required to complete forms P35, P35L and P60 for each employee. A guide to P35 End-of-Year Returns and supplies of all Revenue forms can be obtained from the Revenue's Forms and Leaflets Service (☎ 01-878 0100).

Corporation Tax: Limited companies must also register for Corporation Tax (on form TR2) and are obliged to pay Preliminary Tax on their profits within six months of the end of their accounting period and make a final tax return (CT1) within nine months of the end of that period. They are also required to supply certain trading details to the Revenue Commissioners by completing form 11F CRO within 30 days of starting trading.

The Revenue Commissioners publish a series of booklets explaining the various taxes (see above) and can provide you with a *Business Start-up Pack*, which is available from tax offices (see page 104).

Non-EU Nationals: Non-EU nationals wishing to start a business in Ireland must demonstrate that they will be creating jobs on a long-term basis for EU nationals (e.g. by showing a commitment to training). Businesses that create jobs are welcomed with open arms, particularly in areas with high unemployment.

Avoiding Problems: In addition to any problems you may have with the Irish authorities, you may have to contend with people of doubtful business ethics, although these are far less common in Ireland than in many other countries as trust is still an important part of doing business. However, it's probably wise to have a healthy suspicion regarding the motives of anyone you do business with (unless it's your mum or spouse), particularly your fellow countrymen. It's usually best to avoid partnerships as they rarely work and can lead to disaster. In general, you should trust nobody and shouldn't sign anything or pay any money before having a contract checked by a solicitor. It's a sad fact of life that there are foreigners in most countries who prey on their fellow countrymen. In most cases you're better off dealing with a long-established Irish company with roots in the local community (and therefore a good reputation to protect), rather than your compatriots. Note that if things go wrong with a 'foreign' partnership, you may not be protected by Irish law.

Research: BEWARE! If you aren't prepared to thoroughly research the market and obtain expert business and legal advice, then you shouldn't even think about starting a business in Ireland (or anywhere else for that matter). The key to starting or buying a successful business in Ireland is exhaustive research, research and yet more research (plus innovation, value for money and good service). It's an absolute must to check out the level of competition in a given area. Note that even when competition is light, there may be insufficient business to sustain another competitor. In some areas there's already a saturation of trades and services and your chances of making a living are practically zero. If you're convinced that you have what it takes, don't burn your bridges and sell up abroad, but rent a home in Ireland and spend some time doing research before taking the plunge. You should also lease your business premises (at least initially) rather than buying them outright. However, before doing so it's imperative to ensure that you fully understand your rights regarding possible future rent increases and the renewal and termination of a lease.

Some foreigners start businesses in Ireland on a whim and a prayer with little business acumen or money. They're simply asking for trouble. It's no good following your dream of living in Ireland if you end up working all hours of the day and night struggling to make a living from a business that's doomed to failure. Bear in mind also that when a couple operate a business together it can put an intolerable strain on their relationship and many marriages fail under the pressure.

Wealth Warning: Whatever people may tell you, working for yourself isn't easy and it requires a lot of hard slog (self-employed people generally work much longer hours than employees); a sizeable investment and sufficient operating funds (underfunding is the major cause of business failure); good organisation (e.g. bookkeeping and planning); excellent customer relations; and a measure of luck (although generally the harder you work, the more 'luck' you'll have). Don't be seduced by the apparently relaxed way of life in Ireland – if you want to be a success in business, you cannot play at it.

However, although there are numerous failures for every success story, many foreigners *do* run successful businesses in Ireland. Those who make a go of it do so as a result of extensive market research, wise investments, excellent customer relations and most important of all, a lot of hard work.

KEEPING IN TOUCH

A recent US$5 billion investment in a state-of-the-art telecommunications network has ensured that communications, both within Ireland and with other countries, aren't only modern and efficient (with all the latest technology such as ISDN, VPN, SMDS, etc.), but also among the cheapest in Europe.

Telephone

Until recently the Irish telephone service was operated exclusively by Telecom Éireann, better known as simply TE. Although a state-controlled company, TE is to be floated on the stock market in 1999 when up to 30 per cent of the company will be sold. In 1994 the corporate sector was deregulated and two new telecommunications companies were started by Irish entrepreneurs: TCL, recently taken over by the US telecom giant WorldCom, and Esat Telecom, which has already established a national fibre optic network along CIÉ railway lines and has recently launched an 'Esat Home' scheme offering cheap international calls to domestic customers. Another Irish company, ITL, already provides discounts on international calls and calls to mobile phones, and has set up the country's first local call alternative to Telecom Éireann, offering savings of up to 20 per cent. Cable & Wireless and a joint venture between ESB and British Telecom are also contemplating entering the market. Full deregulation is due to come into effect at the end of 1998, a year ahead of the original EU deadline, but until then all domestic services will be provided by TE.

Nevertheless, the competition has already benefited TE customers in better quality service. On average, new customers are connected within ten days (TE aims to reduce this to five days) and 97 per cent of faults are remedied within two working days. Impending deregulation has also inevitably brought down prices. Over the past few years Telecom Éireann has dramatically reduced its long-distance and international call charges and has recently announced further price cuts, including savings of up to 50 per cent on calls to Australia, 40 per cent to the USA and 30 per cent on UK calls. It's even possible that by the end of the century users will be able to make free local calls.

Installation: When moving into a new home in Ireland with a telephone line, you must have the account transferred to your name. If you're planning to move into a property without an existing telephone line, you'll need to get one installed (although it isn't compulsory!). You can have a telephone installed or reconnected without even visiting your local TE office. All they need to know is your name and address and the existing telephone number of the property (if there is one). If you're renting, you'll need to pay a deposit or find someone with a TE account to act as a guarantor. If you're taking over a property from the previous occupants, you should arrange for the telephone account to be transferred to your name from the day you take possession. Before buying a property, check that all the previous telephone bills have been paid, otherwise you may find yourself liable for them.

It can take up to five weeks to get a telephone line installed in Ireland, although it usually takes just a week (five working days) or two in most areas. The cost of getting a private telephone line installed is IR£99 and the charge for taking over an existing line (which takes up to a week) is IR£35. Unless you set up a direct debit for bill payments, a deposit of IR£200 is required or a guarantee from someone with a TE account.

Using the Telephone: Main towns and their surrounding areas have area codes consisting of two to four digits, as listed below:

Arklow	0402	Enniscorthy	054	Roscommon	0903
Athlone	0902	Galway	091	Rosslare	053
Ballina	096	Kilkenny	056	Shannon	061
Bandon	023	Killarney	064	Sligo	071
Bundoran	072	Letterkenny	074	Thuries	0504
Carlow	0503	Limerick	061	Tipperary	062
Castlebar	094	Longford	043	Tralee	066
Cavan	049	Mallow	022	Tuam	093
Clonmel	052	Monaghan	047	Tullamore	0506
Cork	021	Mullingar	044	Waterford	051
Donegal	073	Naas	045	Westport	098
Drogheda	041	Navan	046	Wexford	053
Dublin	01	Nenagh	067	Wicklow	0404
Dundalk	042	Portlaoise	0502	Youghal	024
Ennis	065	Rathluire	063		

Numbers beginning with 02 denote areas in Cork City and County, those beginning with 04 eastern areas, 05 the south-east, 06 the south-west and mid-west, 07 and 09 the west and north-west, and 01 the Dublin area. Each of these seven areas is covered by one of the 'white pages' telephone books published by Telecom Éireann. Dublin's Golden (or yellow) Pages classified directory is published as a separate volume. In all other areas the Golden Pages are included with the white pages. A separate fax directory for Ireland is available from TE (☎ 01-800 202 020 or 353-1-874-8888 from outside Ireland), although many fax numbers are also listed in telephone books. TE also publishes a CD ROM containing all phone and fax numbers in Ireland, which is updated annually and costs around IR£20 (it's obtainable by calling the above numbers). An Internet version will soon be available, but in the meantime business numbers can be found on the Europages Online Directory or the Kompass Directory.

Touch-tone dialling is universally available on the public network. Telecom Éireann uses the European caller-id standard, therefore telephones and other devices operating on the North American caller-id standard won't deliver caller-id information when used in Ireland. When making a domestic call to a place with the same area code as the number you're calling from, you don't dial the code. However, to make a call to a place with a different code, the appropriate area code must be dialled. When making an international call to Ireland, dial your international access code followed by 353 for Ireland, then the area code minus the initial 0 and the subscriber's number. A call to Dublin, for example, would begin 00-353-1. In Ireland you dial 10 for the operator, 114 for the international operator, and 1190 for domestic directory enquiries. The emergency number is 999 or 112.

Costs: Rental and call charges in Ireland are among the lowest in Europe. Line rental is IR£12.10 per month and rental of a standard telephone set IR£1.33 per month; both charges are payable bi-monthly. Call management services (i.e. call answering, call waiting, call forwarding and three-way calling) are free.

Payphones: Payphones are widespread in Ireland, where there are over 7,000. Unlike some countries, where it's hard to find a public phone which hasn't been vandalised, TE claim that some 95 per cent of their payphones are working at any given time. Card phones are at least as common as coin-operated phones (in fact they usually appear in pairs) and it works out slightly cheaper to use a card phone. The minimum payphone charge for all calls (whether local or international) is 1 unit, which costs 20 pence from a coin phone and 16 to 20 pence from a card phone depending on the value of the card you use. Phone cards (known as CallCards) are sold in four denominations: an IR£2 card buys you ten units (20p per unit), an IR£3.50 card 20 units (17.5p per unit), an IR£8 card 50 units (16p per unit) and an IR£16 card 100 units (16p per unit). CallCards are sold at most post offices and petrol stations and at many shops. Credit card phones accept CallCards as well as the four major international credit cards (Visa, MasterCard, Eurocard and American Express). Note that credit card calls are much expensive than CallCard calls and you're charged an additional fee of 70p for the first unit plus an extra 20p for subsequent units.

You can buy Global Telecards in Ireland, but note that these can be used only for phoning abroad (or phoning Ireland from abroad). Ireland Direct Prepaid Calling Cards are also available for IR£5 or IR£10 for phoning Ireland from abroad. They can be used in 21 countries and offer substantial savings on standard international charges.

Tariffs: The price of a telephone call is determined by the number of 'units' used, which varies according to the time of day, the day of the week and the destination of the call. The price for a single unit is 11.5p (including VAT at 21 per cent). There are generally three rates in Ireland: standard, reduced and weekend trunk call rates. For calls to ordinary phones, the standard rate applies on weekdays (except public holidays) between 0800 and 1800; the reduced rate applies at all other times. Between midnight on Friday and midnight on Sunday and all day on public holidays there's a reduced charge of 11.5p for each 10-minute interval for trunk calls (i.e. calls outside your local area) within Ireland, including Northern Ireland (excluding calls from payphones and operator assisted calls). For calls to mobile phones, the standard rate applies between 0800 and 2000 on weekdays and reduced rate at all other times.

The amount of time allocated per unit for direct dialled calls depends on the distance and the time of a call, as shown in the table below:

Distance	Standard Rate	Reduced Rate	Weekend Trunk Rate
Local	3 minutes	15 minutes	N/A
Up to 56km (A rate)	66.7 seconds	100 seconds	10 minutes
Over 56km (B rate)	46 seconds	69 seconds	10 minutes
Calls to mobiles	25 seconds	37.5 seconds	37.5 seconds

Charges from payphones are as follows:

Distance	Standard Rate	Reduced Rate	Weekend Trunk Rate
Local	3 minutes	3 minutes	N/A
Up to 56km (A rate)	66.7 seconds	100 seconds	3 minutes
Over 56km (B rate)	25 seconds	37.5 seconds	3 minutes
Calls to mobiles	25 seconds	37.5 seconds	37.5 seconds

Note that there's a surcharge for operator connected calls, which are charged as follows:

Distance	Standard Rate	Reduced Rate	Weekend Trunk Rate
Local	72p for first 3 minutes and 11.5p for each subsequent 3 minutes	72p for first 15 minutes and 11.5p for each subsequent 15 minutes	N/A
Up to 56km (A rate)	IR£1 for first 3 minutes and 13p for each subsequent minute	86p for first 3 minutes and 8.5p for each subsequent minutes	N/A
Over 56km (B rate)	IR£1.40 for first 3 minutes and 27p for each subsequent minute	IR£1.11 for first 3 minutes and 17p for each subsequent minute	N/A
Calls to Mobiles	IR£1.80 for first 3 minutes and 40p for each subsequent minute	IR£1.40 for first 3 minutes and 27p for each subsequent minute	N/A

Operator assisted calls from payphones are charged as follows:

Distance	Standard Rate	Reduced Rate	Weekend Trunk Rate
Local	70p for first 3 minutes and 20p for each subsequent 3 minutes	70p for first 3 minutes and 20p for each subsequent 3 minutes	N/A
Up to 56km (A rate)	IR£1.30 for first 3 minutes and 80p for each subsequent 3 minutes	IR£1 for first 3 minutes and 50p for each subsequent 3 minutes	N/A
Over 56km (B rate)	IR£2 for first 3 minutes and IR£1.50 for each subsequent 3 minutes	IR£1.50 for first 3 minutes and IR£1 for each subsequent 3 minutes	N/A
Calls to Mobiles	IR£2.10 for first 3 minutes and IR£1.60 for each subsequent 3 minutes	IR£1.60 for first 3 minutes and IR£1.10 for each subsequent 3 minutes	N/A

Note that the above charges apply to Northern Ireland, but not to the rest of the UK.

You can buy or rent a telephone with a built-in counter, which records the units used, or have a separate counter installed to monitor the cost of calls or check unauthorised use, e.g. by baby-sitters, guests, burglars or children (alternatively you can buy a telephone lock). Or you can ask the operator the cost and duration of a call for a fee of 36p per time. The charge for a directory enquiries call (for a maximum of three enquiries) for anywhere in the world is 34.5p, except for calls from payphones and Éircell mobile phones, which are free. TE customers are allowed two free directory enquiries calls a month.

International Calls: International Direct Dialling (IDD) calls can be made from Ireland to most countries, from both private and public telephones. A full list of IDD country codes is shown in the information pages of your local white pages directory, plus area codes for main cities and tariffs. The international access code is 00, which must also be used for calling the UK. For example, to call the central London number 123-4567 from Ireland you would dial 00-44-171-123-4567. To dial a Northern Ireland number, however, use the prefix 080 followed by the area code (minus the initial 0). International Directory Enquiries are on 1197 (for the UK) and 1198 (for the rest of the world) and cost the same as Directory Enquiries for Ireland (see above). To make a call to a country where there isn't international direct dialling (IDD), you must dial 114 for the international operator.

There are no fewer than ten different charge bands for international calls: Band 1 for the UK (excluding Northern Ireland); Band 2 for near Europe (i.e. Andorra, Belgium, France, Germany, Luxembourg, Monaco and the Netherlands); Band 3 for mid-Europe (from Portugal and Spain to Greece); Band 4 for far Europe and North Africa; Band 5 for the USA and Canada; Band 6 for Mexico and the Caribbean; Band 7 for Australia and New Zealand; Band 8 for the Middle East and South Africa; Band

9 for the Pacific Rim; and Band 10 for the rest of the world. There are also two additional bands for Inmarsat and Skyphone calls.

As with domestic calls, there are three rates: standard, reduced, and economy. These apply at the following times: standard rate 0800 to 1800 weekdays (Bands 1–4), 1200 to 2000 weekdays (Bands 5 and 6), 0800 to 1400 and 2000 to 0000 weekdays (Band 7), at all times (Bands 8 to 10); reduced rate 1800 to 0800 weekdays and all day, at weekends and holidays (Bands 1 to 4), 0800 to 1200 and 1800 to 2200 weekdays (Bands 5 and 6), 1400 to 2000 and 0000 to 0800 daily (Band 7); economy rate 2200 to 0800 daily (Bands 5 and 6 only).

The approximate charges per minute for direct dialled calls are as follows:

Band	Rate	Private Phone	Payphone
1	Standard	24p	63p
	Reduced	22p	48p
2	Standard	39p	75p
	Reduced	33p	67p
3	Standard	48p	£1
	Reduced	41p	75p
4	Standard	73p	£1.43
	Reduced	63p	£1.22
5	Standard	36p	£1.45
	Reduced	34p	£1.24
	Economy	31p	£1.11
6	Standard	66p	£1.35
	Reduced	61p	£1.24
	Economy	54p	£1.11
7	Standard	88p	£1.91
	Reduced	68p	£1.47
8	Standard	£1.09	£3.03
9	Standard	97p	£2.52
10	Standard	£1.74	£3.03

As part of a recent price-reduction package, Telecom Éireann has announced reductions of up to 50 per cent in the cost of international calls, in addition to a new weekend rate (midnight Friday to midnight Sunday) of 19p per minute. Note that there's a high surcharge for operator connected international calls. International reverse charge calls can be made by dialling the international operator on 114 (or 1800-457 457 from a payphone).

Ireland subscribes to a Home Direct service that allows you to call a number giving you direct and free access to an operator in the country you're calling, e.g. for Britain you dial 1800-55 00 44. The operator will connect you to the number required and will also accept credit card calls. Countries with a Home Direct service include Australia, Belgium, Brazil, Canada, Chile, Denmark, Finland, France, Germany,

Guatemala, Hong Kong, Indonesia, Japan, South Korea, Norway, the Netherlands, Portugal, Spain, Sweden, the United Kingdom, Uruguay and the USA.

Internet 'Telephone' Services: The success of the Internet is built on the ability to gather information from computers around the world by connecting to a nearby service for the cost of a local telephone call. If you have relatives, friends or business contacts who are connected to the Internet, you can make international 'calls' for the price of a local telephone call to an Internet provider. Once on the Internet, you usually have a choice between paying for the time you spend 'online' as you do with your telephone or fax and paying a set fee for unlimited use (which doesn't, however, include the local call charges). The fee varies according to which provider you use. Most providers offer a free trial period, usually a month, with so many free hours of Internet access. Internet users can buy software (costing around IR£50) that effectively turns their personal computer into a voice-based telephone (both parties must have compatible computer software). You also need a sound card, speakers, a microphone, a modem and access to a local Internet provider. While the quality of communication isn't as good as using a telephone (it's similar to using a CB radio) and you need to arrange call times in advance, making international calls costs virtually nothing.

Fax: Fax machines can be purchased (but not rented) from TEIS, a division of Telecom Éireann, and purchased or rented from private companies and stores. Shop around for the best price. Before taking a fax machine to Ireland, check that it will work there (i.e. is compatible) or that it can be modified. Usually foreign fax machines will send but not receive messages in Ireland. Note also that getting a fax machine repaired in Ireland may be impossible unless the same machine is sold there.

Mobile phones: Over the past couple of years the use of mobile phones has increased dramatically in Ireland, where there are now over half a million mobile phone users (one in seven of the population). You may bring your mobile phone to Ireland, although the older analogue phones may not work (American analogue phones, for example, aren't compatible with the Irish network). Cellular mobile communications in Ireland are regulated by the Office of the Director of Telecommunications Regulation (ODTR), the national regulatory authority established in 1996. There are two GSM mobile networks, Éircell and ESAT Digifone, both of which use the international standard 900Mhz system. Éircell, a subsidiary of Telecom Éireann, is the state mobile phone company which has over 300,000 customers, whereas ESAT Digifone (a private company) has only a third as many.

The Digifone service is cheaper for most calls and provides better coverage, particularly in congested urban areas. It offers a choice of two 'plans': DigiMax, which has a higher monthly fee but lower call charges for medium to heavy users, and DigiLite, with a lower monthly fee and higher call charges for light users. Digifone bills international calls on a per second basis, whereas the minimum charge using Éircell is one minute. On the other hand, Éircell have more 'roaming' agreements (102 in 61 countries compared with Digifone's 74 in 52 countries). Note, however, that roaming charges can be substantial (particularly when receiving calls) and it's best to check the charges before using your mobile phone outside Ireland. A cheaper option is to use the SMS (short message service) system, for which the cost is the same whether the message is delivered to Dublin or Delaware. Messages are restricted to 160 characters, but there's no limit on the number of messages that can be sent and it's possible to reach countries with minimal mobile phone coverage. Éircell operate an older analogue network than Digifone (at 900Mhz), but this is being wound down to comply with EU regulations.

The ODTR plans to license a third GSM network in 1998, which will be a hybrid network using both 900Mhz GSM and 1,800Mhz GSM/PCS. Subscribers to other GSM networks can use the Irish networks freely, providing that they have a roaming agreement with the foreign network. Prepaid GSM cards are available from Éircell at IR£20 each with national call charges of 50p/min. peak and 20p/min. off-peak. It's also possible to rent a GSM phone at Dublin airport. You can send and receive e-mail via a mobile phone on both the Éircell and Digifone networks. The messages are displayed like paging messages. Outgoing e-mail messages use the SMS system and are charged at 15p each by Éircell and 12.4p a minute by Digifone.

Post Office Services

There's a post office in most towns, main railway stations, major airports and ports in Ireland. In addition to the usual post office services, main post offices provide a range of other services including telegrams, fax and telex transmissions, and domestic and international giro money orders (postal orders can be purchased at any post office). Business hours at ordinary post offices are usually from 0900 until 1300 and from 1400 until 1730 Monday to Friday, and from 0900 to 1300 on Saturdays. Main post offices in major towns don't close for lunch and may also provide limited services outside normal business hours. The General Post Office in O'Connell Street, Dublin, is open from 0800 to 2000 Monday to Saturday and 1000 to 1830 on Sundays and public holidays, when only stamps and foreign exchange are available. There are also post offices at international airports, which are generally open during normal office hours. Sub-post offices in small towns and villages usually close one day a week at 1300.

The Irish postal service is operated by the state-controlled *An Post*, but the impending liberalisation of the postal market will mean that around a quarter of postal services will be privatised by the year 2003. International courier companies such as TNT and UPS are likely to be among the first to offer letter post services as soon as it's permitted. In the meantime, *An Post's* service is as efficient, reliable and inexpensive as any in Europe.

Domestic post is known as 'first class' mail (there's no second class!) and 90 per cent is delivered the next day, providing it's posted before the specified latest posting time (which varies depending on the area). Letters weighing up to 25g cost 30p (the rate was reduced from 32p in April 1998), but there's no longer a reduced rate for open letters (the 'standard letter' and 'printed paper' services have been amalgamated, so all letters should be sealed). However, there are reduced rates for newspapers and magazines. Swiftpost is a guaranteed next day service (before 1230 in town centres and industrial estates), which is also subject to latest posting times, costing IR£2 for letters up to 100g. Registered post is tracked (so that if it doesn't arrive you can find out where it has gone) and you're compensated for loss or damage. You pay a surcharge on top of the normal first class letter rate according to how much compensation you require: IR£1.70 for up to IR£100, IR£2.20 for up to IR£500, and IR£2.70 for up to IR£1,000.

An Post provides numerous other services including Private Box (your mail is addressed to a PO Box and held until collected); Private Posting Box (*An Post* collects from you for an annual fee); Collection Service (you pay for each collection); Private Bag (your post is delivered in a locked bag); Callers Service (you collect from your nearest post office); Retention (your post is held for collection); Redirection (if you have recently moved); Diversion (to another address in the same area); poste restante (non-residents' post can be held for up to three months free of charge); and Freepost.

International letter rates depend on the destination and whether letters are sent by air or surface mail. All overseas mail should have either a green 'economy' label or a blue 'priority' label. Surface mail (up to 50g) costs 35p to Britain and 40p to the rest of the world. In fact postal charges to Britain are the same as within Ireland, i.e. 30p for postcards and letters up to 25g. Postcards are 32p to European countries and 45p to the rest of the world, but packs of five pre-paid postcards for Ireland or Britain can be bought for IR£1.40 (i.e. 28p each). Airmail letters up to 25g are 32p to European countries and 45p to the rest of the world. International Swiftpost (priority handling to meet the first available despatch to the country of destination) costs a minimum of IR£2 extra for items up to 100g. Aerogrammes are available from post offices and cost IR£2.20 for a pack of five and can be sent anywhere in the world. An International Registered service is also available, as are Sorted and Unsorted Services for bulk mail; M-Bags (for a large volume of mail sent to one address); Direct Entry (processed as local mail in the country of destination so as not to appear to have been sent from abroad); International Business Reply Service (an international Freepost); and International Reply Coupons.

International parcels are handled by a branch of *An Post* called Special Delivery Services (SDS). As with letters there are two rates: economy for surface mail and priority for air mail. A 1kg parcel sent to the UK costs IR£4 economy or IR£9.90 priority up to IR£16 economy or IR£20.20 priority to the Far East. EMS (express mail services) is a guaranteed and insured service costing an additional IR£8 to IR£10 depending on the destination.

Note that all post to countries outside the EU (unless it contains only letters, documents, etc.) must be accompanied by the appropriate customs declaration form(s). For goods worth up to IR£250 this means form CN22, which is an adhesive green label on which you describe the contents of the letter or parcel. For goods valued over IR£250 you list the contents on form CN23, which accompanies the top tear-off portion of form CN22.

Courier Services: The only guaranteed way to send something urgent (if it cannot be faxed or e-mailed) is by courier. Express mail and courier services are provided by SDS, Irish railways and airlines, and international (e.g. DHL and UPS) and domestic courier companies. One of the most economical ways to send urgent international parcels is via SDS's EMS service serving around 200 countries. Mail sent within Ireland or to major European cities is guaranteed to arrive before noon the next day and to other European towns/regions within 24 or 48 hours (depending on the country), while mail to New York is guaranteed to arrive within 48 hours. The maximum delivery time to any country is three or four days. SDS also offer a Business Special service, which usually guarantees delivery of parcels within Ireland in less than 24 hours, and a 'regular' service without a delivery guarantee.

GETTING THERE

Although it isn't so important if you're planning to live permanently in Ireland and stay put, one of the major considerations when buying a holiday home there's the cost of getting to Ireland from your home abroad. How long will it take to get to a home in Ireland, taking into account journeys to and from airports, ports and railway stations? How frequent are flights or ferries at the time(s) of year when you plan to travel? Are direct flights available from an airport near you? Is it feasible to travel by car (bearing in mind the high cost of ferries)? What's the cost of travel from your home country to the region where you're planning to buy a home in Ireland? Are off-season discounts or inexpensive charter flights available? Are costs likely to rise or fall in the future? If a long journey is involved, you should bear in mind that it may take you a day or two to recover, e.g. from jet-lag after a long flight. Obviously the travelling time and cost of travel to a home in Ireland will be more important if you're planning to spend frequent long weekends there, rather than a few long stays each year.

Airline Services: There are nine airports in the Republic of Ireland: Donegal in the north, Sligo; Knock (also called Connaught or Connacht), Galway (or Connemara Airport), Shannon, and Kerry in the west; Cork and Waterford in the south; and Dublin in the east. Dublin and Shannon are the main international 'gateway' airports and are served by scheduled flights from most European capitals and major cities. These are operated by Alitalia, British Airways, British Midland, City Jet, Crossair, Air France, Iberia, Jersey European, Lufthansa, Manx Airlines, Romanian Airlines, Ryanair, SAS (Scandinavian Air Systems), Swissair, TAP Air Portugal, and Viva Air. Aer Lingus, Ireland's national airline, also operates a large number of flights to and from Europe and, with its hostesses' lilting Irish accents and emerald green uniforms, will give you a taste of Ireland even before you arrive. You can fly direct to Dublin from Alicante, Amsterdam, Barcelona, Berlin, Bonn, Brussels, Copenhagen, Dusseldorf, Faro, Frankfurt, Hamburg, Helsinki, Lisbon, Madrid, Malaga, Malta, Milan, Moscow, Munich, Nice, Palma, Paris, Rome, Stockholm, Stuttgart and Zurich.

There are also direct flights to Dublin from the five main London airports (including City Airport) as well as from most regional British airports. Shannon is served direct from Heathrow, Gatwick, Belfast, Birmingham and Manchester, as well as Bucharest, Dusseldorf, Jeddah, Minsk, Paris, Stuttgart, Zurich, and of course, Dublin. Cork has direct flights from Belfast, Birmingham, Bristol, Exeter, Isle of Man, Jersey, Heathrow, Gatwick, Stansted, Manchester, Newquay and Plymouth, in addition to Amsterdam, Frankfurt, Paris, Rennes and Rotterdam. There are flights to Kerry from Luton and Manchester, and to Knock and Waterford from Stansted and Manchester. Donegal, Galway and Sligo have flights from Dublin only.

Dublin and Shannon are the only airports handling flights from North America. Direct scheduled services operate from Atlanta, Boston, Chicago, Newark and New York into both airports. Apart from Aer Lingus, the major carriers are Delta Air Lines and Continental, who operate direct services from New York and Newark into Shannon and Dublin. Perhaps the most unlikely service is from Miami to Shannon with the Russian airline Aeroflot. Many other airlines fly to major European cities (such as London) from where connecting flights to Ireland are available. There's a wide range of promotional air fares available to Ireland. Super Apex fares can be had from London for as little as GB£69 return, and Aer Lingus, British Midland and Ryanair all offer advance booking discounts. Conversely, many airlines operate a late booking service, but this isn't advisable if you want to be sure of a seat. There are weekend return fares from most London airports to Dublin or Cork costing between IR£70 and IR£90 with most airlines. Some people even 'commute' to London from homes in Ireland in preference to buying property in the London suburbs, which would cost two or three times as much! Students with an International Student Identity Card (ISIC) can obtain discounts on certain flights, e.g. between Britain and Ireland, as well as on transatlantic flights.

Charter Flights: A number of companies in North America offer inexpensive charter flights to Ireland, such as American Holidays, American Trans Air, JWT, Keytours, Pleasure Break Vacations, Sceptre Charters, Tour America, and Translift Leisure from the USA, and Air Transat Holidays, Canada 3000, CIÉ Tours, Regent Holidays, and Sunquest Vacations from Canada. However, make sure that you read the small print as there are often drawbacks such as heavy cancellation charges and restrictions on changing the dates of your flights. Sometimes charter companies will reserve the right to cancel your flight or change the dates and times of travel, or even add 'fuel surcharges' after you have paid the standard fare. If you're flying onto other destinations, it's usually cheaper to pay for your onward travel at the same time as your transatlantic flight. Seasonal charter flights are also available from various parts of Europe: CIÉ Tours operate from a number of German airports; Euralair, Falcon/JWT from Spain; GO Holidays, Star Europe, and TAT from France; Maersk Air from Denmark; Transwede from Stockholm; TAP from Faro in Portugal; and Crossair from Zurich. There are also special charter flights to Knock from Basle, Frankfurt, Hamburg and Zurich during the summer. If you arrive in Ireland on a one-way ticket and need to buy your flight home in Ireland, you'll need to pay a departure tax (IR£10 for North America and IR£5 for Europe), which is usually included in the ticket price.

Shannon Airport, 26km (16mi) west of Limerick, lays claim to the world's first (and, some say, finest) duty-free shop (established in 1947) where you can purchase a wide variety of goods duty-free including traditional Irish products such as cut glass, Connemara rugs and marble, Donegal tweed, etc. If you don't want to be weighed down by all your purchases during your stay in Ireland, you can buy them as you leave, in which case everything will be loaded straight onto the plane without you even having to pay surplus baggage charges. Note, however, that duty-free within the European Union is due to be abolished in mid-1999, which may mean that fares will increase by up to 20 per cent to compensate for the loss in revenue.

Ferries: Sadly, the days of leisurely transatlantic crossings by liner are gone and the only regular scheduled sea-crossings to Ireland are from France and Britain. As for getting *to* Ireland by sea, less exclusive services operate all year round from Britain and France. From various parts of Wales there's a choice of four routes and three operators: Fishguard to Rosslare (Stena Line), Pembroke to Rosslare (Irish Ferries or Stena Line), Swansea to Cork (Swansea-Cork Ferries), and Holyhead to Dublin (Irish Ferries) or Dun Laoghaire (pronounced 'leary') near Dublin (Stena Line). There's also a Liverpool-Dublin service and a seasonal service to Dublin from the Isle of Man, both operated by the Isle of Man Steam Packet Company (aka Seacat). If you're travelling from Scotland or northern England, it may be easier to cross to Northern Ireland and travel to the Republic by road from there. Stena offer a Stranraer-Belfast service and Irish Ferries a Cairnryan-Larne link (slightly further north). These are the shortest crossings to Ireland from mainland Britain, with Irish Ferries' Jetliner taking just one hour.

Crossing times from the Welsh ports vary from 99 minutes on Stena Line's new HSS (High-speed Sea Service) from Holyhead to Dun Laoghaire and Fishguard to Rosslare (near Wexford), to ten hours on the Swansea-Cork route, allowing you sleep your way to the Emerald Isle. All ferries, including catamarans, take cars and there are between one and six crossings daily in each direction, depending on the route and the time of year. There's little to choose between the different operators for comfort and standard of service, but fares vary considerably depending on the time of year and the amount of time you want to spend on the Irish Sea. Some fares are more than double in mid-summer and you pay a premium for the faster services. Stena's HSS, for example, costs more than twice as much as their three-and-a-half hour ferry crossing at peak times. Most standard fares are for a car, driver and up to four passengers.

Stena's fares are from GB£158 (low season) to GB£169 (high season) return for the Holyhead-Dublin Port ferry and from GB£208 to GB£408 return for the HSS into Dun Laoghaire. There are various special deals to be had, such as a Nightrider, Wednesday Special or Two-Day Return which can cost as little as GB£105. On the Fishguard-Rosslare route you have a choice between a standard ferry and a faster Lynx service. Prices range from GB£108 to GB£298 for the ferry and from GB£128 to GB£438 for the Lynx. The Lynx Summer Return or Summer Sunday Return costs from GB£269.

Irish Ferries' standard fares start at GB£118 for their Pembroke-Rosslare ferry (a four-hour crossing), rising to GB£298 in the summer. The slightly faster (3¼ hours) Holyhead-Dublin Port route costs from GB£158 to GB£338. Again there are special deals such as a Wednesday Special, 48-hour Special and Summer Sunday Special from just GB£105 return. Swansea-Cork's overnight service costs from GB£150 to GB£378 if you're prepared to sleep in a chair (you must pay extra for a cabin). Their special offers include a Weekend Return, Sunday Saver and a Midweek Special starting at GB£129 return. Ferries leave Swansea at 2100 and arrive in Cork at 0700. They run around every two days in each direction in low season (mid-March to mid-June and mid-September to mid-January) and daily in high season (mid-June to mid-September). There are no sailings between mid-January and mid-March. The Seacat service from Liverpool to Dublin runs twice daily and takes four hours. A standard five-day return fare for four people and a car starts at GB£169 in low season, rising to GB£319 in mid-summer. Again there are reductions such as a day return, two-day return and Wednesday special return.

Irish Ferries' services from France operate out of Cherbourg to Rosslare, while Brittany Ferries sail from Roscoff and St Malo to Cork. Crossings take around 14 hours with Brittany Ferries and around 17 hours with Irish Ferries. The Roscoff-Cork service costs from IR£155 (low season) to IR£410 (high season) return for a car, driver and one passenger. Prices on the Cherbourg-Rosslare route are for a car, driver and four passengers and also start at IR£155 for a 9-day return in low season, rising to IR£646 for a standard return in high season. Cabins are extra. There are no sailings between early January and April.

Those who prefer to leave their car at home can let the train take the strain. All ferry services from the UK are scheduled to link with InterCity trains serving Fishguard, Holyhead, Swansea and Stranraer, and at the Irish end some train services connect with incoming ferries. Inclusive train/ferry tickets are available from as little as IR£42 return from Manchester or Liverpool to Dublin. Irish Ferries offer their own train/ferry service with fares from London to Dublin via Holyhead as low as GB£39 (low season) or GB£59 (high season) return per person. As well as being a good deal cheaper than taking the car, the rail route can save you time. For example, London (Euston) to Dublin via Holyhead-Dun Laoghaire takes around 11 hours and London (Paddington) to Wexford via Fishguard-Rosslare around 12 hours 30 minutes.

Irish Ferries also offer a coach/ferry service via Holyhead or Pembroke which is even cheaper, London-Dublin fares starting at just GB£29 return per person. Eurolines, a National Express company, operate daily coach/ship services from major UK cities to Cork, Dublin, Limerick, Tralee, Waterford and other main towns, with onward connections to over 100 destinations throughout Ireland. There's a choice of single, return (valid for 6 months) and open-dated return tickets. Prices for the London-Dublin route are similar to those of Irish Ferries. Other bus services are provided by Irish Bus and numerous small companies which can be found on the back pages of Irish newspapers (available in Britain). The disadvantages of coach travel (slowness and relative discomfort) are offset by the advantage of being able to get to parts of Ireland other services cannot reach (sounds like an ad. for a Dutch beer!).

GETTING AROUND BY PUBLIC TRANSPORT

Public transport throughout Ireland is provided by CIÉ (*Coras Iopair Éireann*), the state-subsidised national transport company in addition to various private operators. CIÉ has three subsidiaries, Irish Rail (*Iarnród Éireann*), Irish Bus (*Bus Éireann*), and Dublin Bus (*Bus Átha Cliath*), which together carry over 300 million passengers a year, the highest number since the late '70s. As part of the government's commitment to ease the increasing urban grid-lock caused by cars and commercial vehicles, CIÉ is to invest IR£25M a year in the bus network (over half of which will be swallowed by Dublin Bus), and a massive IR£700M in the railway system between 1999 and 2007.

Public transport is generally good in Ireland, although rail services are sparse or non-existent in many areas and buses are sometimes infrequent. Irish railways provide an efficient and reasonably fast rail service, particularly between cities served by AVE (*Alta Velocidad Española* from Spain) high-speed trains. Ireland has comprehensive intercity bus and domestic airline services and is also served by frequent international coaches, trains and excellent air links. Taxis are common in main towns and cities, although they aren't a cheap form of transport. Urban public transport in major cities, particularly Dublin, is inexpensive and efficient, and includes comprehensive bus and suburban rail networks. Around Dublin, systems are integrated so that the same ticket can be used for all services and a range of commuter and visitor tickets are also available. There are travel agencies in all major cities and large towns, and specialist agencies for young travellers such as USIT.

Bus: The efficient national bus service in Ireland is operated by Irish Bus (*Bus Éireann*), which is part of CIÉ. Buses are generally cheaper than trains and reach even the most remote corners of the country. A return fare from Dublin to Cork, for example, costs as little as IR£16. Irish Bus also operates services in the cities of Cork, Galway, Limerick and Waterford, and has links between Cork Airport and Cork City, and Shannon Airport and Limerick Town. Alternative services are offered by Expressway (which covers the main routes), Nestor Bus (which operates a Galway-Dublin service) and Suirway Bus Service in Waterford, among others. You can obtain an Expressway timetable plus those of certain provincial services from the CIÉ or from tourist offices and some newsagents.

Dublin Bus (*Bus Átha Cliath*), another branch of CIÉ, is a virtual monopoly operating all public bus services in the greater Dublin area (which includes parts of the counties of Wicklow, Kildare and Meath). Dublin Bus has invested heavily in new buses and infrastructure and has had a 15 per cent increase in users over the last ten years. It has also increased its number of routes and introduced new services such as City Imp (high-frequency minibuses operating on six routes); Nitelink (a Thursday to Saturday night service operating hourly between midnight and 3am on 15 routes); Cityswift (operating along ten 'quality corridors' every six minutes at peak times), Cityspeed (a special commuter service with few stops); Airlink (connecting Dublin Airport to the city centre and bus and rail stations and running every 20 minutes from early in the morning to 2300 seven days a week); and Stationlink (between the three main stations: Heuston, Connolly and Tara Street).

An 'autofare' system operates on around half the routes, which means that you need to have the exact fare as drivers don't handle cash. Alternatively you can buy '2 EASY' cards, which are prepaid for two journeys at a certain fare (e.g. 55p or IR£1) and must be used within a month. There's a wide range of other discounted pre-paid tickets, from day tickets to monthly season tickets, which can be purchased at the CIÉ Desk at Dublin Airport, the head office of Dublin Bus at 59 O'Connell Street, or at any of the over 200 bus ticket agencies located throughout the city and its suburbs. Dublin is divided into 'hop' zones for buses and trains: short, medium, long and giant, with fares varying accordingly. There are other regional bus companies (in addition to Dublin Bus) such as Suirway, which operates in the Waterford area.

Note that destinations shown on the front of buses are often in Irish. Dublin, for example, may be shown as *Átha Cliath*, so a timetable comes in handy for translation purposes. But don't try to find a place called *An Lár* – it means town centre! Concessionary bus tickets and Travelsave stamps are covered in the section on rail travel below.

Rail: The Irish rail network is operated by the Irish Rail (*Iarnród Éireann*) arm of CIÉ, which is in a 'serious' financial position, running at a loss of around IR£50M per year and state supported to the tune of some IR£92M per year. Nevertheless, it has an increasing number of passengers, totalling some 30 million in 1998. A major restructuring plan has recently been given EU support.

Most railway lines radiate out from Dublin, so the network isn't much good for travelling up and down the west coast, for example, and there are no lines at all north of Sligo. Trains run frequently between the major airports and nearby city centres, and services are reliable and efficient and fares reasonable. The trains themselves are fairly modern and clean, although taking a trip on Irish railways is like stepping back in time: railwaymen still operate the signals from little signal boxes and even open the gates by hand at level crossings (and the trains stop at every tiny hamlet on the way). There are two categories of tickets: standard and super standard (there are no first and second class people in Ireland!). A standard single from Dublin to Cork costs around IR£30 and a super standard single IR£5 more. The Belfast-Dublin Enterprise service is a new cross-border service (which commenced in September 1997) that's a joint Irish Rail/Northern Ireland Railways initiative supported by the EU as part of its European High Speed Railway Network. Its 90mph diesel trains currently do the 113 mile trip in two hours, which will be reduced to 1 hour 45 minutes when the track has been upgraded.

The Dublin area is served by DART (Dublin Area Rapid Transit) suburban rail system which serves 25 stations around the capital from Howth in the north to Bray in the south. The Arrow service operates from Kildare to Heuston Station. Daily, weekly, monthly and annual tickets are available as well as a Dublin four-day Explorer. Ireland is also a paradise for steam train enthusiasts as more and more narrow gauge line is being opened up.

A number of special rail and rail/bus passes are offered for those planning to do a lot of travelling by public transport. An Irish Explorer ticket entitles you to eight days' travel out of 15 for IR£90 and an Emerald Card provides the same arrangement within Northern Ireland as well as the Republic for IR£105 or 15 days out of 30 for IR£180. An Irish Explorer for Rail Only provides five days' train travel out of 15 for IR£60 and an Irish Rover ticket (which is valid on both Irish Rail and Northern Ireland Railways) the same deal for IR£75. There are concessions on all these tickets for under-16s.

Students and younger travellers are entitled to other special rates. An International Student Identity Card (ISIC), which costs IR£7, provides at least 25 per cent off most standard fares. An ISIC also enables you to buy a Travelsave Stamp (costing a further IR£8) which will save you up to 60 per cent on single and return rail fares, CIÉ provincial bus journeys and the return boat fare to the Aran Islands. Stamps are available from the Union of Students International Travel (USIT) in Dublin or any USIT office, the Irish Bus Travel Centre in Dublin, the Central Buildings in Limerick and Campus Travel in London. Further savings can be obtained on bus and rail travel in and around Dublin with an Education Travel Concession Ticket, available from the Group and Educational Department of Dublin Tourism. An ISIC is available only to full-time students. If you aren't a full-time student but are under 26, you're entitled to a European Youth Card (EYC), which costs IR£7 per year and entitles you to low cost air fares, special travel insurance rates, reduced price maps and guidebooks, and discounts from certain retailers, restaurants and other outlets. The EYC is the Irish member of the European network of youth cards (EURO 26) and is valid in 29 European countries. For an additional IR£7 you can add a FairStamp to your EYC entitling you to up to 30 per cent discount on rail travel in Ireland.

However, you don't need to be a student or young to benefit from travel discounts. Ireland is part of the network covered by the Eurail Pass, which allows any non-European unlimited travel for a fixed fee depending on how many days travel you require (up to a maximum of two months). A Eurail pass, which must be purchased outside Europe, also entitles you to free ferry travel to Ireland from France, providing you don't pass through Britain, which isn't part of the network.

Air: It's possible to fly between major towns in Ireland, although most internal flights are routed via Dublin. In any case the distances involved are quite small: the longest possible flight, from Donegal in the north to Cork in the south (via Dublin), is only 400km (ca. 250mi). Aer Lingus, Ireland Airways and Ryanair offer services between Dublin and Knock, Cork, Donegal, Kerry, Shannon, Galway and Sligo. Aer Árann provides flights to the Aran Islands from Galway Airport. Private aeroplanes and helicopters can be rented from Dublin and Shannon airports. Airlink Airways (☎ 094-23349) and West Air (☎ 061-475166) have small planes for hire and Celtic Helicopters (☎ 01-890 1349) provide helicopters. Note that private aircraft heading for Dublin must land at Dublin Airport as there are no private airfields near the capital.

Boat: Most of the islands off the west coast of Ireland can be reached by boat, although some in the summer months only, where the type of vessel varies from a modern hydrofoil to a converted Second World War landing craft. The Irish Tourist Board publishes details of the various island boat services.

Taxis: Telephone numbers of local taxi companies are listed under 'Taxis & Taxicabs' in the Golden Pages. In Dublin and Cork all taxis have meters (the minimum fare in Dublin is IR£1.90). Elsewhere standard fares generally apply, but as in most countries it pays to confirm the fare before setting off. On the whole, Irish taxis wait at ranks and outside airports, stations and the larger hotels, but some can be stopped in the street. Note that in Dublin you can wait as long as 90 minutes at peak times for a taxi and a 20 minute wait isn't uncommon, although there are moves to increase the number of licensed taxis in the capital over the next few years. Taxi drivers usually expect a tip of around 10 per cent of the fare, but will occasionally round the fare *down* to the nearest punt.

DRIVING IN IRELAND

Motoring in most parts of Ireland contrasts strongly with almost anywhere else in Europe. There's only some 60km (40mi) of motorway (all of it near Dublin) and barely more than twice as much dual carriageway in the whole country. All other roads have just a single lane in each direction, although there's sometimes an extra lane on long hills for slow vehicles. The good news is that there are only two places in Ireland where you'll be charged a toll for using a road: on the M50 ring road around Dublin and on the R131 when crossing the East Link Bridge near the capital. In both cases the charge is less than IR£1.

One particular peculiarity on Irish roads is their 'so-called' hard shoulder, which is indicated by broken yellow lines, so-called because it's used in rather a different way from hard shoulders in most other countries. Instead of being reserved for breakdowns or other emergencies, it's used for overtaking. That doesn't mean that the Irish overtake on the inside, but that when you see a vehicle approaching rapidly from behind with the intention of overtaking, it's expected that you should pull over onto the hard shoulder to let it pass. Even more disconcerting is when you find an oncoming vehicle heading straight towards you on your side of the road and your only option is to veer onto the hard shoulder to avoid a head-on collision. The Irish won't thank you for doing so – not because they are inconsiderate, but because to them it's a completely normal manoeuvre. Another feature of Irish roads is their unevenness. Most are positively bumpy and you need to keep a weather eye out for pot holes, and it's a great relief to come upon one of the rare strips of new or resurfaced road which will reassure you that your suspension is still working properly (or not, as the case may be!).

Outside the cities and towns, roads are often deserted and traffic jams rare. Because there are few ring roads or bypasses, however, most towns suffer from congestion, which is particularly bad in Cork and Dublin. Although statistics state that of the major European capitals Dublin has almost the lowest car-to-population ratio (at 1:3.2), you're no better advised to take your car into the city centre than to drive into London, Paris or Rome. The current growth in Ireland's population and economy, however, is expected to lead to an increase in the number of cars on the roads of more than 50 per cent to 1.6 million (or one car for each 2.75 people) by the year 2006, despite the government's efforts to persuade more people to use public transport.

The speed limit on motorways is 70mph (113kph), 60mph (97kph) on other main roads and 30mph (48kph) in built-up areas, unless otherwise indicated (the speed limit signs are in miles per hour). You can be fined up to IR£150 for the first offence and up to IR£350 for the second for exceeding these limits. If you're foolish enough to be caught a third time within a year of your second offence, you can be imprisoned for up to three months. As in Britain, cars drive on the left side of the road (when not in the middle) and the wearing of seat belts is compulsory for both front and rear seat passengers. The legal limit of alcohol in the blood is 0.08 per cent and it's a law which is strictly enforced; contravention can lead to fines of IR£1,000, a year's disqualification and even a jail sentence.

Road signs, like all signs, are generally in both English and Irish Gaelic, although in some of the more remote western areas (where Irish is in everyday use) English may be dispensed with. Further confusion can be caused by the use of both miles and kilometres on road signs to indicate distances. The newer green and white signs are in kilometres, whereas the traditional black-on-white signs are in miles. Roads are in the process of being renumbered and what used to be T (trunk) and L (link) roads are being converted to N (national) and R (regional) roads – you'll encounter both old and new numbers on road signs.

Petrol stations usually stay open until around 2000 and in villages they open after Sunday Mass. If you've run out of petrol or are about to and you cannot find a station open, a knock on the door and a polite request will generally get the pumps going. All grades of petrol and diesel are widely available in Ireland, where prices tend to be a little lower than in Britain.

Yellow lines along the road indicate parking or waiting restrictions. In Dublin you'll need to park at a meter or in a multi-storey car park (where the charge is around IR£1.30 per hour), whereas in the centre of Cork and most other main towns a disc system is used to control parking. Discs can be bought, usually in books of ten, at shops or garages near the town centre. Those with vehicles registered in Ireland will need to pay motor tax, which is done at the Motor Tax Office (not at post offices) and is charged on a sliding scale according to a vehicle's engine capacity, from IR£92 for engines up to 1,000cc up to IR£800 for engines over 3,000cc. These rates are set to rise by 6 per cent from 1st January 1999, the first increase since 1992. There's no compulsory testing of older vehicles as there is in most other EU countries, although it's likely to be introduced in the near future.

Because of the relative scarcity of traffic in Ireland, motorists tend not to be as aggressive as those found in many other countries nowadays. However, that isn't to say that they are necessarily good or even patient drivers. Although a booklet entitled *The Rules of the Road* is obtainable from any post office for just IR£1, few drivers seem to possess a copy or to have assimilated its contents. In fact, Irish drivers tend to fall into two categories: fast or very slow. Nevertheless, outside the main cities you'll rarely hear a horn sounded in anger, and if 'raised fingers' are a common sight, they invariably indicate thanks rather than rudeness. It's common also to encounter animals on the road, particularly sheep which will happily graze at the roadside inches from passing traffic. Quite often you'll find yourself following tractors or other farm machinery or one of those very slow drivers (who are usually wearing tweed caps), who may pull onto and off the road without warning or signals at that unhurried pace which is the norm in rural Ireland.

If your car breaks down there's no need to worry or feel embarrassed as you might at home. You're unlikely to be left standing at the side of the road for long and the next vehicle will probably stop to find out what's wrong and help you to get to a garage or at least seek out a mechanic to get you back on the road. Breakdown services are available from the AIT (☎ 01-800 667788) and FIA (☎ 01-800 535005) motoring organisations.

If you're unfortunate enough to be involved in a road accident, you're required by law to stop immediately and to remain at the scene of the accident long enough to inform the *Gardaí* (police) and give your name, address (and those of the vehicle's owner if it isn't yours), registration number and insurance details to anyone else involved in the accident. You should also, of course, obtain the same information from them as well as the details of any witnesses. Before leaving the scene of the accident it's advisable to take photographs or make drawings of the scene and note any relevant information, such as the date, time and location of the accident; the weather and road conditions; the speed of the vehicles involved; any road signs or markings; and, if appropriate, details of any injuries sustained.

Driving Licences

The minimum age for driving in Ireland is 17 for a motor car or a motorcycle with an engine capacity over 125cc and 16 for a motorcycle up to 125cc. There's no maximum age for obtaining your first licence and it has been known for people in their late 70s to take driving lessons for the first time. Anyone can drive in Ireland on a foreign or international driving licence for up to 12 months, even in an Irish-registered vehicle. Drivers of EU-registered vehicles don't require a green card, although it's recommended (see below). Those living permanently in Ireland, on the other hand, must obtain an Irish driving licence within one year of taking up residence. Citizens of the EU, Australia, Iceland, Japan, Liechtenstein, South Africa and Switzerland can exchange their national licences for an Irish one (it's expected that this won't be necessary for EU nationals by the end of 1999).

All other foreigners must apply for a provisional Irish driving licence (valid for two years) and take an Irish driving test. Presently this consists of a practical test only, but a written test similar to the British one is to be introduced some time in 1999. The cost of a driving test is IR£30. No medical examination is necessary unless you wish to obtain a truck or bus licence or are suffering from a recognised illness (e.g. diabetes) or disability. If it's your first driving test, however, you'll need to produce an eyesight report. Driving licences aren't issued for life (as, for example, in the UK) and must be renewed every ten years at a cost of IR£20. This isn't simply because they wear out, but so that you can be recognised more easily from your photograph, which must be replaced at the same time.

Car Insurance

Under Irish law, all motor vehicles plus trailers and semi-trailers must be insured when entering Ireland. However, it isn't mandatory for cars insured in most European countries to have an international insurance 'green card' (see below) in Ireland. Motorists insured in an EU country, the Czech Republic, Hungary, Liechtenstein, Norway, Slovakia and Switzerland are automatically covered for third-party liability in Ireland. There are essentially two categories of car insurance available in Ireland: third-party and comprehensive.

Third-Party: Third-party insurance is compulsory and is the minimum required by law. A third party is anyone apart from the driver, including your own passengers, and you must be insured against third-party claims for personal injury and damage to property. There's no limit to your liability if you have third-party insurance, although it won't usually cover you against natural hazards such as rocks falling on your car. Additional cover can be purchased to protect against personal accidents as well as fire, theft (of the car or your possessions inside it), windscreen damage, roadside assistance, etc. Personal accident cover, for example, costs an additional IR£10 to IR£20 per year.

Comprehensive: Comprehensive insurance usually covers all risks listed above and includes damage to your own vehicle irrespective of how it's caused. It usually includes theft of factory-fitted stereo systems and may also cover legal expenses in the event of a court case. Comprehensive cover is usually available on all vehicles irrespective of age, but cars over four years old may need to be inspected before insurance is granted. Note that comprehensive cover may be compulsory for lease and credit purchase contracts. Irish insurance doesn't always pay for a replacement car when yours is being repaired after an accident, although this is becoming more common.

Premiums: Insurance premiums in Ireland vary enormously according to numerous factors including the kind of insurance; type and make of car; your age and sex; accident record; and the area where you live. A policy which costs IR£200 for a middle-aged female with a good driving record living in the country may cost a young Dublin man with a poor record IR£3,000. There are some 25 companies providing car insurance in Ireland, each offering different packages and rates. Some companies separate cars into insurance brackets or groups (as in the UK), although most vary their rates according to the value, age and engine size of a car. Some won't insure high performance vehicles, while others offer special low-cost policies for experienced older drivers, e.g. those aged over 50 or 55, with a good safety record. Your annual mileage, on the other hand, won't usually affect the price you pay. Most companies in Ireland charge men and women different rates (women generally pay less). If you've been driving for a year or more without an insurance claim, you may be entitled to a 'no-claims bonus', which is usually transferable from one insurance company to another providing you furnish sufficient evidence of no claims. You should therefore shop around or, better still, use an insurance broker such as National Insurance Ltd. (☎ 01-874 5392) to do it for you.

In addition to the many Irish insurance companies, car insurance is also available from a number of foreign insurance companies registered in Ireland. In general the Irish car insurance market is quite stable and there are few 'cowboy' operators to be avoided. Short-term policies for periods of less than one year are available for a small premium from a few companies in Ireland. There's no VAT on insurance premiums, but there's a government levy of 2 per cent which goes towards a fund to pay for injuries caused by uninsured drivers.

Green Cards: All Irish insurance companies and most other insurance companies in Western Europe provide an automatic 'green card', which extends your normal insurance cover (e.g. comprehensive) to most other European countries. This is available on request and is usually free. The exception is Britain, where insurance companies usually provide only third-party cover in other EU countries and charge for a green card which is only issued for limited periods (i.e. 30 to 45 days) and for a maximum number of days a year, e.g. 90. (This is to discourage the British from driving abroad, where they are a menace and a danger to all road users, as most don't know their left from their right – particularly the politicians!) However, you should shop around, as some companies allow drivers a green card for up to six months a year. If you're British and have comprehensive insurance, it's wise to have a green card when visiting Ireland.

If you drive a British-registered car and spend over six months a year in other EU countries, you may need to take out a special (i.e. expensive) European insurance policy or obtain insurance with a European company. Another alternative is to insure your car with a British insurance company in Ireland. Note that from 1995, EU rules have required that all vehicles be insured in their country of registration. For example, if you keep a British-registered car in Ireland, you can insure it through an insurance agent in Ireland, but it must be with a UK-based insurance company. If you want to insure your car with an Irish company, you'll need to re-register it in Ireland. Similarly, if you have an Irish-registered car, it must be insured with an Irish insurance company (or a foreign insurance company registered in Ireland). Irish residents are obliged to display a valid insurance disc on their cars and failure to do so can result in a fine of IR£50.

Car Crime

All European countries have a problem with car crime, i.e. thefts of and from cars, but happily Ireland's is less severe than most, except perhaps in Dublin, where quite a lot of cars are stolen (often by young joyriders). It goes without saying that you should always lock your car and never leave any valuables inside it. If you drive anything other than a worthless heap you should have theft insurance, which includes your car stereo and personal belongings. If you drive a new or valuable car, it's wise to have it fitted with an alarm, an engine immobiliser (the best system) or another anti-theft device, plus a visible deterrent such as a steering or gear stick lock. It's particularly important to protect your car if you own a model that's desirable to professional car thieves, e.g. most new sports and executive models, which are often stolen by crooks to order.

Few cars are fitted with deadlocks and most can be broken into in seconds by a competent thief. However, even the best security system won't prevent someone from breaking into your car (which usually takes expert thieves a matter of seconds) and may not stop your car being stolen, but it will at least make it more difficult and may persuade a thief to look for an easier target. If you buy an expensive stereo system, you should choose one with a removable unit or with a removable (face-off) control panel that you can pop into a pocket or bag. However, never forget to remove it (and your mobile telephone), even when parking for a few minutes. Some manufacturers provide stereo systems that won't work when they're removed from their original vehicles or are inoperable without a security code.

Thieves often smash windows to steal stereo systems and other articles from cars, even articles of little value such as sunglasses or cigarettes. When leaving your car unattended, store any valuables (including clothes) in the boot (trunk). Note, however, that storing valuables in the boot isn't foolproof, as when a car is empty a thief may be tempted to force open the boot with a crowbar. Some people leave the boot of their car unlocked (and empty) to avoid having it broken open, as it can be expensive to repair. It's never advisable to leave your original car papers in your car (which will help a thief dispose of it). When parking overnight or when it's dark, it's advisable to park in a secure overnight car park or garage, or at least in a well-lit area. If possible, avoid parking in insecure long-term car parks as they are favourite hunting grounds for car thieves. Foreign-registered cars, particularly camper vans and mobile homes, are popular targets, particularly when parked in ferry ports.

If your car (or any of its contents) is stolen, report it to the police in the area where it occurred. You can report it by telephone, but must go to the station to complete a report. Don't, however, expect the police to find it or even take any interest in your loss. Report a theft to your insurance company as soon as possible.

Car Rental

Renting a car in Ireland isn't cheap. Although there's considerable competition among rental companies, demand for rental cars has increased over the last few years as more and more people visit Ireland. At best the rates are comparable with those in France and the UK, but high by US standards. A small family car (group A), for example, costs from around IR£135 per week compared with IR£95 in Spain, IR£140 in France, and IR£145 in the UK. Seasonal variations, on the other hand, are smaller than in some other countries. If you're paying IR£135 for a week's rental of a small car in the low season, you should expect to pay only an extra IR£20 or IR£30 in the summer. Major international companies such as Avis, Hertz and Budget have offices at major airports and in main towns, as do local companies such as Murrays Europcar

(☎ 01-614 2830). Car rental companies are listed in the Golden Pages under Car Hire.

While smaller companies may offer cheaper rates, they usually charge extra for leaving the car anywhere other than where you hired it (particularly if it's in the middle of nowhere), whereas the multi-nationals allow you to do so for free, at least on a week's hire or longer (you'll need to pay around IR£30 extra for the same facility on a day's hire). You can often save money by booking in advance (which is always advisable at peak times), particularly if you take a fly-drive or sail-drive package through an airline, ferry company or tour operator. If you're coming from America and have credit card insurance (though not with American Express), you can save as much as IR£60 on a week's car rental.

You need to be aged at least 21 to hire a car in Ireland, but most companies have a minimum age limit of 23 and some 25, 26 or even 27. Some companies charge extra for 21 to 24 year-olds and there's usually an upper age limit too, which varies between 65 and 75. You also usually need to have held a driving licence for at least 12 months without endorsements. When booking in advance, you should specify an automatic model if you're unused to a manual (stick-shift) gearbox as most rental cars are manual – but note that these are often more expensive (by as much as 25 per cent in some cases).

Prices generally vary quite a bit, so shop around. Most companies have special low rates for weekend hire and for rentals of 14 days or longer. When comparing rates, check what's included in the price. Basic third-party insurance is usually included in the hire charge, but make sure that you check exactly what you're covered for. In some cases you can be liable for the cost of damage to a car unless you pay an additional Collision Damage Waiver (CDW) premium of between IR£3 and IR£5 per day (although this is usually included these days). Personal accident insurance can usually be taken out for a similar premium and a second driver can be added for between IR£10 and IR£15 a week. Some companies don't offer unlimited mileage and provide a certain number of 'free' kilometres (or miles) after which there's a charge per kilometre, which usually works out more expensive unless you plan to drive a relatively short distance only. Theft protection is usually included, but VAT at 12.5 per cent may or may not be.

If required, check that you're permitted to take a car out of Ireland, e.g. to Northern Ireland, as you may need extra insurance, although there's usually no additional charge. For an extra fee you may be able to obtain extras such as baby seats and roof racks. Note also that there's usually an accident 'excess' of at least IR£150 but which can be as high as IR£400. In other words, if you crash the car you may need to pay that amount even if you're properly insured. About 30 car hire companies are members of the Car Rental Council of Ireland (CRCI), which means that they have been approved by the Irish Tourist Board (a list is available from the CRCI, ☎ 01-676 1690).

When choosing a rental car, bear in mind that if you're touring you should ensure that you have sufficient power for mountain driving, e.g. at least a 1.6 litre engine for two people and their luggage. When parking overnight or at any time in cities, don't leave any valuables in your car (see page 52). Always check the car (e.g. for body damage and to ensure that everything works) and the contract carefully before setting out.

Drivers must produce a valid licence (a copy isn't acceptable) and some drivers require an international driving licence. If more than one person will be driving, all the drivers' names must be entered on the rental agreement. Unless you use a credit card, you'll usually need to pay a cash deposit equivalent to the excess and possibly the whole rental in advance. When paying by credit card, carefully check your bill and statement as unauthorised charges aren't unknown. It may be possible to sign a credit card authorisation slip and pay cash when you return a car. However, if you do this, you must make sure that you obtain (and destroy) the credit card payment slip.

2.

FURTHER
CONSIDERATIONS

This chapter contains important considerations for most people planning to buy a home in Ireland, particularly those planning to live there permanently or semi-permanently. It includes information about climate, geography, health, insurance, shopping, pets, TV and radio, and learning English and Irish.

CLIMATE

Hardly surprisingly, Ireland's climate isn't the overwhelming attraction for most foreigners. Ireland is one of the wettest countries in Europe, with average annual rainfall in parts of the west coast (where it rains on at least half the days of the year) as high as 20cm a month and nowhere is it much less than 5cm a month. The driest regions are in the east and in low-lying areas. Influenced by the relatively warm waters of the Gulf Stream and the prevailing south-westerly winds from the Atlantic, Ireland enjoys generally mild temperatures. Winters are cool and summers warm, although extremes of temperature are rare. July and August usually bring the highest temperatures, around 14°C to 24°C, and most of the country enjoys an average of at least six hours of sunshine a day between May and August. Nevertheless, you're unlikely to encounter lengthy spells of dry, sunny weather, and bright intervals between showers are more common as are what the locals refer to as 'soft' days, when the rain is like a fine mist. The best advice is to expect constant rain and then you'll be pleasantly surprised when the sun appears, as even the wettest days often have sunny intervals. Perhaps this is why the Irish are habitually optimistic about the weather.

If summer is rarely hot, winter is seldom severe, with only occasional snow except on high ground. Spring tends to be relatively dry and autumn mild until as late as the end of November. The coldest months are January and February, when average temperatures are usually between 4 and 7°C. The 'reward' for all that rain is, of course, the lush green vegetation for which Ireland is famous. The Irish are almost as obsessed by the weather as the British and frequent weather forecasts are given on TV and radio and in daily newspapers.

GEOGRAPHY

The Republic of Ireland (*Poblacht na hÉireann* or simply *Éire*) forms the greater part of the island of Ireland in the Atlantic Ocean to the west of Britain (encompassing England, Scotland and Wales) lying between 51½° and 55½° north latitude and between 5½° and 10½° west longitude. The island, which is one of the British Isles, also includes Northern Ireland, part of the United Kingdom. The Republic is sometimes referred to as Southern Ireland, although that's a misnomer as the most northerly point on the island, Malin Head in County Donegal, is within the Republic. The island is separated from the British mainland by the Irish Sea. While Northern Ireland is only some 30km (19mi) from the coast of Scotland and is easily visible on a clear day, the nearest point to the Irish Republic in southern Britain is St David's Head in South Wales, which is some 80km (50mi) away across St George's Channel. The Republic of Ireland covers an area of 70,282km² (27,136 sq. mi.) and measures 486km (303mi) from north to south and 303km (189mi) from east to west.

Overall, Ireland resembles a shallow bowl with hills and mountains forming a rim around the coast where often dramatic cliffs are interspersed with sandy beaches (or strands). Ireland's highest mountain, Carrantuohill, rises to 1,041m (3,414ft) in a range called Macgillicuddy's Reeks in County Kerry in the extreme south-west. Other mountain ranges are to be found higher up the west coast in the counties of Donegal and Galway. The most spectacular cliffs are also in the west, the highest plunging nearly 2,000 ft (650m) into the sea at Slieve League in Co. Donegal.

The central part of Ireland consists of a flat or gently rolling limestone plain, occasionally interrupted by low hills (called *drumlins*) and liberally scattered with lakes (or *loughs*) and bogs where the land is below the water table. This is where Ireland's famous peat comes from, while its equally famous lush grass grows on the higher ground, which is covered with rich, light soil. The gently winding River Shannon is Ireland's longest river, almost dividing the country in half. Other major rivers include the Erne in the north, and the Slaney, Barrow, Sluir and Blackwater in the south. There are literally hundreds of lakes on the island, the two largest being in Northern Ireland. The most attractive, Lough Corrib, Lough Mask and Lough Conn, are in the west of Ireland, not forgetting Loughs Allen, Derg and Ree, through which the River Shannon flows on its leisurely way to Limerick and the sea. There are also numerous tiny islands just off the west coast of Ireland, the best-known being the Aran Islands in Galway Bay (not to be confused with the Isle of Arran off Scotland's west coast, where the wool comes from).

Ireland is divided into four provinces of roughly equal size: Munster (south), Connacht (west), Ulster (north) and Leinster (east). These derive from pre-Christian times (roughly corresponding to the divisions made by the Fir Bolg invaders) and have no political significance. Part of Ulster, for example, is in Northern Ireland and part in the Republic. They are, however, socially and culturally important: Ulster is supposedly the land of battle, Munster the land of music, Leinster of prosperity, and Connacht of learning. How true this is today is open to question. The capital, Dublin (*Baile Átha Cliath*) lies on the east coast and has a population of around one million. It's the only really large city in Ireland, the next biggest being Cork with a population of around 130,000. No other town exceeds 60,000 and more than half the population lives in rural areas.

Like Britain, Ireland is on GMT (i.e. five hours ahead of US eastern time and one hour behind standard European time) from late March until late October. For the other half of the year Ireland is on GMT plus one hour, i.e. six hours ahead of US eastern time.

HEALTH

One of the most important aspects of living in Ireland (or anywhere else for that matter) is maintaining good health. The quality of health care and health care facilities in Ireland is generally excellent, although facilities are limited in some rural areas. There are around 1,650 GPs (general practitioners) in Ireland and the number of people per doctor (approximately 680 on average) is about the same as in the UK, although higher than in most of the rest of Europe. However, the number of public hospitals is limited. Irish medical staff are highly trained and major hospitals are equipped with the latest equipment. Since 1970, Ireland's public health system has been administered by eight Regional Health Boards, which come under the jurisdiction of the Department of Health and Children. The Department's four-year plan, 'shaping a healthier future', is due to end in 1998 when a wide-ranging review of health services will take place.

Ireland and the UK are the only EU countries where you can obtain public health care without having to make social security contributions. In Ireland your entitlement to benefits is determined solely by your residence status. The Health (Amendment) Act 1991 introduced the concept of 'ordinary residence', which is the minimum requirement for eligibility. In order to be 'ordinarily resident' in Ireland, non-EU nationals must be able to show that they intend to remain in Ireland for a minimum of one year. This means producing an Alien's Registration Book or residence/work permit, proof of property purchase or rental (including evidence that it's your principal residence), confirmation of registration with a school or college, or details of an Irish bank account. Note that if you establish ordinary residence, your dependants won't necessarily be eligible for public health care unless they are also ordinarily resident. EU citizens who are resident in Ireland but insured in another EU or EEA country are automatically eligible for health care as are their dependants, although if you're self-employed you'll receive few benefits (see page 52). If you're ordinarily resident in Ireland and receiving a social security pension from another EU country, you're entitled to public health care providing you don't also have an Irish Department of Social Welfare pension and aren't earning over IR£2,500 per year from employment or self-employment in Ireland.

Unemployed people seeking work need form E119 and students form E109 to qualify for public health care. Temporary EU visitors can obtain free emergency treatment on production of form E111 (see below). Irish nationals returning to Ireland who aren't covered by EU regulations are regarded as ordinarily resident if they're employed or self-employed in Ireland, or provide evidence that they intend to remain in Ireland for a minimum of one year. If they have been abroad for less than three years, they may be entitled to benefits in any case. Anyone who doesn't meet any of the above criteria will usually have to pay the 'commercial rate' for medical treatment and other benefits, although the Health Board may authorise urgent treatment at a reduced rate or even free in certain cases.

There are two categories of entitlement to public health care in Ireland. Category 1 eligibility (a 'medical card') entitles you to the full range of medical services without charge; Category 2 entitles you to only a limited range of services without charge. EU citizens resident in Ireland but insured in another EU country automatically receive a medical card, as do pensioners and those seeking work in Ireland (see above). Otherwise, eligibility for medical cards is means tested, i.e. assessed according to your income. The upper income limit is adjusted annually in January and varies according to age, family status and other factors, but in general Category 1 eligibility applies to those with low incomes (officially around 36 per cent of the population). A medical card entitles you to free GP services; prescribed drugs and medicines; in-patient and out-patient services in a public hospital; dental, optical and aural services and appliances; and maternity and infant care during pregnancy and for up to six weeks after birth.

Everyone else who's entitled to public health care falls into Category 2, which means that they must pay for medicines and prescriptions, routine dental, optical or aural treatment, in addition to for visits to a doctor (IR£18 to IR£20 for a routine consultation). Maternity care and public hospital out-patient services are free, but a daily charge of IR£25 is payable for in-patient accommodation and IR£20 for a visit to an accident and emergency department (unless referred by a doctor). Those who don't usually qualify for public health care but have achieved a certain level of Irish PRSI (social security) contributions may be entitled to some benefits. The required levels are 39 weeks' PRSI contributions for those aged under 25 and 260 weeks for those over 25.

If you aren't entitled to a medical card, you're usually sent a letter by the Department of Health and Children confirming your entitlement to Category 2 benefits. You will then be free to register with any doctor who can accommodate you. Medical card holders are sent a list of 'approved' doctors from which to choose and can switch to another doctor in the same area, depending on the availability of places. Note that even if you're entitled to free hospitalisation, you have the option to pay for private or semi-private accommodation, which costs from IR£60 a day.

There are various schemes designed to offset the cost of drugs and medicines for those with serious or long-term illnesses. Under the 'drug refund scheme', you may claim a refund if you spend over IR£90 on prescribed drugs within three months. The 'drugs cost subsidisation scheme' assists those without a medical card who are certified as having a long-term (i.e. more than 12 months) medical condition that requires drugs costing over IR£32 a month. If you suffer from certain long-term conditions such as diabetes, epilepsy, multiple sclerosis or Parkinson's Disease, you can obtain a long-term illness book which entitles you to free medication. Each Health Board is responsible for ambulance services and some make a charge.

The cost of private nursing homes is high in Ireland, as is the demand for places. However, if you're paying nursing home fees for your spouse (or, in certain cases, another relative), you may be entitled to tax relief, and those on lower incomes may qualify for assistance such as a Nursing Homes Subvention. There's a dependent relative allowance of IR£110 and a small amount of tax relief available to those with dependent relatives living with them. Children are entitled to free immunisation up to the age of 15 months and annual school dental check-ups.

Various benefits are available to those with disabilities, although most are means tested. There's a disability allowance for those aged 16 to 66 with a long-term (i.e. more than 12 months) disability and a blind welfare allowance for those over 18. Disabled drivers can obtain a government grant to help them buy or adapt a car and in certain cases are exempt from motor tax and vehicle registration tax, plus VAT and duty on fuel. A new kind of parking permit for those with disabilities was introduced in December 1997, which applies to the person rather than the vehicle and can therefore be used by any vehicle transporting a disabled passenger. Further details of entitlements for those with disabilities can be obtained from the National Social Service Board (☎ 01-605 9099), and information about equipment and resources from the Disability Resource Centre (☎ 01-874 7503) and the Irish Wheelchair Association (☎ 01-833 8241).

Short-term visitors to Ireland (i.e. those who aren't ordinarily resident) from EU countries are entitled to free urgent medical treatment. Unless you're a UK national, you need to produce form E111 (which you should obtain from your own health authority before travelling). Non-EU visitors are entitled to nothing free!

In general, the Irish are as healthy as any other Europeans and have an average life expectancy of 73 for men and 79 for women (Guinness is good for you). The infant mortality rate of eight deaths under the age of 5 per 1,000 births is also comparable with the rest of Europe. However, according to the National Council on

Ageing and Older People, almost half of Irish citizens over 65 have major health problems (which doesn't of course mean that if you move to Ireland you'll necessarily have a greater chance of incurring such problems!). Cardiovascular disease is the major cause of death in Ireland, which has the highest death rate for heart disease in the EU – almost double the EU average. Deaths from cancer, the second most frequent cause of death, are also above the EU average, although only slightly. The number of deaths from accidents, on the other hand, is well below the EU average.

The Irish are particularly health conscious and health education is part of children's schooling. The Health Promotion Unit of the Department of Health and Children organises campaigns such as 'Smokebusters', a smoking prevention programme for youngsters, 'Smoking Cessation and Reduction Programme' (SCRAP) and 'On My Own Two Feet', a substance abuse prevention scheme, in addition to national Healthy Eating Weeks and No Smoking Days. Employers are also aware of the value of good health (and the cost of ill health). It's estimated that 15 per cent of employers provide free private health insurance as a standard benefit for employees and some 70 per cent make a contribution. Many employers also offer subsidised fitness club membership or provide 'in-house' fitness facilities.

As in many other countries, the use of illegal drugs is on the increase in Ireland, particularly that of heroin and other opiate drugs. The problem is largely confined to the Dublin area, but there's also some drug abuse in Cork and Limerick. The smoking of cannabis is also fairly widespread, as is solvent abuse, although the use of other drugs such as LSD, amphetamines and cocaine is at quite low levels. The use of *legal* drugs (i.e. tobacco and alcohol), on the other hand, is as high as anywhere else in the world, particularly among the young. Between 1980 and 1990, alcohol consumption increased in Ireland faster than in any other European country except Holland, although it has since slowed and Ireland now has the highest percentage (25 per cent) of people in the EU aged 15 and over who *don't* drink alcohol.

Cigarette smoking is also on the decline, with only some 30 per cent of adults being regular smokers. Nevertheless, an amazing 20 per cent of all Irish consumer spending is on tobacco and alcohol products, and it's estimated that almost 30 per cent of the population is dependent on either nicotine or alcohol. As in other countries, there's a growing anti-smoking movement in Ireland. Not only are there strict advertising controls, but smoking is forbidden in many public places including cinemas, theatres, schools and other public buildings, as well as in buses, trains and taxis. There's also a strong anti-drugs campaign led by the Drugs Task Force, the Department of Education and the National Parents Council. This has been partially successful in controlling the extent of drug abuse among children, although a recent Department of Health Survey indicated that almost 20 per cent of secondary-level school children have taken some kind of drug or substance.

According to statistics published by the Department of Health and Children, there has been an annual average of around 27 deaths from AIDS in Ireland since the epidemic began to be monitored in 1986. This equates to around one in 130,000 people, which is similar to the UK figure, where the death rate is around 300 per year (down from 1,000 a year in the mid-'90s) out of a population of some 55 million.

Health & Retirement

From a psychological point of view, Ireland's slower pace of life is beneficial to those who are prone to stress (it's difficult to remain up-tight while gazing out over green fields listening to the bleating of sheep), although it takes many foreigners some time to adjust. The climate and lifestyle in any country has a noticeable effect on mental health and this should be taken into account when considering buying a home in Ireland.

Maintaining good health is an important issue for anyone retiring to Ireland. Many people are ill-prepared for old age and the possibility of health problems, although you're better provided for in Ireland than in many other countries. All retirees over 65, whether or not they have a medical card, are entitled to regular visits by a public health nurse and, if required, occupational therapy. Meals on wheels and a home help service are provided by voluntary organisations on behalf of the Health Board, usually for a small fee. A few hospitals are 'day hospitals', where services such as physiotherapy are available for a lower fee than at in-patient departments. A number of public hospitals have specialised geriatric departments, although these aren't intended for long-term care. For this you'll need to be admitted to either a geriatric hospital or a welfare home. In both cases you'll be expected to make a means-related contribution towards your keep (known as 'extended-stay maintenance charges', which are determined by Regional Health Boards). If you need to be admitted to a nursing home and there's no space at a state home (e.g. there are only eight in the Dublin area), the Health Board will pay a subvention of up to IR£120 per week towards the cost of accommodation in a private home (of which there are over 100 in Dublin).

There are also grants for security devices for elderly people living alone, although these aren't usually paid directly to individuals. Other schemes offer home improvement grants, free draught proofing and insulation (in some parts of the country), and house alterations for disabled people. The only universal benefit for elderly people is free travel, for which everyone over 66 qualifies, but even that has various conditions attached. Note that, in general, to obtain any benefits in Ireland you must apply for them. No one is going to come along and offer them to you! On the other hand, a number of private establishments such as cinemas, theatres and other places of entertainment, as well as hairdressers, dry-cleaners and certain shops, offer reductions to pensioners, and anyone over 60 can take advantage of 'Golden Holidays' (contact the Tourist Board for details).

Ireland's provision for handicapped travellers is improving as awareness of the need for such facilities increases. New building regulations introduced in 1991 require all public buildings to be wheelchair accessible, so that all modern hotels and restaurants (etc.) have good access. The Irish Wheelchair Association (☎ 01-833 8241) has a database of accessible buildings and will provide a list on request.

Pre-Departure Check: If you're planning to take up residence in Ireland, even for just part of the year, it's wise to have a health check (medical or screening, eyes, teeth, etc.) before your arrival, particularly if you have a record of poor health or are elderly. If you're already taking regular medication, you should note that the brand names of drugs and medicines vary from country to country, and should ask your doctor for the generic name. If you wish to match medication prescribed abroad, you'll need a current prescription with the medication's trade name, the manufacturer's name, the chemical name and the dosage. Most drugs have an equivalent in other countries, although particular brands may be difficult or impossible to obtain in Ireland. It's possible to have medication sent from abroad, when no import duty or value added tax is usually payable. If you're visiting a holiday home in Ireland for a limited period, you should take sufficient medication to cover your stay. In an emergency a local doctor will write a prescription which can be filled at a local pharmacy. It's also advisable to take some of your favourite non-prescription drugs (e.g. pain killers, cold and flu remedies, lotions, etc.) with you, as they may be difficult or impossible to obtain in Ireland or may be more expensive. If applicable, take a spare pair of spectacles, contact lenses, dentures or a hearing aid with you.

There are no special health risks in Ireland and no immunisations are required. However, although you're unlikely to get sunburn, you can suffer badly from midge bites on warm summer evenings, particularly on the west coast, so it's as well to stock up with insect repellent. Wasps, hornets and horseflies can also be quite persistent in the summer months. You can safely drink the water anywhere in Ireland (but the stout tastes *much* better!). Note that the telephone number to dial in emergencies is 999 or 112.

INSURANCE

An important aspect of owning a home in Ireland (or anywhere else) is insurance, not only for your home and its contents, but also travel and health insurance for your family when visiting Ireland. If you live in Ireland permanently, you'll require additional insurance. It's unnecessary to spend half your income insuring yourself against every eventuality from the common cold to being sued for your last penny, although it's important to insure against any event that could precipitate a major financial disaster, such as a serious accident or your house being demolished by a storm. The cost of being uninsured or under-insured can be astronomical!

As with anything connected with finance, it's important to shop around when buying insurance. Simply collecting a few brochures from insurance agents or making a few telephone calls can save you a lot of money. Note, however, that not all insurance companies are equally reliable or have the same financial stability, and it may be better to insure with a large international company with a good reputation rather than with a small local company, even if this means paying a higher premium. Read all insurance contracts carefully and make sure that you understand the terms and the cover provided before signing them. Some insurance companies will do almost anything to avoid paying out on claims and will use any available legal loophole, therefore it pays to deal with reputable companies only (not that this provides a foolproof guarantee). Note that Irish insurance companies can compel you to renew your insurance for a further year if you don't give adequate written notice (e.g. up to three months) of your intention to terminate it, although most companies allow policy holders to cancel on renewal. Check in advance.

In all matters regarding insurance, you're responsible for ensuring that you and your family are legally insured in Ireland. Regrettably you cannot insure yourself against being uninsured or sue your insurance agent for giving you bad advice! Bear in mind that if you wish to make a claim on an insurance policy, you may be required to report an incident to the local police within 24 hours (this may also be a legal requirement). The law in Ireland may differ considerably from that in your home country or your previous country of residence and you should *never* assume that it's the same. If you're unsure of your rights, you're advised to obtain legal advice for anything other than a minor claim. Under EU rules, an insurance company registered in an EU member country can sell its policies in any other EU country.

The following pages contain information about health insurance, household insurance, third-party liability insurance and travel insurance. See also **Car Insurance** on page 51.

Health Insurance

If you're visiting, living or working in Ireland and aren't entitled to public health care (see page 59), it's extremely risky not to have private health insurance for your family, because if you're uninsured or under-insured you could be faced with some *very* high medical bills. When deciding on the kind and extent of health insurance, make sure that it covers *all* your family's present and future health requirements in Ireland. A health insurance policy should cover you for *all* essential health care whatever the reason, including accidents (e.g. sports accidents) and injuries, whether they occur in your home, at your place of work or while travelling. Don't take anything for granted but check in advance. Note, for example, that BUPA's health insurance covers car accidents whereas VHI's doesn't, although it's available for a small premium (see below).

Even if you're eligible for public health care, it's advisable (if you can afford it) to take out private health insurance, which provides a wider choice of medical practitioners and hospitals, and more importantly, frees you from public health waiting lists. Under the state system you may need to wait six months for a routine (non-urgent) operation, whereas with private insurance you can expect to be treated within two or three weeks. In many areas there are also long waiting lists for dental treatment. Some 40 per cent of Irish people have private health insurance, mainly to bypass waiting lists.

Proof of health insurance must usually be provided when applying for a visa or permission to set up a business in Ireland, so that the authorities can be sure you won't be a burden on the state if you require medical treatment. Visitors to Ireland should have holiday health insurance (see page 68) if they aren't covered by a reciprocal agreement. Note that some foreign insurance companies don't provide sufficient cover to satisfy Irish regulations and therefore you should check the minimum cover necessary with an Irish consulate in your country of residence. Long stay visitors should have travel or long stay health insurance or an international health policy (see **Health Insurance for Visitors** on page 68). If your stay in Ireland is limited, you may be covered by a reciprocal agreement between your home country and Ireland (see page 69). When travelling in Ireland you should carry proof of your health insurance with you at all times.

We're not in business to make money.

VHI is a not-for-profit organisation.

Any surplus is used to provide a better service for our members.

Over 40 years ago, VHI was founded on the principle that every man, woman and child in the community should have access to independent health care.

We're here to make a difference.

This principle still stands today.

To 1.4 million Irish people, VHI continues to make a great deal of sense, because it still makes a real difference.

VHI's new *Option* plans offer you an even wider choice of healthcare cover. For more details on how you can share the security of VHI's 1.4 million Members, call 1-850 444 844 (calls charged at local rate).

 The Better Way

Dublin: VHI House, Lower Abbey Street, Dublin 1. Tel: (01) 872 4499. Cork: VHI House, 70 South Mall. Tel: (021) 277188.
Dun Laoghaire: 35/36 Lower George's Street. Tel: (01) 280 0306. Galway: VHI House, 10 Eyre Square. Tel: (091) 563715.
Limerick: Gardner House, Charlotte Quay. Tel: (061) 316122. Website: http://www.vhi.ie/ E-mail: info@vhi.ie

Private Health Insurance for Residents

The two main private health insurers in Ireland are the Voluntary Health Insurance (VHI) board and the British-based BUPA. If you're already covered by private health insurance abroad, you may be able to transfer to VHI or BUPA in Ireland (both companies have reciprocal agreements with other insurance companies including Blue Shield, Blue Cross and PPP). EU legislation requires insurers to allow members to transfer to another provider without penalty. Both VHI and BUPA premiums are calculated on the basis of 'community rating', which means that all members pay the same amount and premiums don't increase with age. This does mean that younger people are generally paying more than they would under a purely risk-based system. There is, however, a lower rate for those aged under 21 with BUPA or aged under 18 with VHI. You must be under 65 to join BUPA, but once you're a member there's no upper age limit. The same is true for the normal cover offered by VHI, but over 65s can be accepted onto 'Plan P', which covers the cost of routine hospitalisation (for which you would normally be charged IR£25 per night for the first ten nights).

Neither BUPA nor VHI require new policy holders to have a medical examination, but both organisations impose a 'waiting period' of 26 weeks for those under 55 and 52 weeks if you're over 55, during which you're unable to make claims. If you become pregnant within 52 weeks of joining, you won't be entitled to maternity benefit. If you have a 'pre-existing' medical condition, you'll need to have been a member for at least five years (seven years if you're aged over 55 but under 60 and ten years if you're over 60) before being able to claim for treatment for that condition. These conditions are standard among all private health insurance companies in Ireland, but they are also 'transferable', i.e. if you have been a member of VHI for 26 weeks and transfer to BUPA (or vice versa), you'll be entitled to claim immediately.

VHI is a non-profit organisation established in 1957 with some 1.4 million members. The Irish insurance market was deregulated in July 1994 and BUPA services became available in November 1996. Although BUPA doesn't disclose membership figures, it's estimated to have at least 30,000 members in Ireland. Some of BUPA's early plans, such as cash plans, subsequently had to be revised and are no longer available. It offers a choice of three plans (Essential, Essential Plus and Essential Gold), whereas VHI has no fewer than ten to choose from (A to E with options on each). Although VHI claims 50 per cent lower running costs than UK health insurers, its premiums are similar to BUPA's. BUPA's lowest child rate, for example, is around IR£50 compared with VHI's Plan A rate of around IR£60 and adult charges start at IR£188 with BUPA and IR£182 with VHI. Both companies operate group schemes (for six or more members) for companies and organisations providing a 10 per cent reduction off individual rates. BUPA's group rates start at around IR£155, VHI's at around IR£180. Private health insurance is provided by many employers in Ireland, although in most cases employees are required to make a contribution. Note that tax relief at the standard rate (26 per cent) is available to those paying private health insurance.

The conditions and benefits offered by the two companies, however, are slightly different. For example, VHI covers around 100 hospitals compared with BUPA's 75 (BUPA's coverage is rather sparse in Connacht, and Ulster has just three hospitals to choose from), and BUPA provides full hospital cover whereas (in some cases) VHI pays only some 90 per cent of hospital bills. Both companies provide help towards maternity costs (up to IR£300), as well as offering an allowance for mothers who choose to give birth at home. BUPA also provides the option of certain 'approved' alternative therapies such as acupuncture. VHI charges an annual excess of up to IR£250 on claims for doctors' visits, X-rays, consultant and hospital out-patient fees, and certain other costs. BUPA charges an excess of IR£50 for certain kinds of hospital accommodation on its Essential Plus scheme, but there's no excess on the Gold scheme. Both VHI and BUPA operate a world-wide emergency medical assistance scheme (VHI call theirs 'VHI Assist'), which is included in the normal cover. Note that the rules applicable to both VHI and BUPA can change at any time, so you should check the current situation. BUPA Ireland is based at Mill Island, Fermoy, Co. Cork (☎ 025-42121) and VHI has offices in Dublin, Cork, Dun Laoghaire, Galway and Limerick (Dublin office ☎ 01-872 4499)

Changing Employers or Insurance Companies: When changing employers or leaving Ireland, you should ensure that you have continuous health insurance. If you and your family are covered by a company health plan, your insurance will probably cease after your last official day of employment. If you're planning to change your health insurance company, you should make sure that important benefits aren't lost; existing medical conditions, for example, won't usually be covered by a new insurer. When changing health insurance companies, it's advisable to inform your old company if you have any outstanding bills for which they are liable.

Health Insurance for Visitors

Visitors spending short periods in Ireland (e.g. up to a month) should have a travel health insurance policy (see page 68), particularly if they aren't covered by an international health policy. If you plan to spend up to six months in Ireland you should take out either a travel, special long stay or an international health policy (which should cover you in your home country and when travelling in other countries). Note that premiums vary considerably and it's important to shop around. Most international health policies include repatriation or evacuation (although it may be optional), which may also include shipment (by air) of the body of a person who dies abroad to his home country for burial. An international policy also allows you to decide to have non-urgent medical treatment in the country of your choice.

Most international insurance companies offer health policies for different areas, e.g. Europe, world-wide excluding North America, and world-wide including North America. Most companies also offer different levels of cover, for example basic, standard, comprehensive and prestige. There's always a limit on the total annual medical costs, which should be at least IR£250,000 (although many provide cover of up to IR£1M) and some companies also limit the charges for specific treatment or care such as specialists' fees, operations and hospital accommodation. A medical examination isn't usually required for international health policies, although existing health problems are excluded for a period, e.g. one or two years. Claims are usually settled in all major currencies and large claims are usually settled directly by insurance companies (although your choice of hospitals may be limited). Always check whether an insurance company will settle large medical bills directly, because if you're required to pay bills and claim reimbursement from an insurance company, it can take several months before you receive your money (some companies are slow to pay). Most international health insurance companies provide emergency telephone assistance.

The cost of international health insurance varies considerably depending on your age and the extent of cover. Note that with most international insurance policies, you must enrol before you reach a certain age, e.g. between 60 and 80 depending on the company, in order to be guaranteed continuous cover in your old age. Premiums can sometimes be paid monthly, quarterly or annually, although some companies insist on payment annually in advance. When comparing policies, carefully check the extent of cover and exactly what's included and excluded from a policy (often indicated only in the *very* small print), in addition to premiums and excess charges. In some countries, premium increases are limited by law, although this may apply only to residents in the country where a company is registered and not to overseas policy holders. Although there may be significant differences in premiums, generally you get what you pay for and can tailor premiums to your requirements.

The most important questions to ask yourself are: does the policy provide the cover required and is it good value for money? If you're in good health and are able to pay for your own out-patient treatment, such as visits to a family doctor and prescriptions, then the best value is a policy covering specialist and hospital treatment only.

Reciprocal Health Agreements: If you're entitled to social security health benefits in another EU country or in a country with a reciprocal health agreement with Ireland, you'll receive free or reduced cost medical treatment in Ireland. For emergency treatment, EU residents (other than UK citizens) should apply for a certificate of entitlement to treatment (form E111) from their local social security office before they travel to Ireland. The E111 form can officially be used for a stay of three months' duration only (although many people use them for much longer periods). If you use the E111 in Ireland, you must apply for reimbursement to Irish social security (instructions are provided with the form), which can take a number of months. Note, however, that you can still receive a large bill from an Irish hospital, as your local health authority assumes a percentage of the cost only. For example, although serious illnesses and accidents are totally reimbursed, minor ailments and injuries are reimbursed at 20 per cent only for out-patient treatment and 35 per cent for ambulance costs.

UK citizens don't require form E111 but need to show evidence of UK residence (e.g. a passport or driving licence). Note that a form E111 issued abroad (i.e. not in Ireland) isn't valid in Ireland if you're an Irish resident. Participating countries include all EU member states and most other European countries, excluding Albania, Switzerland and Turkey. The USA doesn't have a reciprocal health agreement with Ireland and therefore American students and other Americans who aren't covered by Irish social welfare *must* have private health insurance in Ireland. UK visitors and those planning to live in Ireland can obtain information about reciprocal health treatment from the Department of Social Security, Overseas Branch, Newcastle-upon-Tyne, NE98 1YX, UK (☎ 0191-225 3699).

Household Insurance

Household insurance in Ireland generally includes the building, its contents and third-party liability, all of which are contained in a multi-risk household insurance policy. Policies are offered by both Irish and foreign insurance companies, and premiums are similar, although foreign companies may provide more comprehensive cover.

Building: Although it isn't compulsory, it's wise for owners to take out property insurance (usually referred to as buildings insurance) that covers damage to a building due to fire, smoke, lightning, water, explosion, storm, freezing, snow, theft, vandalism, malicious damage, acts of terrorism, impact, broken windows and natural catastrophes (such as falling trees). Insurance should include glass, external buildings, aerials and satellite dishes, gardens and garden ornaments. Note that if a claim is the result of a defect in building or design, e.g. the roof is too heavy and collapses, the insurance company won't pay up (another reason why it's advisable to have a survey before buying a home).

Property insurance is based on the cost of rebuilding your home and should be increased annually in line with inflation. Make sure that you insure your property for the true cost of rebuilding. It's commonly thought that a property should be insured for its market value (i.e. the price it would fetch if put up for sale), but in fact the market value of a property often bears little relationship to the cost of rebuilding. The Society of Chartered Surveyors (☎ 01-676 5500) in Ireland publishes a *Guide to House Rebuilding Costs*, according to which the minimum rebuilding cost of properties in and around the three main cities is between IR£61 (for bungalows in the Galway area) and IR£75 (for terraced houses in Dublin) per square foot. It's particularly important to have insurance for storm damage in Ireland, which can be severe in some areas. If floods are one of your concerns, make sure you're covered for water coming in from ground level, not just for water seeping in through the roof. Always read the small print of contracts. Note that if you own a home in an area that has been hit by a succession of natural disasters (such as floods), your household insurance may be cancelled.

Contents: Contents are usually insured for the same risks as a building (see above) and are insured for their replacement value (new for old), with a reduction for wear and tear for clothes and linen. Valuable objects are covered for their actual declared (and authenticated) value. Most policies include automatic indexation of the insured sum in line with inflation. Contents insurance may include accidental damage to sanitary installations, theft of money, credit cards, bicycles, garden furniture, satellite dishes, replacement of locks following damage or loss of keys, frozen food, alternative accommodation, and property belonging to third parties stored in your home. Some items are usually optional, e.g. contact lenses, caravan and camping equipment, musical instruments, emergency assistance (plumber, glazier, electrician, etc.), redecoration, garaged cars, replacement pipes, loss of rent, and the cost of emergency travel to Ireland for holiday home owners. Many policies include personal third-party liability, e.g. up to IR£250,000, although this may be an option. Items of high value (e.g. over IR£1,500) must usually be itemised and documentation (i.e. a valuation) provided. A photograph may be required of anything worth over IR£5,000. Some companies even recommend or insist on a video film of belongings.

When claiming for contents, you should produce the original bills if possible (always keep bills for expensive items) and bear in mind that replacing imported items in Ireland may be more expensive than buying them abroad. Contents policies always contain security clauses and if you don't adhere to them a claim won't be considered. If you're planning to let a property, you may be required to inform your insurer. Note that a building must be secure with key operated locks on ground-floor windows and patio doors. Most companies give a discount if properties have high security locks and alarms (particularly alarms connected to a monitoring station), but only if they're installed to certain recognised standards. An insurance company may send someone to inspect your property and advise on security measures. Policies pay out for theft only when there are signs of forced entry and you aren't covered for thefts by a tenant (but may be covered for thefts by domestic personnel). All-risks policies offering a world-wide extension to a household policy covering jewellery, cameras and other items aren't usually available from Irish insurance companies, but are available from a number of foreign companies.

Leasehold Properties: If you own a leasehold property, such as an apartment or flat, buildings insurance will be arranged by your landlord or the management company (it's worth checking that it's adequate), so you'll be responsible only for insuring the contents of a property. Household insurance policies in Ireland usually include third-party liability up to a maximum amount, e.g. IR£250,000.

Holiday Homes: Premiums are generally higher for holiday homes, due to their high vulnerability, particularly to burglaries. Most policies include restrictions if a property is unoccupied for more than 30 days at a time. Premiums are usually based on the number of days a year a property is inhabited and the interval between periods of occupancy. Cover for theft, storm, flood and malicious damage may be suspended when a property is left empty for an extended period. Note that you're generally required to turn off the water supply at the mains when vacating a building for more than 72 hours. It's possible to negotiate cover for periods of absence for a hefty surcharge, although valuable items are usually excluded (unless you have a safe). If you're absent from your property for long periods, e.g. longer than 30 days a year, you may be required to pay an excess on a claim arising from an occurrence that takes place during your absence (and theft may be excluded). Note that (where applicable) it's important to ensure that a policy specifies a holiday home and not a principal home. In areas with a high risk of theft (e.g. major cities), an insurance company may insist on extra security measures. It's unwise to leave valuable or irreplaceable items in a holiday home or a property that will be vacant for long periods. Note that some insurance companies will do their utmost to find a loophole making you negligent and relieving them of liability. You should ensure that the details listed on a policy are correct, otherwise your policy could be void.

Rented Property: Your landlord will usually insist that you have third-party liability insurance. A lease requires you to insure against 'tenants' risks', including damage you may make to the rental property and to other properties if you live in an apartment, e.g. due to floods, fire or explosion. You can choose your own insurance company and aren't required to use one recommended by your landlord.

Premiums: Premiums are usually calculated on the size of a property, its age and type of construction, but the amount you'll pay may vary considerably according to a property's location and the measures you take to protect it from accidental damage and burglary. Smoke detectors, window locks and security alarms, for example, can reduce your insurance bill by as much as 15 per cent, and participation in a local Community Alert scheme by a further 5 per cent. If you're aged over 50 or 55, you may qualify for an extra discount of 10 per cent. Some companies also offer 'no-claims' bonuses of up to 20 per cent. Several companies offer a combined buildings and contents insurance with the contents automatically insured for 50 per cent of the value of the building. Some companies offer discounts (for alarms, community alert, etc.) only if you take out a combined policy, while others offer an extra 30 per cent discount on buildings and/or contents insurance if they also insure your car. A typical three-bedroom house in a Dublin suburb valued at IR£90,000 and fitted with smoke detectors and security alarms would cost around IR£200 a year to insure. For a similar property outside Dublin you may pay up to 30 per cent less. The contents of such a house should cost around IR£100 a year to insure. There's usually an excess of IR£50 or IR£100 (which may be reduced on payment of an additional premium). All insurance premiums are subject to a government levy of 2 per cent.

As policies and prices vary, it pays to shop around or to use a broker to do so on your behalf. The 600 members of the Irish Brokers Association (IBA) offer an independent service and are bound by a code of conduct as well as being required to offer a minimum compensation bond of IR£50,000 should you suffer financial loss as a result of their actions. Further details of the IBA and its members can be obtained on ☎ 01-661 3061.

Claims: If you wish to make a claim, you must usually inform your insurance company in writing (by registered letter) within two to seven days of an incident or 24 hours in the case of theft. Thefts should also be reported to the local *Gardaí* (police) within 24 hours, as the police report, of which you receive a copy for your insurance company, constitutes irrefutable evidence of your claim. Check whether you're covered for damage or thefts that occur while you're away from your property and are therefore unable to inform the insurance company immediately.

Take care that you don't under-insure your house contents and that you periodically reassess their value and adjust your insurance premium accordingly. You can arrange to have your insurance cover automatically increased annually by a fixed percentage or amount by your insurance company. If you make a claim and the assessor discovers that you're under-insured, the amount due will be reduced by the percentage by which you're under-insured. For example, if you're insured for IR£5,000 and you're found to be under-insured by 50 per cent, your claim for IR£1,000 will be reduced by 50 per cent and you'll lose IR£500.

Insuring Abroad: It's possible and legal to take out buildings and contents insurance in another country for a property in Ireland (some foreign insurance companies offer special policies for holiday home owners), although you must ensure that a policy is valid under Irish law. This may seem like a good option for a holiday home in Ireland, although it can be more expensive than insuring with an Irish company and can lead to conflicts if, for example, the building is insured with an Irish-registered company and the contents with a foreign based company. Most experts advise that you insure an Irish home and its contents with an Irish insurance company through a local agent.

Holiday & Travel Insurance

Holiday and travel insurance is recommended for all who don't wish to risk having their holiday or travel ruined by financial problems or to arrive home broke. As you probably know, anything can and often does go wrong with a holiday, sometimes before you even get started (particularly when you *don't* have insurance). The following information applies equally to both residents and non-residents, whether they are travelling to or from Ireland or within Ireland. Nobody should visit Ireland without travel (and health) insurance!

Travel insurance is available from many sources including travel agents, insurance companies and agents, banks, automobile clubs and transport companies (airline, rail and bus). Package holiday companies and tour operators also offer insurance policies, some of which are compulsory, too expensive and don't provide adequate cover. You can also buy 24-hour accident and flight insurance at major airports, although it's expensive and doesn't offer the best cover. Before taking out travel insurance, carefully consider the range and level of cover you require and compare policies. Short-term holiday and travel insurance policies should include cover for holiday cancellation or interruption; missed flights; departure delay at both the start *and* end of a holiday (a common occurrence); delayed, lost or damaged baggage; personal effects and money; medical expenses and accidents (including evacuation home); flight insurance; personal liability and legal expenses; and default or bankruptcy insurance, e.g. against a tour operator or airline going bust.

Health Cover: Medical expenses are an important aspect of travel insurance and you shouldn't rely on insurance provided by reciprocal health arrangements (see page 69); charge and credit card companies; household policies; or private medical insurance (unless it's an international policy), none of which usually provide adequate cover (although you should take advantage of what they offer). The minimum medical insurance recommended by experts is IR£250,000 in Ireland and most of the rest of Europe, and IR£1m for the rest of the world (many policies have limits of between IR£1m and IR£2m). If applicable, check whether pregnancy related claims are covered and whether there are any restrictions for those over a certain age, e.g. 65 or 70 (travel insurance is becoming increasingly expensive for those aged over 65, although they don't usually need to worry about pregnancy!).

Always check any exclusion clauses in contracts by obtaining a copy of the full policy document, as not all relevant information is included in an insurance leaflet. High risk sports and pursuits should be specifically covered and *listed* in a policy (there's usually an additional premium and 'dangerous' sports are excluded from most standard policies). Third-party liability cover should be IR£2m in North America and IR£1m in the rest of the world. Note that this doesn't cover you when you're using a car or other mechanically propelled vehicle.

Cost: The cost of travel insurance varies considerably, depending on where you buy it, how long you intend to stay in Ireland and your age. Generally the longer the period covered, the cheaper the daily cost, although the maximum period covered is usually limited, e.g. six months. With some policies an excess must be paid for each claim; with others the excess applies only to certain items such as luggage, money and medical expenses. As a rough guide, travel insurance for Ireland (and most other European countries) costs from around IR£20 for one week, IR£30 for two weeks and IR£45 for a month for a family of four (two adults and two children under 16). Premiums may be higher for those aged over 65 or 70.

Annual Policies: For those who travel abroad frequently, whether on business or pleasure, an annual travel policy usually provides the best value, but always carefully check exactly what it includes. Many insurance companies offer annual travel policies for a premium of around IR£100 to IR£150 for an individual (the equivalent of around three months insurance with a standard travel insurance policy), which are excellent value for frequent travellers. Some insurance companies also offer an 'emergency travel policy' for holiday home owners who need to travel abroad at short notice to inspect a property, e.g. after a severe storm. The cost of an annual policy may depend on the area covered, e.g. Europe, world-wide (excluding North America) and world-wide (including North America), although it doesn't usually cover travel within your country of residence. There's also a limit on the number of trips a year and the duration of each trip, e.g. 90 or 120 days. An annual policy is usually a good choice for owners of a holiday home in Ireland who travel there frequently for relatively short periods. Again, carefully check exactly what's covered (or omitted), as an annual policy may not provide adequate cover.

Claims: If you need to make a claim, you should provide as much documentary evidence as possible to support it. Travel insurance companies gladly take your money, but they aren't always so keen to pay claims and you may need to persevere before they pay up. Always be persistent and make a claim *irrespective* of any small print, as this may be unreasonable and therefore invalid in law. Insurance companies usually require you to obtain a written report and report a loss (or any incident for which you intend to make a claim) to the local police or carriers within 24 hours. Failure to do so may mean that a claim won't be considered.

SHOPPING

Shopping in Ireland is unusually pleasurable because you're never made to feel as if you need to buy something, so you can browse as much as you like. Shop assistants won't stand over you or watch your every move, but politely ignore you until you're ready to buy or need help. Generally prices are comparable with other European countries and similar to the UK, apart from a few items such as books, which are significantly more expensive. Nevertheless, Ireland isn't an inexpensive country and the cost of living (see page 128) has risen considerably in the last few years. As in many other countries, there was a huge downturn in consumption during the recession in the early '90s. In recent years, however, there has been a strong recovery (retail sales rose by around 10 per cent during 1996-1997) and a wealth of specialist Irish food shops and boutiques have sprung up in the last few years.

Small family-run stores still constitute the bulk of Irish retailers and the invasion of shopping centres and hypermarkets has for the most part been successfully resisted. They are, however, more common nowadays than they were a few years ago, particularly on the outskirts of the three major cities (Dublin, Cork and Galway). Recently there has also been an influx of British and other foreign supermarket chains into Ireland. Marks & Spencer, for example, now challenges the Irish-owned Dunne's, Penny's and Roches stores, which have outlets in all the main towns. Tesco is making inroads on the food front, while US stores like Gymboree children's wear have recently opened attractive outlets. Chains such as Benetton and the Body Shop are now a familiar sight and high street shopping in Ireland is quite a different experience from ten years ago. On the other hand, the Irish value quality and are far less 'discount mad' than most other Europeans; a large discount superstore which opened recently in Cork was forced to close due to lack of custom!

It's worth shopping around and comparing prices in Ireland as they can vary considerably, not only between small shops and supermarkets, but also among supermarkets in the same town. Note, however, that price differences often reflect different quality, therefore ensure that you're comparing similar products. The best time to have a shopping spree is during the winter and summer sales in January-February and July-August respectively. You won't, however, find shops advertising sales all year round as in the UK. Among the best buys in Ireland are the diverse handicrafts which include lace, linen, tweed, knitwear, pottery, glass, and silverware, all of which are well made, although not cheap. Handicrafts can be found in most towns as well as in the many craft centres which have been set up recently by the Craft Council of Ireland (mostly in Industrial Development Authority parks).

You'll invariably be warmly received in small shops where you're a regular customer and many shopkeepers will even allow you to pay another day if you don't have enough money with you. In major cities, particularly Dublin, and tourist areas you must be wary of pickpockets and bag-snatchers, particularly in markets and other crowded places. *Never* tempt fate with an exposed wallet or purse, or by flashing your money around.

Irish shops are usually open from 0900 to 1730, Monday to Saturday, although newsagents and 'all-purpose' shops are often open for longer hours and even on Sundays. Craft shops generally also open on Sundays. Many towns have late night shopping (until 2000 or 2100) on Thursdays or Fridays (or both days). In small towns and villages there's usually an early closing day (usually Wednesday) when shops close at 1300. A number of supermarkets in the larger urban areas are now open on Sundays from 1200 to 1800 and large shopping centres (which have sprung up on the outskirts of towns such as Cork and Galway) usually open from 0900 to 1800 each day.

Although Ireland is gradually going metric, you'll still find items sold in pounds and ounces as well as kilos and grams, and of course the Guinness still comes in pints!

Furniture & Furnishings

The kind of furniture you buy for your Irish home will depend on a number of factors including its style and size, whether it's a permanent or holiday home, your budget and, not least, your personal taste. Properties are occasionally sold furnished (for example, if they were previously rented or if the vendors are intending to buy new furniture for their new home) or you may be able to persuade the vendor to part with some or all of his furniture if you make a suitable offer. Ex-rental furniture used to be cheap and nasty, but now it often tends to be of reasonable or even good quality, so buying a furnished property can represent a bargain as the cost of the furnishings usually isn't reflected in the price. In the case of new properties, agents and developers won't normally get involved in furnishing them (as in some other countries), so you'll need to either buy or import your own furniture.

If you plan to furnish a holiday home with antiques or expensive modern furniture, bear in mind that you'll need adequate security and insurance. If you own a holiday home in Ireland, it may be worthwhile shipping surplus items of furniture you have in your home abroad (but not if you live in Australia!). If you intend to live permanently in Ireland in the future and already have a house full of good furniture abroad, there's little point in buying expensive furniture in Ireland. Nevertheless, many foreigners who decide to live permanently in Ireland find that it's better to sell their furniture abroad and buy furniture locally.

A wide range of modern and traditional furniture is available in Ireland, although it tends to be of good quality and therefore isn't cheap. The best time to buy furniture and furnishings (and all expensive items) is during sales, when prices of certain items are reduced. It's possible for residents to pay for furniture (and large household appliances) over a period of up to 12 months. Payment over three months is usually interest-free, but you'll be charged interest on a 12-month payment period and may need to pay a 25 per cent deposit. It may also be worthwhile comparing the cost of furniture in Northern Ireland or England with that in Ireland.

If you're looking for antique or mock-antique furniture, there's no shortage of genuine and reproduction antique furniture shops in Ireland. There are also a number of second-hand furniture dealers for those on a tight budget (look under 'Furniture – Used' in the Golden Pages). Note that do-it-yourself hypermarkets such as are common in other European countries aren't easy to find in Ireland, where most things must be purchased in smaller specialist shops.

Household Goods

Household goods in Ireland are generally of high quality and the choice is as wide as in most other European countries. Bear in mind when importing household goods that aren't sold in Ireland, that it may be difficult or impossible to get them repaired or serviced locally (however, should you need to get something repaired, there are strict rules to protect consumers). If you import appliances, don't forget to bring a supply of spares and consumables such as bulbs for a refrigerator or sewing machine, and spare bags for a vacuum cleaner (unless you have a Dyson!). Note that the standard size of kitchen appliances and cupboard units in Ireland may not be the same as in your own country and it may be difficult to fit an imported dishwasher or washing machine into an Irish fitted kitchen. Check the size *and* the latest Irish safety regulations before shipping these items to Ireland or buying them abroad, as they may need expensive modifications.

If you already own small household appliances, it's worthwhile bringing them to Ireland, as usually all that's required is a change of plug. However, if you're coming from a country with a 110/115V electricity supply such as the USA, you'll need a lot of expensive transformers (see page 193) and it's usually better to buy new appliances in Ireland. Small appliances such as vacuum cleaners, grills, toasters and irons aren't expensive in Ireland and are of good quality. Don't bring a TV or video recorder without checking its compatibility first, as TVs made for other countries often don't work in Ireland without modification (see page 80). You won't usually be able to hire electrical goods in Ireland, with the exception of TVs and video recorders. Tools and do-it-yourself equipment can, however, be rented in most towns. If you need kitchen measuring equipment and cannot cope with decimal measures, you'll need to bring your own measuring scales, jugs, cups and thermometers (etc.).

Shopping Abroad

Shopping 'abroad', i.e. outside Ireland, is generally limited to day trips to Northern Ireland, although shopping excursions to mainland Britain and France are possible. A day trip across the border makes an interesting day out for the family and can save you money, depending on what and where you buy and the exchange rate between punts and pounds. Most shops in towns near the border (such as Newry) will accept Irish punts and may even give you a better exchange rate than the banks (some offer a 'punt for pound' rate, which is currently to the advantage of visitors from the Republic). Whatever you're looking for, always compare prices and quality before buying. Bear in mind that if you buy goods that are faulty or need repairing, you may need to return them to the place of purchase.

From 1st January 1993 there have been no cross-border shopping restrictions within the European Union for goods purchased duty and tax paid, providing that all goods are for personal consumption or use and not for resale. Although there are no official restrictions, there are 'indicative levels' for items such as spirits, wine, beer and tobacco products, above which goods may be classified as commercial quantities.

Never attempt to import illegal goods into Ireland and don't agree to bring a parcel into Ireland or deliver a parcel to another country without knowing exactly what it contains. A popular confidence trick is to ask someone to post a parcel abroad (usually to a poste restante address) or to leave a parcel at a railway station or restaurant abroad. THE PARCEL USUALLY CONTAINS DRUGS! Many truck drivers are languishing in foreign jails having been the unwitting victims of drug traffickers (who conceal drugs in shipments of goods).

Duty-Free Allowances

Under European Union (EU) rules, duty-free shopping within the EU is to remain until 30th June 1999. Ireland has the fourth highest duty-free sales per capita in the EU and stands to lose millions of punts and hundreds of jobs when duty-free is abolished. Until then duty-free allowances are the same whether or not passengers are travelling within the EU or from a country outside the EU. On each journey to an EU member state, travellers aged 17 or over (unless otherwise stated below) are entitled to import the following duty-free goods:

- one litre of spirits (over 22° proof) *or* two litres of fortified wine, sparkling wine or other liqueurs (under 22° proof);
- two litres of still table wine;
- 200 cigarettes *or* 100 cigarillos *or* 50 cigars *or* 250g of tobacco;

- 60cc/ml of perfume;
- 250cc/ml of toilet water;
- other goods including gifts and souvenirs to the value of IR£73.

Note that travellers under 17 aren't entitled to tobacco or drinks allowances. Duty-free allowances apply on both outward and return journeys, even if both are made on the same day, and the combined total (i.e. double the above limits) can be imported into your 'home' country.

Your local customs regulations apply to the goods you take home from Ireland. Residents of the USA may take goods up to the value of US$400, including their tobacco and alcohol allowance, without having to pay duty. Canadians can take home up to C$300 worth of goods, excluding tobacco and alcohol, in a year. Britons should note that they aren't allowed to bring fresh meat, vegetables or plants into the UK. Non-EU residents can reclaim VAT (at up to 21 per cent) on goods purchased in Ireland providing they are taken out of the EU within three months of purchase and that their total value exceeds IR£50. You will need a Tax-free Shopping Cheque (also known as a 'cashback' voucher), which needs to be stamped by the retailer and by customs before you leave Ireland. You can either present your vouchers at the cashback desk at airports or ports for an instant refund (less a service charge of around 4 per cent) or send them to Customs and Excise on your return home. For more information on VAT refunds contact Cashback Ltd. (☎ 091-83258). With certain purchases, particularly large items, it's better to have them shipped directly abroad, when VAT won't be added.

PETS

Irish quarantine regulations are under review, so it's advisable to check with your local embassy or consulate or directly with the Department of Agriculture's (DoA) quarantine section in County Dublin (☎ 01-840 1776) before making any decisions regarding importing pets into Ireland. In any case, you should contact the Department of Agriculture at least four months in advance of your move in order to ensure you obtain the necessary paperwork in time.

At present all dogs and cats imported from all countries except the UK (including the Channel Islands and the Isle of Man) must spend at least six months in quarantine, during which time they must be given an anti-rabies vaccination. Quarantine space won't usually be made available for animals imported on a temporary basis, therefore you should only consider importing pets if you intend to stay in Ireland permanently or at least for an extended period. You should bear in mind not only the expense of quarantining an animal, but also the distress it can cause (to you as well as your pet!). There's only one approved public quarantine centre, which is in Dublin (Lissenhall Quarantine Kennels and Catteries, ☎ 01-840 1776). Pets arriving from certain countries may be permitted to be quarantined privately, providing that they have a current rabies vaccination certificate. They will still need to spend a minimum of one month at Lissenhall, but may then be transferred to your own (permanent) residence for a further five months 'private quarantine'. This is subject to a satisfactory blood test on the animal and to the DoA's inspection and approval of the quarters in which it will be quarantined (you must submit a detailed plan to the DoA at least three months in advance of importation – the conditions for approval are available from the DoA on request). Transportation from the port of arrival to Lissenhall (and, if appropriate, to your home for private quarantine) must be undertaken by Irish Rail's Road Freight Section (☎ 01-703 4262), which is the only authorised carrier.

Public quarantine fees for dogs vary according to size and breed, but are in the region of IR£1,200 for the average dog. There's a fixed fee for cats of IR£1,000. These fees don't of course include transport to Ireland or to and from the quarantine centre, which must be arranged by owners. You must obtain an import licence; if your local embassy doesn't have the necessary forms, write to the Department of Agriculture, Veterinary Division, Kildare Street, Dublin 2. You will also need a Form of Declaration and Health (Form PQB), which must be completed by your vet and a magistrate, notary public or commissioner for oaths. Note that an import licence won't be granted until the necessary bookings have been made with both the public quarantine centre and Irish Rail. The import licence must accompany an animal in transit to Ireland and be presented to Customs and Excise on arrival. Animals must be sent by air as 'manifested freight' and arrive at Dublin, Cork or Shannon airports (if they are sent to Cork or Shannon, they will need to be air-freighted to Dublin for quarantine).

There are no restrictions on cats and dogs imported from the UK and no documentation is required, providing that they have spent the previous six months there. Note, however, that if you need to return to Britain prematurely, even after a few hours in Ireland, your pet will need to go into quarantine in Britain (although this is likely to change in the near future, if the UK abolishes quarantine, as expected).

Similar regulations apply to the import of other kinds of pets. Animals such as gerbils, guinea pigs, chinchillas and mice require an import licence and must be quarantined for at least six months unless imported from the UK. All birds imported into Ireland must have a health certificate in accordance with EU directives. In general, whatever kind of pet you plan to take to Ireland, it's important to check the latest regulations and to ensure that you have the correct papers, not only for Ireland, but for any countries you'll pass through to reach Ireland.

If you're transporting a pet to Ireland by air or sea, you should obtain a certificate from your vet that the pet is fit to travel, as this may be required by the airline or shipping company. In you're travelling by sea you should notify the shipping company as some insist that pets are left in vehicles (if applicable), while others allow pets to be kept in cabins. If your pet is of nervous disposition or unused to travelling, it's best to tranquillise it on a long sea crossing.

If you intend to live permanently in Ireland, most vets recommend that you have pets vaccinated against rabies before you leave home, which saves you having to get them vaccinated on arrival in Ireland. It's also advisable to have them vaccinated against the most common contagious diseases, particularly if they are likely to spend some time in a cattery or kennels. You should obtain advice from your vet as to the best way to protect your pets. Note that there are no animal diseases which are peculiar to Ireland.

All dogs kept in Ireland must have a licence, which is available from any post office for IR£5 (you can be fined IR£100 for not having one). Dogs (with the exception of guide dogs) are prohibited from entering certain public places, particularly restaurants and cafés. Some breeds must be muzzled and kept on a strong lead or chain in any public place and accompanied by a person aged over 16, in addition to wearing a collar containing the name and address of the owner. These include bulldogs and bull mastiffs, bull terriers and pitbull terriers, rottweilers, doberman pinschers, German shepherds (alsations), Rhodesian ridgebacks, and Japanese akitas and tosas. Note also that there may be discrimination against pets when renting accommodation, particularly when it's furnished, and the statutes of community properties can legally prohibit pets. Many hotels accept pets such as cats and dogs, and the Irish Tourist Board's guides to hotels and bed & breakfast accommodation indicates whether pets are allowed.

TELEVISION & RADIO

Television

Irish TV (and radio) services are operated by RTÉ (*Radio Telefís Éireann*), the public broadcasting company, which transmits nationally on three channels: RTÉ 1, Network 2 television and *Teilifís na Gaeilge* (the Irish Gaelic station). There's also a local TV station in Cork city, imaginatively called 'The Local Channel'. The country's first independent national TV station, TV3 (part-owned by the Canadian communications group, CanWest), is to be launched in late 1998. The publicity material describes TV3's target audience as the 15 to 44 age group with a 'psychographical make-up of affluent acquirers, liberal sophisticates, young aspirers and comfy full nesters'! It plans to offer a highly original mix of news, sport, movies and imported soaps! British radio and TV (including Ulster TV) are also widely available, as are satellite and cable services (see below).

NICAM digital stereo sound is available on most TV programmes and a limited number of RTÉ programmes are now being transmitted in wide screen format on a trial basis. Aertel Teletext is carried on both TV networks and a few pages of Teletext information are also available on the Internet. RTÉ 1 television provides European news each day between 0500 and 0730 and shows several of the same 'soaps' broadcast on British TV in addition to programmes originating in Northern Ireland. Network 2 shows a lot of sport and also a number of British programmes. Irish broadcasting and the local taste in programmes is similar to most other countries, with the most popular inevitably including 'soaps' such as Coronation Street and Home and Away, each of which is screened no fewer than four times a week. An annoying tendency in Ireland is for TVs and radios to be blaring away in places such as pubs and hotels, where they are even more intrusive than the usual background music.

Although RTÉ is a commercial station (i.e. programmes are interspersed with advertising), you're required to have a TV licence in Ireland. This costs IR£70 per year and can be purchased at post offices. TV programmes are listed in all Irish newspapers and in special TV guides such as the *RTE Guide* (the best-selling publication in Ireland). Irish TV programmes are also listed in newspapers and magazines, along with satellite TV programmes.

Standards: The standards for TV reception in Ireland aren't the same as in some other countries. Ireland, like Britain, uses the PAL I standard, therefore TVs and video recorders (VCRs) operating on the French (SECAM) or North American

(NTSC) systems won't work. Machines operating on the European PAL B/G system can be converted for around IR£40. It's also possible to buy a multi-standard European TV (and VCR) containing automatic circuitry that switches between different systems. Some multi-standard TVs also include the North American NTSC standard and have an NTSC-in jack plug connection allowing you to play back American videos. Grundig is the only make generally available in Ireland and prices are high – almost twice as much as standard TVs/VCRs. Some people opt for two TVs, one to receive Irish TV programmes and another (e.g. SECAM or NTSC) to play back their favourite videos.

British-made TVs need a 'televerter' so that they can receive VHF as well as UHF signals (most cable transmissions are in VHF as are RTÉ's broadcasts in certain areas). This is an external, mains-powered unit costing around IR£80. If you decide to buy a TV in Ireland, you'll find it advantageous to buy one with Aertel Teletext, which, apart from allowing you to display programme schedules, also provides a wealth of useful and interesting information. In fact most new TVs (apart from very basic ones) come with Aertel Teletext. A small portable colour TV can be purchased in Ireland from around IR£170. A 55cm (21 inch) TV costs between IR£250 and IR£300 depending on the make and features, and one with Nicam stereo around IR£350. Interest-free credit for up to 12 months can be obtained on some makes of TV and VCRs.

It's possible to rent a TV, VCR or video camera in Ireland. The cost of renting a standard 55cm (21 inch) TV is around IR£11 to IR£13 a month for a 12-month contract. The same TV plus VCR costs around IR£20 per month and a 65cm (25 inch) TV and VCR around IR£25. Note, however, that it's cheaper to buy a TV over the long term as you can buy a small portable TV for around IR£170 and could easily sell it for half this amount or more if it was no longer required. If you need a TV for a short period only, some companies rent them by the month, but obviously the charges are much higher, e.g. up to IR£25. Usually no deposit is required when renting but you must pay a month in advance and non-residents are usually required to give the name and address of their employer or some other guarantor. VAT at 21 per cent is included in all rental rates.

Satellite TV: Some 25 geostationary satellites are positioned over Europe, carrying over 200 TV stations broadcasting in a variety of languages. All the European satellite TV services can be received throughout Ireland; the Astra and Eutelsat satellites provide a particularly strong signal which requires only a small dish. The Eutelsat satellite also links up with digital TV and radio broadcasts from Europe.

Astra: Although it wasn't the first in Europe (which was Eutelsat), the European satellite revolution really took off with the launch of the Astra 1A satellite in 1988 (operated by the Luxembourg-based *Société Européenne des Satellites* or SES), positioned 36,000km (22,300mi) above the earth. TV addicts (easily recognised by their antennae and square eyes) are offered a huge choice of English and foreign-language stations which can be received throughout most of Ireland with a 60cm (or smaller) dish and receiver. Since 1988 a number of additional Astra satellites have been launched, increasing the number of available channels to 64. An added bonus is the availability of foreign radio stations via satellite, including all the popular British Broadcasting Corporation (BBC) stations (see **Cable & Satellite Radio** on page 85).

Among the many English-language stations available on Astra are Sky One, Movimax, Sky Premier, Sky Cinema, Film Four, Sky News, Sky Sports (three channels), UK Gold, Channel 5, Granada Plus, TNT, Eurosport, CNN, CNBC Europe, UK Style, UK Horizons, The Disney Channel and the Discovery Channel. Other stations broadcast in Dutch, German, Japanese, Swedish and various Indian languages. The signal from many stations is scrambled (the decoder is usually built into the receiver) and viewers must pay a monthly subscription fee to receive programmes. You can buy pirate decoders for some channels. The best served by clear (unscrambled) stations are German-speakers (most German stations on Astra are clear).

Eutelsat: Eutelsat (owned by a consortium of national telephone operators) was the first company to introduce satellite TV to Europe (in 1983) and it now runs a fleet of communications satellites carrying TV stations to over 50 million homes. Until 1995 they had broadcast primarily advertising-based, clear-access cable channels. Following the launch in March 1995 of their Hot Bird satellite, Eutelsat hoped to become a major competitor to Astra, although its channels are mostly non-English. The English-language stations on Eutelsat include Eurosport, Euronews, BBC World, European Business News, CNBC Europe and Worldnet. Other channels broadcast in Arabic, French, German, Hungarian, Italian, Polish, Portuguese, Spanish and Turkish.

Sky Television: You must buy a Videocrypt decoder, an integral part of the receiver in most models, and pay a monthly subscription to receive all Sky stations except Sky News (which isn't scrambled). Various packages are available costing from around IR£12 for a basic package to IR£30 a month for the premium package offering all movie channels plus Sky Sports. When you sign your contract (for a minimum of one year), you'll be sent a satellite viewing card (similar to a credit card), which must be inserted in the decoder to switch it on (cards are frequently updated to thwart counterfeiters). Sky have an office in Ireland, so you won't need a friend or relative in Britain to subscribe for you.

Digital Television: Digital TV was launched on 1st October 1998 by Sky Television in the UK. The benefits include a superior picture, better (CD) quality sound and widescreen cinema format. To watch digital TV you require a Digibox and a (digital) Minidish, which in 1998 could be purchased for a subsidised GB£159.99 for existing Sky customers (GB£199.99 to new customers), including installation. Customers must sign up for a 12-month subscription and agree to have the connection via a phone line (to allow for future interactive services). In addition to the usual analogue channels (see above), digital TV offers BBC 1, BBC 2 and Channel 4 (but not ITV or ITV2), plus many new digital channels (a total of 200 with up to 500 possible later). ONdigital launched a rival digital service on 15th November 1998, which although it's cheaper, provides a total of 30 channels only (15 free and 15 subscription) including BBC, ITV, ITV2, Channel 4 and Channel 5. Cable & Wireless also plan to launch a digital service in 1999. Widescreen digital TVs cost around GB£1,000, but will inevitably become cheaper as more models become available and the demand increases. Digital TV will also be available via cable and terrestrial aerials in the near future. Contact your local TV store for further information and installation.

BBC Worldwide Television: The BBC's commercial subsidiary, BBC Worldwide Television, broadcasts two 24-hour channels: BBC Prime (general entertainment) and BBC World (24-hour news and information). BBC World is free-to-air and is transmitted via the Eutelsat II F1 satellite. No subscription fee or decoder is needed. BBC Prime, on the other hand, is a subscription channel (GB£75 plus VAT per year). It's available in analogue or digital format and the analogue signal can be received from Telenor Satellite Services satellite position Intelsat 707. The signal is encrypted and you'll need a D2-MAC decoder and a smartcard costing GB£12, which will be sent to you when you register.

Note, however, that Telenor plan to provide BBC Prime in digital format sometime in 1999 and the analogue broadcast is expected to be terminated shortly afterwards. Otherwise, BBC Prime can already be received in digital format from the Eutelsat II F1 satellite, so that both Prime and World can be received using the same source. One or both channels may also be available via cable and you should contact your local cable operator to check. For more information and a programming guide contact BBC Worldwide Television, Woodlands, 80 Wood Lane, London W12 0TT, UK (☎ UK 0181-576 2555). The BBC publishes a monthly magazine, *BBC On Air*, giving comprehensive information about BBC Worldwide Television programmes. A programme guide is also listed on the Internet (www.bbc.co.uk/schedules) and both BBC World and BBC Prime have their own websites (www.bbcworld.com and www.bbcprime.com). When accessing them, you need to enter the name of the country (e.g. Ireland) so that the schedules appear in local time.

Equipment: A satellite receiver should have a built-in Videocrypt decoder (and others such as Eurocrypt, if required) and be capable of receiving satellite stereo radio. In most parts of Ireland you'll need a 1.2m or 1.5m dish to receive satellite broadcasts from outside Europe. A basic fixed satellite dish (which will receive programmes from one satellite only) costs around IR£275 and a motorised dish (which will automatically adjust its orientation so that you can receive programmes from all satellites) will set you back IR£1,200. If you wish to receive satellite TV on two or more TVs, you can buy a satellite system with two or more receptors. To receive stations from two or more satellites simultaneously, you need a motorised dish or a dish with a double feed antenna (dual LNBs). There are numerous satellite sales and installation companies in Ireland (listed under 'Television' in the Golden Pages). Shop around and compare prices. Alternatively you can import your own satellite dish and receiver and install it yourself. Before buying a system, ensure that it can receive programmes from all existing and planned satellites.

Location: To receive programmes from any satellite, there must be no obstacles between the satellite and your dish, i.e. no trees, buildings or mountains must obstruct the signal, so check before renting or buying a home. Before buying or erecting a satellite dish, check whether you need permission from your landlord or the local authorities. In general, dishes of up to 1m in diameter don't require planning permission providing that they aren't positioned on the front wall or roof and don't protrude above the top of the roof, and that there's only one per house. Dishes can usually be mounted in a variety of unobtrusive positions and can be painted or patterned to blend in with the background. New blocks of flats or apartments are generally fitted with at least one communal satellite dish. Less expensive blocks may only have CATV, which provides seven or eight popular satellite channels to each apartment, whereas the more expensive ones will often have SMATV, which allows each apartment to have its own control unit ('flave').

Programme Guides: Many satellite stations provide Teletext information and most broadcast in stereo. Sky satellite programme listings are provided in a number of British publications such as *What Satellite, Satellite Times* and *Satellite TV* (the best), which are available on subscription. Satellite TV programmes are also listed in expatriate newspapers and magazines in Ireland. The annual *World Radio and TV Handbook* (Billboard) contains over 600 pages of information and the frequencies of all radio and TV stations world-wide.

Cable TV: Most households in urban areas subscribe to a cable service, which provides a range of TV (and radio) programmes from other European countries including the UK, France, Germany, Italy and Spain, as well as from the USA (e.g. CNN and CNBC). Ireland is divided into eight franchise areas, each allocated to a cable company. Cablelink, for example, operates in the counties of Dublin, Galway and Waterford where it provides a choice of 17 TV channels and 17 FM radio channels for a basic monthly fee of IR£8.50. Various 'premium packages' enable you to receive Sky Sports and four movie channels. The minimum subscription period is six months. Those in remote areas (where cables haven't been laid) can receive the same service via a microwave signal (called MMDS), that can be received with an ordinary aerial. The only disadvantage of this method of reception is that the signal can be interrupted by obstacles such as buildings and mountains.

Radio

Irish radio (and TV) services are operated by RTÉ (*Radio Telefís Éireann*), the public broadcasting company, which transmits nationally in English on three radio channels: Radio 1 (news, current affairs, chat and 'middle-of-the-road' music), 2FM (popular music) and FM3. Radio 1 is also available on the Astra satellite across Europe and on the Internet. FM3 broadcasts in Irish between 0800 and 2000, after which it's dedicated to classical music (RTÉ plans to introduce a dedicated classical music channel in 1999). Irish speakers are served by RTÉ's dedicated radio channel *Raidió na Gaeltachta* and RTÉ also has a local radio station called Cork Radio based in Cork city. 1998 saw the launch of a national independent radio station called Today FM (formerly Radio Ireland), which provides round-the-clock music, news and entertainment. Since the Radio and Television Licensing Act of 1988, a number of independent regional and community radio stations have emerged throughout the country. Atlantic 252 is a commercial popular music station which broadcasts from Ireland on long wave and is targeted at the British market. RTÉ's FM signals (as well as those of some local stations) incorporate RDS (radio data service) signals, which are particularly useful for in-car listening.

BBC: The BBC World Service is broadcast on short wave on several frequencies (e.g. 12095, 9410, 7325, 6195, 3955, 648 and 198 khz) simultaneously and you can usually receive a good signal on one of them. The signal strength varies depending on where you live in Ireland, the time of day and year, the power and positioning of your receiver and atmospheric conditions. All BBC radio stations, including the World Service, are available on the Astra satellite. The BBC publish a monthly magazine, *BBC On Air*, containing comprehensive information about BBC World Service radio and TV programmes. For a free copy and frequency information write to BBC On Air, Room 205 NW, Bush House, Strand, London WC2B 4PH, UK (an annual subscription costs GB£24).

Cable & Satellite Radio: If you have cable or satellite TV system you can also receive many radio stations via your cable or satellite link. For example, BBC Radio 1, 2, 3, 4 and 5, BBC World Service, Sky Radio, Virgin 1215, plus many foreign-language stations are broadcast via the Astra satellites. Satellite radio stations are listed in British satellite TV magazines such as the *Satellite Times*. If you're interested in receiving radio stations from further afield you should obtain a copy of the *World Radio TV Handbook* (Billboard). See also **Cable TV** above.

LEARNING ENGLISH & IRISH

Although Irish is the first 'official language' of Ireland (see below), the second official language and *lingua franca* of Ireland is English, which is spoken by almost everyone. If you don't speak English fluently, you may wish to enrol in a language course. If you want to make the most of the Irish way of life and your time in Ireland, it's absolutely essential to learn (or improve your) English as soon as possible, preferably before your arrival. For those living in Ireland permanently, learning English isn't an option, but a necessity. Although it isn't always easy, even the most non-linguistic person can acquire a working knowledge of English. All that's required is a little hard work, some help and perseverance. **Note that your business and social enjoyment and success in Ireland will be directly related to the degree to which you master English.**

Most people can teach themselves a great deal through the use of books, tapes, videos and even CD-ROM computer-based courses. However, even the best students require some help. Teaching English is a thriving business in Ireland, with classes offered by language schools, colleges and universities, private and international schools, foreign and international organisations, local associations and clubs, and private teachers. Tuition ranges from language courses for complete beginners, through specialised business or cultural courses, to university-level courses leading to recognised diplomas. Most Irish universities provide language courses and many organisations offer residential holiday courses all year round, particularly for children and young adults (it's best to stay with a local Irish family). If you already speak English but need conversational practice, you may prefer to enrol in an art or craft course at a local institute or club. Contact an Irish embassy or tourist office or contact Marketing English in Ireland (☎ 01-475 3122) for information about language schools.

Irish: The official language of Ireland is Irish Gaelic, one of the most ancient languages in Europe. It's closely related to Scottish Gaelic, Welsh and Breton, and is claimed to be the purest of the Celtic tongues. Until the early 19th century, Irish Gaelic was spoken by the vast majority of the population, but within a hundred years more than 85 per cent of people were speaking English. The establishment of an independent Irish State in 1921 led to a cultural revival and an attempt to revive the Gaelic language. However, although civil servants and the police are required to know at least some Irish, the majority of the population don't speak it at all. A recent survey found that only around a third of adults have any knowledge of the language. On the other hand, virtually everyone speaks English (with a distinctive, lilting Irish accent).

In a bid to prevent the extinction of Irish Gaelic, the government provides grants to encourage people to live in the few areas where it's still a living language. These are known collectively as the *Gaeltacht* and are mainly in the west in counties Donegal, Mayo, Galway and Kerry. They tend to be pretty and unspoiled areas – or poor and isolated, depending on your point of view. A state authority, *Údarás na Gaeltachta*, promotes industrial development in these areas, while another state agency, *Bord na Gaelige* (the Irish Language Board) ensures that at least some Irish Gaelic is learnt by all children by making it a core school subject. There's also a growing number of all-Irish schools (*Gaelscoileanna*) and an increase in the number of people enrolling in Irish language courses. *Radio na Gaeltachta* broadcasts nationally in Irish and an Irish language TV channel, *Telefís na Gaelige*, was launched in 1996. The most conspicuous evidence of official support for Irish Gaelic is that all signposts are in both languages, which will help you to pick up a few words of Irish, although as Irish spelling is far from standardised you may encounter different versions of certain words and place names.

As an English speaker, you'll already be familiar with a large number of Irish words, probably without realising it, e.g. cranky, dither, skidaddle, galore, lashings, smidgen, hooligan, brogue and bog all have their origins in Irish Gaelic, as well as more obvious borrowings such as leprechaun and shamrock. There's even a theory that the word sure, as used to mean yes (particularly in North America), derives from the Irish *is sa* (it is). However, the strangest derivation is surely that of the word Tory (as used to describe British Conservative Party politicians), which comes from the Irish *toraidhe* meaning bandit!

There are also one or two other words and phrases deriving from Gaelic with which you'll need to be familiar. Most important perhaps is the word *Garda* (pronounced 'gorda'), which is what the police are called (the police are collectively called the *Garda Síochána* and the plural of *Garda* is *Gardaí*, pronounced 'gordee'). Then there are words such as *ben* for mountain, *caher* (or *cahir*) for fort, *currach* (or *curragh*) for either a grassy plain or a leather boat, *inis* (or *ennis*) for island, *glen* for valley, *knock* (or *cnoc*) for hill, *lough* for lake or inlet, *strand* for beach. *Mór* (or more) means big, *wee* is little, a country lane is a *boreen*, *doley* means lovely, a *mullarkey* is a man, a *wean* (pronounced waain) is a child, and if it's *mizzlin* (as it often is in Ireland) it's raining gently.

Other words that sound familiar are used in strange contexts: a *temple* (or teampull) is a church; a *chick* isn't a young woman but a child; if something is *clever* it fits well; if someone is brave he's a worthy sort, but if he's a caution he's a devil-may-care fellow; to be *cut* is to be insulted, to be *destroyed* is to be exhausted, and to be *scalded* is to be vexed; *fairly* means excellently; *fierce* and *terrible* mean extremely; a *skiff* is a shower of rain; and if it's *soft* – you've guessed it – it's raining! As a *fern* (foreign) homeowner, you'll be known as a blow-in. If you're in *fiddler's green*, you're in a mess, and if an Irishman says to you, "I'm after meeting your wife," he doesn't mean he would like to meet her – he already has!

But if the Irish language is struggling for survival, the Irish way with the words of their adopted tongue is famously vigorous. You will encounter that legendary loquacity wherever you choose to travel, stay or live in Ireland and one word you'll undoubtedly come across is *craic*. *Craic* is in fact derived from the English word crack and means simply a good time: a pleasant atmosphere, agreeable company and something to drink – all of which are in plentiful supply in Ireland!

3.

FINANCE

O ne of the most important aspects of buying a home in Ireland and living there (even for relatively brief periods) is finance, which includes everything from transferring and changing money to mortgages and taxes. If you're planning to invest in a property or a business in Ireland financed with imported funds, it's important to consider both the present and possible future exchange rates. On the other hand, if you live and work in Ireland and are paid in Irish punts, this may affect your financial commitments abroad. Bear in mind that if your income is received in a foreign currency, it can be exposed to risks beyond your control when you live in Ireland, particularly regarding inflation and exchange rate fluctuations.

If you own a holiday or second home in Ireland you can employ a local accountant or tax consultant to look after your financial affairs there and declare and pay your local taxes. You can also have your agent receive your bank statements, ensure that your bank is paying your standing orders (e.g. for utilities) and that you have sufficient funds to pay them. If you let a home in Ireland through an Irish company, the company may perform the above tasks as part of its service.

Although the Irish generally prefer to use cash rather than credit or charge cards, it's wise to have at least one credit card when visiting or living in Ireland (both Visa and Mastercard are widely accepted). Even if you don't like credit cards and shun any form of credit, they do have their advantages: for example, no-deposit car rentals; no pre-paying hotel bills (plus guaranteed bookings); obtaining cash 24-hours a day; simple telephone and mail-order payments; greater safety and security than cash; and above all, convenience. Note, however, that while 'plastic' is now widely accepted in the larger shops, hotels, and restaurants, not all Irish businesses accept credit cards.

Wealth Warning: If you plan to live in Ireland you must ensure that your income is (and will remain) sufficient to live on, bearing in mind possible devaluations (if your income is paid in a foreign currency), rises in the cost of living, and unforeseen expenses such as medical bills or anything else that may reduce your income (such as stock market crashes and recessions!). Foreigners, particularly retirees, shouldn't under-estimate the cost of living in Ireland, which has increased significantly in the last decade. If you're planning to live permanently in Ireland, it's important to seek expert financial advice as it may offer the opportunity to (legally) reduce your taxes significantly.

This chapter includes information on Irish currency; importing and exporting money; banking; mortgages; taxes (income, capital gains, capital acquisition, etc.); and the cost of living.

IRISH CURRENCY

On 1st January 1999 the Euro will become the national currency of Ireland (along with that of Austria, Belgium, Finland, France, Germany, Italy, Luxembourg, the Netherlands, Portugal and Spain). That's to say the currencies of all 11 countries will be locked into a fixed exchange rate with the Euro and consequently with each other. In the meantime, as you're probably aware, the unit of Irish currency is the Irish pound or punt, which will circulate alongside the Euro until 1st January 2002, when it will be withdrawn.

Since Ireland joined the European Monetary System the punt has ceased to be worth the same as the pound sterling (GB£), and at the time of writing was worth around GB£1.15 and was one of the strongest currencies in the ERM. The Irish pound is usually written as IR£ (as in this book) to distinguish it from the pound sterling. Like the pound sterling, the punt is divided into 100 pence (p) and is minted in coins of 1, 2, 5, 10, 20 and 50 pence, and IR£1. Take care not to confuse the 20p coin and the 2p coin, which are of a similar size, although different colours. Bank notes are printed in denominations of 5, 10, 20, 50, and 100 punts.

It's advisable to obtain some Irish coins and notes before arriving in Ireland and to familiarise yourself and your family with them. You should have some Irish money in cash (e.g. IR£50 to IR£100 in small denominations) when you arrive, although you should avoid carrying a lot of cash. This will save you having to queue to change money on arrival at the port or airport (where exchange rates are usually poor). It's best to avoid IR£50 and IR£100 notes (unless you receive them as a gift!) as sometimes they aren't accepted, particularly for small purchases or on public transport.

IMPORTING & EXPORTING MONEY

Exchange controls have been abolished in Ireland as in other EU countries and in principle there are no restrictions on the import or export of funds. However, when you open an account, a bank must routinely inform the Central Bank of Ireland of any large account movements as required by the EU Directive to deter money laundering. Similarly, cash, notes and bearer-cheques in any currency (plus gold coins and bars) may be freely imported or exported by residents and non-residents without approval or declaration. However, if it's possible they you may re-export over IR£10,000, you should declare it as this will certify that the foreign currency was imported legally and will allow you to convert Irish pounds back into a foreign currency without suspicion. If you don't declare it, you may find the bank will contact you to enquire where the money came from.

International Bank Transfers: When transferring or sending money to (or from) Ireland you should be aware of the alternatives and shop around for the best deal. A bank-to-bank transaction can be made by a normal transfer or by a SWIFT electronic transfer. A normal transfer is supposed to take three to seven days, but in reality it usually takes much longer (particularly when sent by mail), whereas a SWIFT telex transfer *should* be completed in as little as two hours. Note that it's usually faster and cheaper to transfer funds between branches of the same bank or affiliated banks than between non-affiliated banks. If you intend sending a large amount of money to Ireland for a business transaction such as buying premises, you should ensure you receive the commercial rate of exchange rather than the tourist rate. Charges for transferring funds to Ireland vary depending on the method of transfer. An electronic transfer, for example, may cost you around IR£12. If a cheque or bank draft is sent, normal bank charges apply (see below). There's usually no difference in charges whether the transfer is made in Irish pounds or foreign currency. However, in many cases the charge is incurred by the bank sending the funds. Always check charges and rates in advance and agree them with your bank (you may be able to negotiate a lower charge or a better exchange rate).

Bank Drafts & Personal Cheques: Another way to transfer money is by bank draft, which should be sent by registered mail. Note, however, that if it's lost or stolen, it's impossible to stop payment and you must wait around six months before a new draft can be issued. Bank drafts are treated as cash in Ireland, therefore they don't need to be cleared like personal cheques, but there's usually a small charge (around IR£3.50). It's possible to pay personal cheques and cheques drawn on a foreign account into an Irish bank account; however the money can take a number of weeks to reach your account as cheques must be cleared with the paying bank. Note that personal cheques from foreign banks aren't accepted by retailers anywhere in Ireland unless they're Eurocheques supported by a Eurocheque card.

Postcheques, Giros & Eurocheques: Giro postcheques for up to IR£5,000 issued by European post offices can be cashed at main post offices in Ireland in local currency or be paid into a post office or bank account in Ireland. You can send larger amounts to Ireland via the Girobank Eurogiro system from post offices in 15 European countries (including Britain), but such payments must be paid into a bank account and funds take some time to clear. Eurocheques can be written in 40 currencies, allowing direct payment and withdrawal of cash at home and abroad. However, bank charges for cashing Eurocheques can be quite high (see below). Eurocheque cards are essential for cashing Eurocheques in Ireland (up to a maximum of IR£140) and can be used to withdraw cash from cash dispensers at most banks (look for the EU symbol). Note, however, that with the advent of the Euro, Eurocheques will probably become a thing of the past and some Irish banks are already beginning to phase them out.

Telegraphic Transfers: One of the fastest (it takes around ten minutes) and safest methods of transferring cash is by telegraphic transfer, e.g. Western Union (UK freephone 0800-833833), but it's also one of the most expensive with very high charges. Western Union will accept Visa or Mastercard but not American Express. Amex card holders can use Amex's Moneygram service to transmit money to the nearest American Express office in Ireland in just 15 minutes.

Obtaining Cash: One of the simplest methods of obtaining (usually relatively small amounts) of cash in Ireland is to draw on debit, credit or charge cards. Many foreigners living in Ireland (particularly retirees) keep the bulk of their money in a foreign account (perhaps in an offshore bank) and draw on it with a cash or credit card in Ireland. This is an ideal solution for holidaymakers and holiday-home owners (although home owners will still need an Irish bank account to pay their local bills). Otherwise, most banks in major cities have foreign exchange windows where you can buy and sell foreign currencies, buy and cash traveller's cheques, and cash Eurocheques. Banks throughout Ireland have cash machines (automated teller machines or ATMs) and you can usually withdraw money directly from a foreign bank account using your usual cash or credit card.

Note that most banks charge around 1 per cent commission on foreign exchange with a minimum charge of IR£1 and a maximum of IR£5. There are numerous private *bureaux de change* in Ireland (including most travel agents), but you should compare exchange rates and fees with banks before changing any money. Post offices, tourist information centres and some stores also provide a *bureau de change* service. Post offices tend to charge a slightly higher commission rate than the banks, e.g. 1.5 per cent. There are also exchange desks at Dublin, Shannon, Cork and Knock airports. Note that *bureaux de change* at airports and ports usually offer the worst exchange rates and charge the highest fees. The Irish pound exchange rate for most European and major international currencies is listed in banks, post offices and daily newspapers, and announced on Irish radio and TV. If you're changing a lot of money you may be able to negotiate a better exchange rate. Always shop around for the best rate and the lowest commission, as they can vary considerably.

UK travellers should note that whereas sterling is widely accepted in the Republic, you won't be able to use Irish pounds in Britain, including Northern Ireland (except perhaps in towns near the border).

Traveller's Cheques: If you're visiting Ireland, it's safer to carry traveller's cheques than cash, although they aren't as easy to cash as in some other countries. They aren't generally accepted by businesses, except hotels and some restaurants and shops, which usually offer a poor exchange rate. Remember that you must show your passport when cashing traveller's cheques. Most banks charge the same commission when cashing foreign currency traveller's cheques as for exchanging foreign cash. Traveller's cheques aren't available in Irish pounds.

Always keep a separate record of traveller's cheque numbers and note where and when they were cashed. Most cheque issuers offer a replacement service for lost or stolen cheques, although the time taken to replace them varies considerably. American Express claim a free, three-hour replacement service at any of their offices world-wide, providing you know the serial numbers of the lost cheques. Without the serial numbers, replacement can take three days or longer. Note that for Europeans travelling within Europe, Eurocheques (or postcheques) are a useful alternative to traveller's cheques (see above).

Footnote: There isn't a lot of difference in cost between buying Irish currency with cash, buying traveller's cheques or using a credit or debit card to obtain cash in Ireland. However, many people simply take cash when visiting Ireland, which is asking for trouble, particularly if you have no way of obtaining more money once you're there, e.g. with a credit card or Eurocheques. One thing to bear in mind when travelling anywhere, is not to rely on one source of funds only!

BANKS & BUILDING SOCIETIES

All towns in Ireland have at least one bank, which is generally housed in the most imposing building in town. Banks are usually open from 0930 until 1230 and from 1330 until 1600 on weekdays, with late opening until 1700 or 1730 on one day (usually market day). In Dublin, for example, the banks close at 1700 on Thursdays and the larger branches stay open during the lunch hour. There are eight different banks in Ireland, the most widespread being AIB Bank (with 327 branches) and the Bank of Ireland (with 300 branches). These two along with Ulster Bank (114 branches) and the National Irish Bank (60 branches) are known as the Associated Banks because they provide a clearing system for all other Irish banks. The remaining four banks are Irish Permanent Bank (91 branches), Trustee Savings Bank (80 branches), ACC Bank (49 branches) and ICC Bank (5 branches).

Banking in Ireland is generally fairly non-bureaucratic and branch managers have greater autonomy and authority than in many other countries (e.g. in granting or denying an overdraft facility or a loan). As elsewhere in the world, banking has become highly automated in recent years and in terms of electronic services Irish banks are at least as sophisticated as those in other European countries. Telephone banking is widespread and in September 1997 the Bank of Ireland introduced the world's first Internet banking service. There are, however, no drive-in banks in Ireland.

Bank charges in Ireland generally compare favourably with those in other European countries. As elsewhere there's a trend towards increasing 'non-interest' income by levying charges against specific services while reducing net interest margins, i.e. the difference between the interest rate paid for deposits and the rate charged to borrowers. All the major banks make charges on personal as well as business accounts, although they vary significantly from bank to bank. AIB Bank, for example, charges IR£3.75 per quarter for account maintenance; IR£3 per year for a cheque card (IR£6 for a Eurocheque card); IR£1.50 each for bank drafts (IR£3.50 for foreign currency drafts); IR£3 for setting up a standing order or processing an incoming foreign payment of more than IR£100; and a minimum of IR£12 for outgoing foreign payments. 'Paper' transactions (such as cheque withdrawals and deposits) are charged at 24p each and automated transactions (such as ATM withdrawals, debit card payments, direct debit payments and direct salary transfers) at 17p each.

There's an additional charge for Eurocheques of 1.6 per cent of their value up to IR£240 (subject to a minimum charge of 90p) or IR£4 for cheques over IR£240. For Eurocheque card ATM withdrawals there's a charge of 0.25 per cent of the amount withdrawn plus around IR£1.27. All these charges are waived if you maintain an average credit balance of IR£100 in your current account or IR£200 in a deposit account or make fewer than 30 transactions per quarter. There are no transaction charges with budget accounts. Full-time students are exempt from most charges and those over 60 or who are retired, widowed or blind qualify for free account transactions and reductions in other bank charges. In fact, over 30 per cent of Irish account holders don't pay bank charges.

In addition to its eight banks, Ireland has three building societies. These are less widespread than the banks but offer an increasing range of services and are open slightly longer hours, generally between 0930 and 1730 Monday to Friday (and in some cases also on Saturdays) and until 1900 or 2000 on at least one day per week. First National Building Society has 77 branches, the Educational Building Society 60 branches and the ICS Building Society seven. ICS is part of the Bank of Ireland group and First National has recently been floated on the stock market as First Active plc. Increasingly, building societies are offering banking services and they generally don't make charges. However, you should check exactly what kind of account you can open, as some societies offer deposit accounts only, which means that you won't be issued with a cheque book.

Another kind of financial institution in Ireland is the credit union, a non-profit, community-based, co-operative organisation offering loans and savings facilities. Interest rates on loans tend to be quite low, while the rates on savings can be as high as those of a conventional bank. However, credit unions don't offer long-term loans or mortgages. Opening times vary, but all credit unions open on some evenings and some also open on Saturday mornings. There are over 500 credit unions in Ireland and you should enquire locally for the names and addresses of your nearest branches. Further information on credit unions can be obtained from the Irish League of Credit Unions (☎ 01-614 6700).

An Post, the Irish postal service, offers a range of savings and investment options, and their savings products have the advantage of being state-guaranteed. Also in their favour is the large number of 'branches' (almost 1,900) throughout the country.

There are a number of foreign banks operating in Ireland, although fewer than in most other European countries. Competition from foreign banks is set to increase, however, as EU regulations now allow any bank trading legitimately in one EU country to trade in another. There are a dozen or so foreign banks in Dublin, although branches are rare in other cities. Most, however, offer corporate services only. The most prominent British bank is the TSB, which is the only one with a national network. Note that foreign banks in Ireland operate in exactly the same way as Irish banks, so you shouldn't expect, for example, a branch of the TSB in Ireland to behave like a branch in Britain.

When choosing a bank you should consider the convenience factor, e.g. how many branches it has, where you can use ATM cards and the international services provided. All banks and most building societies in Ireland provide credit cards, most commonly Visa and Mastercard, but interest rates are steep (APRs usually *start* at 21 per cent). American Express and Diners' Club charge cards are also available, as is the US credit card MBNA, which provides more competitive rates providing you keep the amount owed under control.

Opening an Account

You can open a bank account in Ireland whether you're a resident or a non-resident. It's best to open an Irish bank account in person, rather than by correspondence from abroad. In fact most Irish banks will insist on seeing you in person before they will open an account for you. Ask your friends, neighbours or colleagues for their recommendations and simply go along to the bank of your choice and introduce yourself. You must be aged at least 18 and provide two forms of identification (including one with a photograph, such as a passport) as well as proof of residence in Ireland (e.g. a recent utility bill) if applicable. It's best to set up an account before moving to Ireland so that you can transfer funds in advance. It's also sensible to keep an account open in the country you're leaving to deal with final bills and unexpected expenses.

If you need to open an account with an Irish bank from abroad, you must first obtain an application form, available from foreign branches of Irish banks or direct from banks in Ireland. You'll want to select a branch near to where you will be living in Ireland. If you open an account by correspondence, you need to provide evidence of your place of residence and, if you're depositing a large sum of money, confirmation of where the funds originated.

Credit rating is calculated differently in Ireland from other countries and you should supply as much information as possible about your financial status in your present country. If you're leaving a country where credit rating is important, such as the USA, and to which you may return later, it's worth asking your bank or credit card company if you can maintain a credit card rating whilst resident abroad, as credit cards invoiced in Europe won't show in credit records in the USA. The Irish Credit Bureau (ICB) is a private company operating a credit referencing system. For a small fee (IR£5) you may have access to your own file and challenge or request clarification of any details you believe to be incorrect or potentially misleading.

Non-Residents: Since Ireland became a full member of the European Union (EU), banking regulations for both resident and non-resident EU citizens have been identical, so that even non-resident EU citizens may open an Irish pound account.

Although it's possible for non-resident home owners to do most of their banking via a foreign account using debit and credit cards and Eurocheques, you will still need an Irish bank account to pay your Irish utility and tax bills (which are best paid by direct debit). If you have a holiday home in Ireland, you can have all your correspondence (e.g. cheque books, statements, payment advices, etc.) sent to an address abroad. Most banks offer non-resident savings accounts in which you can deposit money in virtually any major currency without incurring handling or administrative charges.

In addition to ordinary deposit accounts, you may have the option of a term deposit account (in which you must leave your money for an agreed term of up to 12 months) or guaranteed bonds (which are for cash deposits of between 18 and 78 months with a minimum deposit of IR£3,000). Occasionally banks come up with 'special offers' for non-residents like the Bank of Ireland's Double Option account. To open a non-resident savings account, you'll need to provide proof of identity or a reference from your current bank. Note, however, that withdrawals from foreign currency bank accounts attract capital gains tax unless the money is used for the account holder's personal expenditure outside Ireland. This principle will continue to apply even if the foreign currency account becomes a Euro account on 1st January 1999.

Residents: You're considered to be a resident of Ireland if you have your main centre of interest there, i.e. if you live and work there more or less permanently. The procedure for opening a bank account is no different whether you're a resident or a non-resident, but residents are subject to tax on all interest earned whereas non-residents are entitled to earn interest on deposits free of Irish tax (see below). Note that it isn't advisable to close your bank accounts abroad unless you're certain you won't need them in the future. Even when you're resident in Ireland, it's cheaper to keep money in local currency in an account in a country you visit regularly (such as the UK), rather than pay commission to convert Irish pounds. Many foreigners living in Ireland maintain at least two cheque (current) accounts: a foreign account for international and large transactions, and a local account with an Irish bank for day to day business.

Offshore Banking

If you have a sum of money to invest or wish to protect your inheritance from the tax man, it may be worthwhile looking into the accounts and services (such as pensions and trusts) provided by offshore banking centres in tax havens such as the Channel Islands (Guernsey and Jersey), Gibraltar and the Isle of Man (around 50 locations world-wide are officially classified as tax havens). Offshore banking has had a good deal of media attention in recent years. The big attractions are that money can be deposited in a wide range of currencies, customers are usually guaranteed complete anonymity, there are no double taxation agreements, no withholding tax is payable, and interest is paid tax-free. Many offshore banks also offer telephone banking (usually seven days a week).

A large number of American, British and other European banks and financial institutions provide offshore banking facilities in one or more locations. Most institutions offer high-interest deposit accounts for long-term savings and investment portfolios, in which funds can be deposited in any major currency. Many people living abroad keep a local account for everyday business and maintain an offshore account for international transactions and investment purposes. However, most financial experts advise investors not to rush into the expatriate life and invest their life savings in an offshore tax haven until they know what their long-term plans are.

Accounts have minimum deposits levels which usually range from the equivalent of around IR£600 to IR£12,000, with some as high as IR£120,000. In addition to large minimum balances, accounts may also have stringent terms and conditions, such as restrictions on withdrawals or high early withdrawal penalties. You can deposit funds on call (instant access) or for a fixed period, e.g. from 90 days to one year (usually for larger sums). Interest is usually paid monthly or annually; monthly interest payments are slightly lower than annual payments, although they have the advantage of providing a regular income. There are usually no charges providing that a specified minimum balance is maintained. Many accounts offer a cash or credit card (e.g. Mastercard or Visa) which can be used to obtain cash from ATMs throughout the world.

When selecting a financial institution and offshore banking centre, your first priority should be for the safety of your money. In some offshore banking centres, all bank deposits are guaranteed under a deposit protection scheme, whereby a maximum sum is guaranteed should the financial institution go to the wall (the Isle of Man, Guernsey and Jersey all have such schemes). Unless you're planning to bank with a major international bank (which is only likely to fold the day after the end of the world!), you should check the credit rating of a financial institution before depositing any money, particularly if it doesn't provide deposit insurance. All banks have a credit rating (the highest is 'AAA') and a bank with a high rating will be happy to tell you what it is (but get it in writing). You can also check the rating of an international bank or financial organisation with Moody's Investor Service. You should be wary of institutions offering higher than average interest rates; if it looks too good to be true it probably will be – like the Bank of International Commerce and Credit (BICC), which went bust in 1992.

Ireland has its own 'offshore centre' in Dublin's International Financial Services Centre, where there are subsidiaries of both Irish and foreign banks offering a variety of financial services to non-residents, including foreign currency transactions such as non-resident deposits and Euro-currency loans and deposits.

In Ireland there are specific tax rules relating to offshore funds which may negate the tax advantages. When you cash a foreign life assurance policy, for example, you'll be liable to capital gains tax at the full 40 per cent (the reduced rate of 20 per cent doesn't apply). In addition, you won't be entitled to indexation relief or the annual capital gains tax exemption of IR£1,000 (see page 125). Both are, however, available on offshore distributor funds, although income is subject to income tax at the highest rate that applies to you, and, when the units in the policy are sold, the proceeds are liable to CGT at 40 per cent. In the case of non-distributor funds, any gains are subject to income tax, PRSI (see page 117) and levies.

MORTGAGES

Mortgages or home loans (for both residents and non-residents) are usually obtained from Irish banks and building societies. The Irish Mortgage and Savings Association (IMSA), which represents the Irish Permanent, First National, EBS, ICS, Irish Nationwide and Irish Life, has around 60 per cent of the mortgage market and funded nearly 50,000 mortgages in 1997, around 10,000 more than the previous year. Mortgages are also available from foreign banks in Ireland and offshore banks.

Although there are relatively few foreign banks in Ireland, there's speculation that more will enter the mortgage market with the introduction of the Euro on 1st January 1999. British banks in particular are expected to start offering competitive mortgages to Irish homebuyers. The Euro will certainly affect lending criteria. For example, whereas there are high penalties for opting out of a short-term fixed rate (with some lenders demanding as much as five months' interest), lenders will in future be able to obtain funding from the large Euro market instead of the restricted IR£ market and will be in a position to offer more flexible US-style re-mortgage options. If you raise a mortgage outside Ireland for an Irish property, you should be aware of any impact this may have on your foreign or Irish tax liabilities or allowances.

As a result of increased competition, lenders have tended to relax their criteria for borrowing in recent years. Whereas previously you needed to be a long-term saver with a building society, you can now literally walk in off the street and, providing you have the required income, take out a mortgage with more or less any institution.

Mortgages are based on the lending institution's valuation, which is usually below the market value of the property. The maximum mortgage in Ireland is 90 per cent of the valuation (although there's usually a limit of 70 per cent for non-residents), subject to certain conditions, principally that the buyer can demonstrate his capacity to repay the loan over the agreed term. Note that the amount you can borrow isn't necessarily the same as the amount you can afford to borrow! Most institutions will lend up to 250 per cent of annual income in the case of sole applicants or 250 per cent of the main income plus 100 per cent of the second income in the case of joint applicants (e.g. a husband and wife). For example, if one partner is earning IR£25,000 per year and the other IR£15,000, the maximum permitted loan will be IR£77,500. The minimum cash deposit required on agreeing to buy a property is usually 10 per cent of the purchase price, although a 5 per cent deposit is often accepted.

There's a variety of mortgages available in Ireland. The most straightforward is a repayment or 'annuity' mortgage, which is effectively a simple loan which you pay off monthly. In the early stages, a high proportion of your payments are taken up by the interest on the loan and as the amount you owe reduces you begin to pay off more of the capital. This type of mortgage is particularly attractive to first-time buyers because of the tax relief they can obtain on mortgage interest (see below) – a benefit which is greatest during the first few years when they are most likely to be short of cash. With a repayment mortgage, you usually have a choice between fixed rate repayments over a variable term and variable rate repayments over a fixed term. With the former method, the amount repaid each month remains constant regardless of fluctuations in interest rates, but the number of monthly payments varies (if interest rates go up, the term lengthens and vice versa). With the latter method, the reverse applies: the number of repayments is fixed, but the amount repaid each month varies according to the prevailing interest rate.

There are advantages and disadvantages to each option. In the present economic climate, with interest rates as low as 6 per cent, most people are opting to fix their repayments. Variable mortgage rates in Ireland are in the region of 7.5 per cent, although by the time Ireland becomes a member of the Euro on 1st January 1999, they will need to fall by around 2 per cent to bring them into line with those of other single currency countries. After that date the Central Bank will no longer be allowed to adjust interest rates, therefore it could become more advantageous to take out a variable rate mortgage. Note, however, that it's possible to fix the interest rate for a limited period only (usually up to a maximum of ten years). Some banks offer split or combination interest rates, whereby part of the loan is fixed and part at a variable interest rate.

Another option, which is becoming more common, is a capped rate mortgage, whereby you pay a premium to guarantee that your mortgage rate won't rise above the rate originally fixed. You can of course always increase the amount you repay each month or year, either as a fixed percentage or by lump sum payments. Needless to say, few people do so! Note that if you opt for a fixed rate mortgage or one whose rate of increase is limited, you may incur a redemption fee if you sell the property and redeem the loan (or part of it) before the end of the term. Similarly, if you decide to switch from a fixed rate to a variable rate before the end of the fixed rate period, you may need to pay a 'funding fee'.

The vast majority of Irish home-buyers are opting for repayment mortgages (over 95 per cent compared with around 60 per cent in 1992). Another option is an endowment mortgage, which combines the mortgage repayment with savings through a life assurance policy; by the end of the mortgage term, the value of the endowment policy should have grown sufficiently to repay the mortgage and may leave you with a surplus. On the other hand, there's no guarantee that the proceeds of the policy will be sufficient to repay the mortgage loan. AIB Bank also offers a 'Surplus Builder' scheme, combining capital repayment and insurance premiums, as well as more sophisticated options such as pension mortgages, which are only available to those who are self-employed or who work for a company which doesn't offer an occupational pension scheme. A pension mortgage operates in essentially the same way as an endowment mortgage: your monthly repayments cover only the interest on the loan, while separate payments are made into a personal pension plan. At the end of the mortgage term the proceeds of the pension plan pays off the capital and the surplus (hopefully) provides you with a retirement income.

Other options available include a 'deferred start' mortgage, whereby you make no repayments for the first one to three months of the term, which is available only with repayment mortgages; a 'flexible month' whereby you don't make a repayment for one or two months of the year, but pay correspondingly more in the remaining months (available with repayment and endowment mortgages, although the endowment element must be paid each month); and a 'mortgage break' which allows you to suspend your repayments for up to three months in any year (this can be done up to four times, making a total break of 12 months, but the mortgage must still be repaid within the original term). Always shop around for the best offer (or get a mortgage broker to do it for you) and ask the effective interest rate including all commissions and fees.

If you borrow over 70 or 80 per cent (depending on the lender) of the purchase price, you must pay a mortgage indemnity fee (sometimes called a mortgage indemnity bond). This is to safeguard lenders against making a loss if they need to repossess the property and sell it. The fee is usually around 3 per cent of the difference between a specified percentage of the purchase price and the amount borrowed. So, for example, if the purchase price is IR£100,000 and you borrow IR£80,000 from a bank which requires indemnity above 70 per cent, you must pay an indemnity fee of 3 per cent of the difference between IR£70,000 and IR£80,000, i.e. IR£300. To this must be added a 2 per cent government levy, bringing the total to IR£306. Some lenders will spread the cost of the indemnity over the term of the mortgage, while others don't charge an indemnity fee, but impose a higher rate of interest for loans above 80 per cent. If you're buying a property for investment, the indemnity fee is 4 per cent.

A mortgage indemnity fee isn't to be confused with a mortgage protection plan, which is insurance to ensure that you don't lose your home when you're unable to pay the mortgage, e.g. if you lose your job or suffer a major accident or illness, or that your family doesn't lose it in the event of your death. There are various plans available, costing around IR£4.50 per IR£100 monthly repayment. You'll also need to obtain life insurance cover before your lender will agree to advance you a mortgage (a mortgage protection policy is usually the minimum cover required). Note also that in purchasing a property you'll incur expenses and fees totalling at least 5 per cent of the purchase price (see **Fees** on page 158).

Commercial Property: If you're purchasing commercial premises, the mortgage procedure is essentially the same as with a normal home loan, but the lending criteria are usually slightly different. Whereas you may be able to borrow 90 per cent of the value of a residential property, for example, you're usually limited to 75 per cent in the case of commercial property. In general it's less straightforward to obtain a commercial loan, which depends very much on the value of the property and your level of income. The self-employed usually need to provide a copy or their accounts or, in the case of a new business, a business plan in support of a mortgage application. If you're buying a residential property for letting, you must usually take out a commercial loan unless you opt for a fixed rate for ten years.

Mortgage Term: The normal mortgage term in Ireland is 15 years, although mortgages can be repaid over as little as five years or up to 25 years or more. In his recent government report on house prices (published in April 1998), Dr. Peter Bacon called for the introduction of longer-term loans to help young house-hunters gain a foothold on the mortgage ladder. The Irish Permanent was the first to react, introducing a 35-year mortgage in March 1998, and the TSB followed by increasing its maximum term to 30 years. Perhaps not surprisingly, there have been few takers for these new long-term mortgages. In any case, some institutions impose a shorter maximum repayment period on non-residents. Repayments are usually made monthly, but can be made weekly, fortnightly, quarterly or even annually.

Mortgage Application: Mortgages are usually applied for locally. If you live abroad or in a different part of Ireland from where the property you're planning to buy is situated, you'll need to submit written confirmation that you have employment in the area of the property. If you're an employee on Pay As You Earn (PAYE), you'll need to provide a copy of your most recent P60 or PAYE balancing statement and a letter from your employer confirming your basic salary and your employment status. If you have been with your present employer for less than a year, you'll need a reference from your previous employer. If you're self-employed, a copy of your audited accounts for the last three years will be required, with a letter from your accountant confirming that your tax affairs are in order.

If you're buying a new house which is still under construction, full plans, specifications and a site map need to be submitted. You'll also need to produce the original National House Building Guarantee Scheme Certificate (HB47), which will be provided by the builder, or (if you're employing a builder directly) a letter from an architect confirming that he will supervise the construction and certify compliance with planning permission and building regulations. In all cases you'll also need to produce details of any outstanding loans, including your most recent annual bank statement showing all payments made to date, estimates for any proposed work to be done on the property (which should also be taken account of when making the valuation) and any documents relating to separation or divorce (if applicable).

Buying Through a Broker: Between 30 and 40 per cent of all new mortgages in Ireland, plus an increasing proportion of re-mortgages and investment mortgages, are arranged through mortgage brokers. From the borrower's point of view, brokers certainly make the job of choosing a mortgage a lot simpler. They save you the time and trouble shopping around, check the details of all loans available and in some cases even provide a form-filling service, so that all you need to do is sign on the dotted line. If you're self-employed and derive your income from various sources, you may well find it easier to obtain a mortgage through a broker rather than direct from a bank or building society. Note, however, that although brokers insist that they are completely independent, there are cases where they seem reluctant to deal with certain lenders. Banks and building societies pay some brokers more than others for the business they introduce (commission rates vary from nothing to one and a half per cent) and some brokers may even have special deals with particular lenders.

A few estate agents (such as Sherry FitzGerald) have their own brokerage service. Hooke & MacDonald owns 50 per cent of the Irish Mortgage Corporation, one of Ireland's bigger brokers, which also has life and pensions advisory services in addition to a tax consultancy. Such arrangements offer the advantage of a 'one-stop shop' for homebuyers and investors, and in some cases offer a better chance of obtaining mortgage approval before viewing properties, so that meaningful offers can be made on the spot (but they may not necessarily give you the best deal).

Buying Through an Offshore Company: It may be possible to avoid certain Irish taxes by purchasing your property through an offshore company located in a tax haven state such as Jersey or the Isle of Man. For example, you'll still pay the purchase stamp duty, but on resale the buyer will have the option to purchase the shares of the company owning the property and so pay stamp duty at 1 per cent instead of the normal rate, which could be as high as 9 per cent (see page 158).

Mortgages for Second Homes: If you have spare equity in an existing property, either in Ireland or abroad, it may be more cost-effective to re-mortgage that property (or take out a second mortgage on it) than take out a new mortgage for a second home. It involves less paperwork and therefore lower legal fees, and a plan can be tailored to meet your individual requirements. Depending on the equity in your existing property and the cost of your Irish property, this may enable you to pay cash for a second home or take out an unsecured personal loan. The disadvantage of re-mortgaging or taking out a second mortgage is that you reduce the amount of equity available in the property. If you do take out a second mortgage, you'll need to provide a recent statement from your existing mortgage lender. If you've paid off the mortgage on your existing property, you'll be able to 'cross-secure' a loan on a second home. If you let your second home, you may be able to offset the interest on your mortgage against letting income. For example, if you let an Irish property for three months of the year, the income will offset a quarter of your annual mortgage interest.

Foreign Currency Loans: It's also possible to obtain a foreign (i.e. not Irish) currency mortgage, e.g. in pounds sterling, Swiss francs, US dollars, Deutschmarks, Dutch guilders or even 'exotic' currencies such as Japanese yen. Foreign currency mortgages have become increasingly popular in recent years, although the take-up is still relatively small. It is, however, an extremely risky way to borrow money, as interest rate gains can be wiped out overnight by currency swings. On the other hand, if the currency happens to be devalued, the rewards can be huge. Anyone who took out a yen loan a few years ago, for example, is now benefiting from its 20 per cent devaluation. With Ireland joining the Euro in 1999, foreign currency loans will become less attractive as the Euro zone will offer low-interest rates (only a few countries such as Japan and Switzerland will offer lower rates).

If you do decide to take out a foreign currency loan, experts advise that it's in the currency in which you're paid or in the currency of the country where a property is situated (in this case, Irish pounds). In this case if the foreign currency is devalued, you'll have the consolation of knowing that the value of your Irish property will ('theoretically') have increased by the same percentage when converted back into the foreign currency. When choosing between an Irish pound loan and a foreign currency loan, make sure that you take into account all costs, fees, interest rates and possible currency fluctuations. Note that if you have a foreign currency mortgage, you must usually pay commission charges each time you transfer foreign currency into Irish pounds and remit money to Ireland. Note also that most banks 'load' foreign currency loans (e.g. charge high fees). **Regardless of how you finance the purchase of a second home in Ireland, you should always obtain professional advice.**

Payment Problems & Changing Lenders: If you're unable to meet your mortgage payments, lenders are usually willing to re-schedule your mortgage so that it extends over a longer period, thus allowing you to make lower payments. Note that if you simply stop paying your mortgage, your lender will embargo your property and could eventually repossess it and sell it at auction. If you want to change lenders, you may be offered an incentive to do so by an institution that's keen to have your business, although this isn't common in Ireland. Also bear in mind that if you do make a change you'll usually incur solicitor's fees, and no lender will offer to pay those for you! Finally, note that when a mortgage is taken out on an Irish property, it's based on that property and not on the individual, therefore it isn't possible to take over an existing mortgage from a previous owner or pass your mortgage on when you sell a property.

TAXATION

They say there are only two disadvantages to living in Ireland: the weather and the taxes. Nothing can be done about the weather, but taxes – or at least some of them – can be avoided. The Irish have always believed that they are the most highly-taxed people in Europe. In fact, thanks to the biggest tax reduction package in the history of the state in 1997, Irish taxes are slightly below the EU average according to a recent KPMG survey. But even prior to this, the proportion of net earnings (after taxes) had gradually increased, particularly for those in the lower income brackets who are up to 9 per cent better off than they were in 1994 from a tax point of view. Nevertheless, Irish income tax rates are significantly higher than in the UK, the USA and Canada.

   This section explains the general tax situation in Ireland, although before deciding to settle in Ireland permanently you should obtain expert advice regarding Irish taxes. This will (hopefully) ensure not only that you don't make any mistakes that you'll regret later, but also that you take optimum advantage of your current tax status. There are usually a number of things you can do in advance to reduce your tax liability, both in Ireland and abroad. Be sure to consult a tax adviser who's familiar with both the Irish tax system and that of your present country of residence. For example, you may be able to avoid paying tax on a business abroad if you establish both residency and domicile in Ireland before you sell. On the other hand, if you sell a foreign home after establishing your principal residence in Ireland, it becomes a second home and may then be liable to capital gains tax.

   Tax evasion in Ireland is a criminal offence, for which offenders can be heavily fined or even receive a prison sentence. On the other hand, tax avoidance, i.e. legally paying as little tax as possible (if necessary by finding and exploiting loopholes in the tax laws), isn't only legal but highly recommended!

FINANCIAL REPRESENTATION

If you're a non-resident with property in Ireland you should appoint someone locally to look after your financial affairs and declare and pay taxes on your behalf. This person would normally be an accountant or tax consultant, to who all communications will automatically be sent by the Irish tax authorities. You can also have your representative check your bank statements, ensure that your bank is paying your regular bills by standing order (such as electricity, gas and telephone), and that you have sufficient funds in your account to pay them.

Note that if you're a non-resident and are collecting rent on a property in Ireland, you need to appoint a 'collecting agent' of some kind, otherwise your tenants will deduct tax at the standard rate from their rental payments. A collecting agent doesn't need to be an auctioneer, accountant or tax consultant, but can be anyone who's resident (and therefore paying tax) in Ireland.

If you need someone to keep your tax affairs in order and to complete an annual return on your behalf, an Irish accountant or tax consultant will charge around IR£400 a year for this service, depending on the complexity of your finances.

INCOME TAX

Ireland has a PAYE (Pay As You Earn) system of income tax and all paid employees must be registered for PAYE. Irish income tax rates vary between 24 per cent (on net earnings up to IR£10,000) and 46 per cent (above IR£10,000). The first IR£3,150 are exempt (IR£3,550 if you're over 65 and IR£3,650 if you're widowed) and there's a special dispensation for artists, writers and sports stars, who don't pay tax on their royalties. Even if you don't fall into one of those categories, there are various ways to reduce your liability. Belgians, Dutch and Scandinavians will find Irish income tax low, while most other Europeans will pay around the same or less. Paying Irish income tax can even be advantageous, as there are more allowances for some people than there are in other countries. If you're able to choose the country where you're taxed, you should obtain advice from an international tax expert. Employees' income tax is deducted at source by employers and individuals aren't responsible for paying their own income tax, unless they have other sources of income. Self-employed people are liable to tax in the same way as employees, but it's collected differently and there are different rules regarding allowable expenses. If you're self-employed, you must pay a lump sum before 1st November each year and then make a detailed tax return by the end of the following January (see below).

Irish income tax is payable on both earned and unearned income. Taxable income includes salaries, pensions, capital gains, property and investment income (dividends and interest), and income from professional or business activities. It also includes employee perks such as overseas and cost-of-living allowances; contributions to profit sharing plans; bonuses (annual, performance, etc.); benefits-in-kind (such as a company car, preferential loan, health insurance, club subscriptions, free accommodation or meals); stock options; home leave or holidays (paid by your employer); children's private education; and storage and relocation allowances. Note that if you're returning to Ireland and your employer is paying your relocation expenses, you'll need a tax exemption for these payments from the Inspector of Taxes.

If you set up a business in Ireland and hire employees, you must obtain their P45 or tax-free allowance certificate and notify your local tax office that you have employed them. If neither a P45 nor a current year's tax-free allowance certificate is available (e.g. with a first-time employee), you'll need to complete form P46 and operate PAYE/PRSI (see page 104) on an 'emergency basis' until a tax-free allowance certificate is received. This means that employees are given the equivalent of a single person's allowance (IR£3,150 a year) for the first four weeks only (i.e. IR£61 a week) and taxed at 24 per cent on the rest of their earnings. For the next four weeks they are taxed at 24 per cent on all their earnings and thereafter at 46 per cent on all earnings. Employees receive a rebate (as appropriate) once they have obtained a PRSI number and tax-free allowance certificate, depending on their residence status.

If you're an employee and have no P45 or tax-free allowance certificate, you'll be taxed on an emergency basis as described above. Note that if you lose your P45, a copy may not be made and the necessary information must be sent by your employer to the Revenue Commissioners. If you're a director of a limited company, you must submit a P45 or P46 to the tax office yourself. As a company director you may make lower PRSI contributions (see page 117), but are subject to the same PAYE as other employees.

If you're self-employed, you won't need to pay income tax until after your first year of trading. Two months before the year end, you'll be sent a preliminary tax notice informing you when your first payment is due. As a sole trader you pay income tax at 24 per cent on the first IR£20,000 of your annual profit and thereafter at 46 per cent. If you're operating as a company, you pay corporation tax at 25 per cent on your first IR£50,000 profit and thereafter at 32 per cent (unless you qualify for the special 10 per cent manufacturing rate). This means that there can be a considerable tax advantage in carrying on a business through a company instead of as an individual. The rate of corporation tax has been reduced in recent years and is expected to fall even further as the government's stated aim is to reduce it to 12.5 per cent by 2006 (see below).

There are also various tax incentives and reliefs for companies, such as the Business Expansion Scheme (BES) relief, research and development incentives, and film investment relief. On the other hand, there are tax penalties for closely controlled family owned companies ('close' companies) if excess funds are allowed to build up. If your business is expected to make a loss in its early stages, it may be better to operate initially as a sole trader, because losses can be offset against income from other sources (if you have any) and you can then establish a company without immediately incurring high taxes. In terms of individual income, there's a tax advantage in taking a dividend rather than a salary out of the business, but the total tax paid by the individual and the company will be greater, as salary payments are tax deductible for corporation tax purposes.

Corporation Tax: In May 1997, the Irish government announced that a single rate of corporation tax for all companies of 12.5 per cent for trading profits and 25 per cent for non-trading profits would become effective by the year 2006. As a step towards this goal, the main rate of corporation tax was reduced on 1ˢᵗ January 1998 from 36 to 32 per cent. The 'reduced rate', applicable to the first IR£50,000 profit, was cut from 28 to 25 per cent. A special 10 per cent rate for manufacturers was introduced in 1980 to encourage inward investment and is the lowest corporate tax rate in the Organisation for Economic Co-operation and Development (OECD). However, this is due to expire at the end of 2005 for companies operating in the International Financial Services Centre in Dublin and in the Shannon region, and at the end of 2010 for all other companies.

Liability

In general, liability for Irish taxes depends on your residence status. You're considered resident in Ireland for tax purposes if you spend 183 or more days there in a tax year or 280 days in two consecutive tax years. (But if you're in Ireland for 30 days or less in either of those years, they won't count towards the 280 days.) You become 'ordinarily resident' when you have been resident for three consecutive tax years. If Ireland is considered to be your permanent home, you're said to be 'domiciled' there (this is distinct from your legal nationality and your residence status). You may choose to be treated as an Irish resident from the date of your arrival if you intend to remain in Ireland permanently and if you think it will be to your tax advantage (you will need to satisfy the Inspector of Taxes that you'll be resident the following year). Note that the 183-day rule also applies to other EU countries and many countries (e.g. Britain) limit visits by non-residents to 182 days in any one year or an average of 90 days per tax year over a four year period.

If you're returning to Ireland and you're both resident and domiciled in the year of your return, you'll be liable to Irish income tax on all your income, but if you have spent less than 183 days in Ireland during the previous year and are therefore not resident, your employment income earned before your return will be exempt, although your non-employment income may be taxable. Note that Irish residents are liable to tax on both Irish source income and foreign income (including foreign pension income) and that the latter is also liable for taxation in the foreign country. However, Ireland has double taxation agreements with 30 countries (see below), so you will obtain relief if your country of residence is among them.

If you take up employment on your return to Ireland but have not worked there since the start of the current tax year (i.e. 6th April), you'll need to complete Form 12A, which is available from the tax office or from your employer. If you intend to reside in Ireland, you'll probably receive the full income tax allowance, but if you start work part way through the tax year intending only to stay a few months, you may be restricted to a temporary or emergency tax allowance (see above).

If you're a tax resident in two countries simultaneously, your 'tax home' may be determined by the rules applied under international treaties. Under such treaties you're considered to be resident in the country where you have a permanent home; if you have a permanent home in both countries, you're deemed to be resident in the country where your personal and economic ties are closer. If your residence cannot be determined under this rule, you're deemed to be resident in the country where you have a habitual abode. If you have a habitual abode in both or neither country, you're deemed to be resident in the country of which you're a citizen. Finally, if you're a citizen of both or neither country, the authorities of the countries concerned will decide your tax residence between them!

If you intend to live permanently in Ireland, you should notify the tax authorities in your previous country of residence. You may be entitled to a tax refund if you depart during the tax year, which usually necessitates completing a tax return. The authorities may require evidence that you're leaving the country, e.g. evidence of a job in Ireland or of having bought or rented a property there. If you move to Ireland to take up a job or start a business, you must register with the local tax authorities soon after your arrival.

Double Taxation: Irish residents are taxed on their world-wide income, subject to certain treaty exceptions (non-residents are taxed only on income arising in Ireland). Citizens of most countries are exempt from paying taxes in their home country when they spend a minimum period abroad, e.g. one year. Ireland has double taxation treaties with many countries, designed to ensure that income that has been taxed in one treaty country isn't taxed again in another treaty country. The treaty establishes a tax credit or exemption on certain kinds of income, either in the country of residence or the country where the income is earned.

Ireland has double taxation agreements with the following countries: Australia, Austria, Belgium, Canada, the Czech Republic, Cyprus, Denmark, Finland, France, Germany, Hungary, Israel, Italy, Japan, the Republic of Korea, Luxembourg, the Netherlands, New Zealand, Norway, Pakistan, Poland, Portugal, Russia, South Africa, Spain, Sweden, Switzerland, the UK, the USA and Zambia. An agreement with Estonia is expected to be ratified in 1998 and treaties with Latvia and Lithuania are to come into effect on 1st January 1999.

Some of these agreements have recently been or are in the process of being re-negotiated (e.g. with Austria, Belgium, Canada, France, Italy, Norway and the USA), so you should check the current position before making any tax-related decisions. Ireland is also negotiating double taxation agreements with Egypt, Greece, India, Malaysia, Mexico, Romania and the Slovak Republic, and is expected to start negotiations with Argentina, China and Turkey in late 1998. Where applicable, a double taxation treaty prevails over domestic law. For more information on double taxation agreements, ☎ 067-3353.

Even when there's no double taxation agreement between Ireland and your country of residence, you can still obtain relief from double taxation. In these cases overseas tax may be deducted as an expense, but there are certain qualifying criteria. Note that if your tax liability in another country is lower than that in Ireland, you must pay the Irish Revenue Commissioners the difference. If you're in doubt about your tax liability in your home country, contact your nearest embassy or consulate in Ireland. The USA is the only country that taxes its non-resident citizens on income earned abroad (US citizens can obtain a copy of a brochure, *Tax Guide for Americans Abroad*, from American consulates).

Leaving Ireland: When leaving Ireland, foreigners must pay any tax due for the previous year and the year of departure. A tax return can be filed before or after departure and must include your income and deductions from 6th April of the departure year up to the date of departure. When departure is made before 5th April, the previous year's taxes are applied. If this results in overpayment, a claim must be made for a refund. A tax clearance certificate isn't required before leaving Ireland.

Deductions, Allowances & Credits

Before you become liable for income tax, you're entitled to certain deductions, allowances (or reliefs) and credits. Your total earnings (less allowable expenses) is your 'aggregate income' (also referred to as your 'net income' or 'adjusted profit' figure), from which you make deductions to arrive at your 'total income'. Allowances and reliefs are then deducted and the resultant figure is your 'taxable income', on which your social insurance (PRSI – see page 117) contributions and government levies are calculated. From your total tax you may then deduct tax credits and reliefs.

Allowable expenses are those incurred 'wholly and exclusively for the purposes of the trade' (e.g. insurance, accountancy). Business entertainment isn't allowable, although expenditure on staff entertainment can be deducted for tax purposes. Similarly, while depreciation in general isn't an allowable expense, certain capital allowances are tax deductible (see below). It's generally more difficult to justify expenses if you're an employee than if you're self-employed, but the Revenue Commissioners publish a list of flat rate expenses allowable in different kinds of employment.

Deductions

Tax deductions include covenants, interest on certain types of loans and retirement annuity contributions. The maximum allowance for covenants, with the exception of those to permanently incapacitated people, is 5 per cent of total income. Qualifying interest includes loans to invest in companies or partnerships where certain conditions are met, e.g. the company mustn't deal in land and you must be a full or part-time employee and have a minimum share holding in the company. Retirement annuity contributions up to 15 per cent of earnings (20 per cent if you're aged 55 or over) are also tax deductible.

Allowances

Each individual is entitled to a basic personal tax allowance, in addition to which there are allowances for single-parent and widowed parent families. Income tax allowances can also be claimed in respect of children and dependent relatives, age, employment, rent, medical expenses, imported cars, as well as for certain kinds of investment and capital expenditure. There are special allowances for the blind and those who work abroad. On the other hand, if you receive certain benefits with your employment ('benefits-in-kind'), you may be liable for additional tax. The major deductions and allowances are detailed below:

- **Personal Allowance:** The personal tax allowance for 1998/99 is IR£3,150 (IR£3,650 if widowed). There's no tax advantage in being married, the allowance for a married couple being exactly twice the individual allowance.

- **One-Parent Families:** Single parents can claim an additional tax allowance of IR£3,150 so that their total allowance is the same as that of two-parent families. Widowed parents are entitled to an annual allowance of IR£2,650 plus an extra IR£5,000 in the first year after bereavement, IR£4,000 in the second year and so on reducing IR£1,000 in the fifth year.

- **Children and Dependants:** You may claim tax allowances for your children. An allowance of IR£450 is made for each of the first two children and IR£650 for each additional child, which means that a married couple with four children will pay income tax on earnings above IR£8,500 instead of the usual IR£6,300 for a couple without children. If you have an incapacitated child, you're entitled to an allowance of IR£800 and there's also a dependent relative allowance of IR£110. If you care for an incapacitated person, you can claim an allowance of IR£8,500. Special allowances are made for single parents and recently widowed people with dependent children (see below).

- **Age Allowance:** The allowance for those aged over 65 is IR£400.

- **Employment:** Any individual with income taxed under the PAYE system may claim an income tax allowance of IR£800. This also applies to company directors, providing that their share holding is less than 15 per cent, and to the children of self-employed people or company directors who work full-time in their parents' business.

- **Rent:** Tax relief is available on rent paid for private accommodation up to a limit of IR£500 a year for a single person, IR£750 a year for a widowed person and IR£1,000 a year for a married couple.

- **Blindness:** Blind people are entitled to an extra tax allowance of IR£1,000.

- **Medical Expenses:** A tax allowance is available for your own or your family's medical expenses (such as visits to your GP, hospital treatment, prescribed drugs, and other services and appliances prescribed by a doctor) above a certain limit. The limit is IR£100 if the expenses were incurred by only one member of the family and IR£200 if by more than one. Maternity care and routine optical and dental treatment are excluded. If you have private health insurance and your expenses have been reimbursed by your insurer, you cannot claim tax relief.

- **Imported cars:** If you're bringing a car with you from abroad, you may be entitled to relief on vehicle registration tax, providing that the car has been used by you for at least six months before your move to Ireland and that you import it within 12 months of your transfer of residence. If you're granted tax relief, you mustn't sell, hire or even lend the car to anyone within a year of its registration in Ireland. Details of vehicle registration tax relief are available from vehicle registration offices.

- **Capital Allowances:** Capital allowances are tax allowances on fixtures, machinery, etc. used in the operation of a business. The rates are 15 per cent of cost for the first six years and 10 per cent in the seventh year. In other words, capital expenditure can be 'written off' over seven years. The Finance Act 1994 introduced tax allowances for certain urban renewal programmes in Dublin, Cork and Galway, and, as part of a government initiative to regenerate seaside resort areas, the Finance Act 1995 entitled buyers of holiday homes in certain resorts to capital allowances. These allowances are in respect of 100 per cent of the cost of a property (less the proportion attributable to the site) up to a maximum of IR£25,000 per year, of which 50 per cent could be received in the first year and 5 per cent annually over the next ten years. The accommodation must be used solely for letting to tourists between April and October each year and not occupied by any person for more than two consecutive months or more than six months in any year.

The areas granted designated status are parts of Achill, Arklow, Ballybunion, Bettystown, Bundoran, Clogherhead, Clonakilty, Courtown, Enniscrone, Kilkee, Lahinch, Laytown, Mosney, Salthill, Tramore, Westport, and Youghal, while certain other resorts have restricted relief on rental income only. Needless to say, properties in these areas are being snapped up like the proverbial hot cakes, but if you're considering buying a hotel, guest house or holiday home, either for your own use or for rental, and can commit to an 11 year investment, it may be worth investigating (a 'Guide to the Renewal Scheme for Traditional Irish Seaside Resorts' is available from most banks). Note, however, that most of the Urban Renewal programmes have now expired and the Seaside Resort Renewal scheme is due to expire on 30th June 1999.

- **Working Abroad:** If you're resident in the Republic and work abroad (except in the UK) for 90 days or more (in blocks of at least 14 days at a time) in any tax year, you can claim a Working Abroad Deduction (WAD) in income tax proportional to the number of days spent abroad. You may also be eligible for a reduction in benefit-in-kind from a company car that you're unable to use while abroad (see below). If you work abroad for a continuous period of at least 13 weeks but spend at least one day each week in the Republic, you can pay tax on your earnings in the foreign country providing that it's one with which Ireland has a double taxation treaty (see above). You may not claim a Working Abroad Deduction as well as Cross Border Relief (CBR). In fact, since CBR in practice applies only to people working in Northern Ireland and WAD isn't available for work in the UK, it's unlikely that you could be eligible for both.

If you're going to be working outside Ireland for a period of six months or more, you're permitted by the Finance Act 1997 to invest in special tax-free policies with companies based in the International Financial Services Centre in Dublin. On your return to Ireland, you may cash the policies and benefit from any profit tax-free; alternatively you can keep the policies, in which case you won't pay tax on any profit made during the period you were outside Ireland (but will pay tax at 24 per cent on the remaining period when you cash the policy). If you agree not to cash the policy until you're aged 60 or over, you can claim 25 per cent of the fund tax-free (see **Pensions** on page 114).

● **Benefits-In-Kind:** A benefit-in-kind is when employees' are given benefits or when expenses are borne by their employer in lieu of salary, e.g. a company car, accommodation, low interest loans, medical insurance and club subscriptions. The taxable value of such benefits varies: the last two are valued at the actual amount paid by the employer; the others are more complex. Company cars are taxed according to their 'open market value' (OMV), which may be up to 10 per cent less than their normal retail price. The maximum taxable value (or 'cash equivalent'), if the employer bears all the running costs (i.e. insurance, servicing, repairs, road tax and fuel), is 30 per cent of the OMV; the minimum cash equivalent, if the employee pays all the running costs, is 18.5 per cent of the OMV. There are further reductions if your business mileage exceeds 15,000 a year or if you spend 70 per cent or more of your working time away from your normal place of work.

There are various ways of reducing the benefit-in-kind from a company car. 'Mileage reimbursement' is a scheme whereby you provide your own car and claim reimbursement for business mileage at revenue approved rates. Your employer gains a tax benefit compared with paying company car running costs and passes it onto you as additional salary. This scheme favours those who have a less expensive car and do between 16,000km (10,000mi) and 32,000km (20,000mi) a year on business. 'Employee contribution', on the other hand, favours those who have a more expensive car (i.e. worth over IR£15,500), where the employee makes a contribution to the cost of the car equivalent to the benefit-in-kind and the employer pays the employee the tax saving on running costs. Pooled cars can be exempt from a benefit-in-kind charge, providing they are used by several employees and for minimal private mileage, and are usually kept at the business premises.

The benefit of accommodation is equivalent to the open market rent of the property plus any expenses borne by the employer (e.g. utilities and cable TV). The Revenue Commissioners use 8 per cent of the market value of property as a guideline rent, but in practice the benefit is often calculated on the actual rent paid by the employer to the landlord. Preferential rate loans become a benefit-in-kind if the interest rate is less than the 'specified rate' (7 per cent for home loans and 11 per cent for other loans). The employee is then taxed on the difference between the specified rate and the preferential rate.

● **Investments & Savings:** Normally Irish residents must pay Deposit Interest Retention Tax (known as DIRT!) on all interest earned from investments and savings. The rate of DIRT is 24 per cent. Non-residents can earn interest free of Irish tax, providing that the appropriate revenue declaration (available from post offices and banks) has been completed. Once DIRT has been deducted, no further income tax is payable, but the interest earned must be included in your income tax return, and PRSI (see page 117) and levies are payable on it. However, certain investments are taxed at lower rates, some of which are listed below:

 − Special Savings Accounts (SSAs) attract 'only' 20 per cent tax on interest earned and aren't subject to PRSI or other levies, so earnings don't need to be entered on your income tax return. The maximum permitted investment in an SSA is IR£50,000 per person.

- Special Investment Products (SIPs) are available from insurance companies, stockbrokers and unit trust promoters. Providing at least 55 per cent of your SIP investment is in Irish stocks and shares, income is taxed at 10 per cent. Your total investment in SIPs and SSAs may not exceed IR£75,000. So, for example, if you have the maximum permitted IR£50,000 invested in SSAs, you can invest only a further IR£25,000 in SIPs.

- *An Post* offers Savings Bonds and Savings Certificates and you may invest up to IR£60,000 in each. Returns are reasonable and tax-free. Bonds will earn you 12 per cent tax-free after three years (equivalent to 3.85 per cent per annum) and Savings Certificates 25 per cent tax free after five years and six months (equivalent to 4.14 per cent per annum). An even better investment are *An Post's* Instalment Savings, which earn 30 per cent tax-free over six years (equivalent to 4.89 per cent per annum), but these are limited to a total of IR£3,600.

- Small investments of IR£3,000 and upwards may be made with life insurance companies. Earnings needn't be declared on your income tax return because tax at the standard rate of 24 per cent is deducted by insurance companies and no PRSI (see page 117) or levies are due. In general you may access your money – or at least part of it – immediately (unless you invest in Tracker bonds, which usually tie up your money for between three and six years). In theory you're buying a life insurance policy, but in practice you may cash it in for its full value.

- Tax relief is also available on shares purchased by employees of Irish companies up to a lifetime limit of IR£5,000. The shares must be retained for a minimum of three years. Tax relief of up to IR£25,000 a year is available if you invest in shares in a Business Expansion Scheme (BES) company, but they must be retained for at least five years. BES funds are operated by most financial institutions, who usually spread the risk involved by investing in a number of qualifying companies. Tax relief up to the same amount is available for investments in certain film projects, but only on 80 per cent of the investment made. However, you need retain the investment for one year only.

Credits

Your taxable income is taxed at 24 per cent up to IR£10,000 and thereafter at 46 per cent. PRSI (see page 117) and government levies (see below) are then applied to the total tax figure, from which can be deducted certain tax credits and reliefs for dividends, DIRT deducted by the bank (see above), mortgage interest, Section 23 (see below), private health insurance, local authority service charges and any PAYE tax paid.

- **Dividends:** Tax credits on dividends from companies paying corporation tax at the full rate (i.e. not at the 10 per cent manufacturing rate) are at the rate of 11/89ths (12.36 per cent), but these are to be abolished on 6th April 1999.

- **Mortgage Interest:** You're entitled to claim tax relief at 24 per cent on the interest charged on your mortgage, although the amount you can claim has been reduced in recent years and is likely to fall further. Currently you can claim relief on 80 per cent of the interest paid, less IR£100 per person (IR£200 for a married couple). If you're a first-time buyer, you're entitled to 100 per cent tax relief on interest up to IR£2,500 per annum (IR£3,600 for a widowed person), but this only applies to mortgages taken out after 6th April 1994 and will cease to apply in 1999. As a result of recent government measures designed to make residential property a less attractive investment (and so curb rising prices), tax relief is no longer available on the interest paid on borrowings to purchase or build property for letting. Note, however, that non-Irish nationals can buy Irish property for investment and claim mortgage interest relief at home. There's also restricted tax relief on loans for repairs or improvements to residential property.

- **Section 23:** Tax relief (called 'section 23') is available on residential properties in designated areas that were constructed or refurbished during a predetermined period, meet certain size and quality requirements, and are let for at least ten years.

- **Insurance:** You're entitled to tax relief at 24 per cent on private health insurance premiums paid during the previous tax year (life insurance premiums are no longer tax deductible).

- **Local Authority Service Charges:** The credit due on local authority service charges is calculated according to the amount paid in the previous calendar year (i.e. 1st January to 31st December 1997 for the tax year 1998/99) and is limited to IR£36 (i.e. 24 per cent of IR£150).

Any personal income taxes paid in another country can also be deducted from your tax base under double taxation agreements (see page 107). Note, however, that if you pay higher tax abroad than would have been paid in Ireland, you won't receive a rebate from the Irish tax authorities!

Pensions

Pension income is generally taxable in the same way as other income (there are certain exemptions for non-resident pensioners). Occupational pensions are usually taxed at source, but all other pensions must be declared on your annual tax return. There are various kinds of state pensions available to retired or elderly people in Ireland, of which the three main types are retirement pensions, old age contributory pensions and old age non-contributory pensions. To qualify for an Irish state retirement pension you must:

- be aged over 65;

- have ceased full-time work (you may still work part-time);

- have started paying PRSI contributions (or their equivalent abroad) before the age of 55 (see page 117);

- have made 156 weeks' PRSI contributions and an annual average of at least 48 weeks between 5th April 1979 and the end of the tax year immediately preceding your retirement;

- have paid an annual average of at least 24 weeks' PRSI from 1953 (or the date you started work) until 5th April 1979;

Retirement pensions aren't means tested and are therefore independent of any other income you may have. You don't need to be retired to qualify for an old age contributory pension, for which the conditions (since 21st November 1997) are that you:

- are aged over 66;

- started paying PRSI contributions (or their equivalent abroad) before the age of 55 (see page 117);

- made a total of 260 weeks' PRSI contributions between 1953 (or the date that you started work) and the end of the tax year immediately preceding your retirement, with an annual average of at least ten weeks' PRSI contributions.

The old age contributory pension is therefore likely to benefit people who worked in Ireland for a short time before emigrating and working for a long period abroad, as well as women who have only spent short periods working.

Those over 66 who have not made sufficient PRSI contributions to qualify for an old age contributory pension may still be entitled to an old age non-contributory pension, which is subject to a means test. If you're aged over 66, regardless of your pension situation, you're entitled to free travel (subject to certain conditions) and possibly also allowances for electricity, TV and telephone rental, plus other benefits. If you're aged over 66 and living alone or are over 80, you may also be entitled to additional benefits such as a fuel allowance and rent/mortgage interest assistance.

The state pension in Ireland is extremely low, representing only some 25 per cent of the average industrial wage. The maximum non-contributory pension is IR£70.50 per week and the maximum contributory or retirement pension is IR£83 per week. The living alone allowance is an extra IR£6 per week and fuel allowances vary between IR£5 and IR£8 per week. The government has stated that it intends to raise the level of pension benefits to IR£100 per week by the year 2002, but even this would only be a small increase in real terms. In fact, with the impending 'greying' of the population, the level of state pensions is unlikely to increase very much, so it's important to consider taking out a private pension as well as ensuring that your state pension is kept 'topped up'. Various personal savings schemes are available, but only an approved pension plan allows you to claim tax relief at the highest available rate and to take part of your pension fund tax-free on retirement.

Private Pensions: To be eligible for a private or personal pension you must be resident in Ireland for tax purposes (see page 106) and your income must be 'earned', i.e. you cannot take out a personal pension with, for example, rental income or income from investments. If you cancel your pension plan within the first year, you'll derive no benefit from it, but if you cancel it after the first year it will remain 'paid up', which means that the amount you have contributed remains invested and you can use it to buy a pension on retirement. The same happens if you join a company with an occupational pension scheme. You cannot withdraw funds from your pension before the age of 60 except under special circumstances, e.g. serious illness.

Over 95 per cent of companies in Ireland have employee occupational pension schemes, the average cost of which is between 10 and 20 per cent of employees' salaries, depending on whether the scheme is funded entirely by the employer or whether employees make a contribution. The total pension payable is typically one-sixtieth of the final salary for each year of service, totalling two-thirds of final salary (the maximum private pension allowed by the Revenue Commissioners) after forty years' service. The employee's contribution can be either compulsory or voluntary (around three-quarters of company pension schemes involve compulsory employee contributions). Under a voluntary scheme, employees may make additional voluntary contributions (AVCs) of up to 15 per cent of their earnings, although the usual contribution is between 5 and 7.5 per cent. However, as you're entitled to tax deduction for all contributions, it's worthwhile making as high a level of AVCs as you can afford. You should, however, take professional advice before making any AVCs.

There are essentially two kinds of occupational pension scheme in Ireland: defined benefit (sometimes called a 'final salary' scheme), where the employee's pension is defined in advance, and defined contribution (also known as a 'money purchase' scheme), where the employer's contribution is defined in advance. In defined contribution schemes, a percentage of your total base salary is contributed by the employer, whereas in defined benefit schemes your 'pensionable' salary means your salary after a portion has been offset in respect of your state pension. There are also differences in the extent to which, as a pension scheme member, you can influence the value of your eventual pension. Investment decisions for defined benefit schemes are made by the pension trustees, whereas in defined contribution schemes members make a choice between cash and managed funds, and their pension operates like a pension bank account. Around three-quarters of company pension schemes in Ireland are defined benefit, although smaller and more recently established companies have tended to prefer defined contribution schemes.

There are several tax advantages to making occupational pension contributions. Not only do you qualify for full rate income tax relief on your contributions, but your employer's contributions are treated as a non-taxable benefit. You also won't have to pay tax on the growth of funds you have invested in your pension. Finally, on retirement you'll be able to take a cash lump sum from your pension fund (see below).

Members of occupational pension schemes in Ireland pay a small annual fee (IR£3) to the Pensions Board, the body responsible for setting standards for company pension schemes and supervising them. There's no levy on personal pensions, but some pension companies make charges to manage private pension plans. These may be as high as 1.25 per cent, per annum plus a monthly 'contract charge' of IR£3. Before taking out a personal pension, you should check the charges.

If you're self-employed or aren't a member of a company pension scheme, you can of course still contribute to your own pension fund (although it's estimated that 75 per cent of self-employed people in Ireland don't) and you're also entitled to tax relief on payments into a personal pension plan up to 15 per cent of your 'net relevant earnings' (20 per cent if you're 55 or over). A number of organisations, including the Irish Small and Medium Enterprises Association (ISME ☎ 01-662 2755) and the Small Firms' Association (SFA ☎ 01-660 1011), offer schemes for the self-employed.

When you retire, you're entitled to a tax-free lump sum of up to 25 per cent of your pension fund. You may then receive the remainder of the pension fund as income over a period of up to ten years. In many schemes, pensions are guaranteed for a minimum period, but this may be for five years only and you should check whether you have the option to extend the period of payment. If you opt for 'escalating' payments, the amount you earn is calculated to increase annually in line with inflation. If you die before the term you've selected, your pension will continue to be paid to your dependants or, if you have chosen a 'spouse's pension', to your spouse. As it's income, your annual pension is liable to income tax. You may also be subject to PRSI and government levies, depending on your level of income (see below). If you die before you retire, the value of your pension fund at the time of your death will be paid to your dependants, who may then be liable for capital acquisition tax (see page 126). Many schemes allow you to give up part of your pension to provide for a dependant if you die after retirement. In general, the younger the dependant, the more you'll need to give up.

The usual investment options for private pension schemes are equities (domestic and international), gilts, property and managed funds, which are a mixture of the other three types. You may also be able to invest in with-profit funds, which is a less volatile option particularly suitable for those nearing retirement. If you're a member of a large company pension scheme, you may have no choice in the matter, but if you run your own company or are self-employed you can influence the kind of investment or even set up a small self-administered scheme that allows specific stock selection. When choosing a pension scheme, you should ask the following questions:

● How is my pension likely to relate to my final pay?

● Will my pensionable service be long or short?

● Will I receive the maximum permitted lump sum on retirement?

● What pension will be left after I've taken my lump sum?

● Who will my dependants be when I retire (e.g. are my children likely to be still dependent)?

● What provision is made for them if I die before or after retirement?

● Can I make extra provision for them?

● What increases can I expect to receive on my pension after retirement?

● What happens if I have to retire early?

A range of booklets explaining pensions in Ireland is available from the Pensions Board (☎ 01-676 2622).

Pay Related Social Insurance (PRSI)

Almost all employed and self-employed people in Ireland pay Pay Related Social Insurance (PRSI) and levies for health, employment and training. If you're employed, your first IR£100 per week (IR£5,200 per year) is exempt but earnings between IR£5,200 and IR£24,200 per year are subject to PRSI at 4.5 per cent. No PRSI is payable on earnings above this level. Government levies (a health contribution of 1.25 per cent and a training and employment levy of 1 per cent) are payable on your whole salary (there's no upper limit), unless you earn less than IR£10,750 a year or have a medical card, in which case you're exempt from both levies. Your employer also contributes to PRSI at 8.5 per cent if you earn less than IR£14,040 per year or at 12 per cent if you earn between IR£14,040 and IR£29,000. Your employer isn't required to make any PRSI contributions on your salary above

IR£29,000. PRSI and levies are payable on income from all sources with the exception of benefits-in-kind.

In general, PRSI contributions for the self-employed are lower than those for salaried employees, but they receive fewer benefits. If your income is below IR£2,500 a year and you've been advised by the Inspector of Taxes that you don't need to make a tax return, you're nevertheless liable for a flat-rate social insurance contribution of IR£124 per year. Once your total income from a business (and any other employment you may have) exceeds IR£2,500 per year, you become liable to PRSI at 5 per cent (compared with the total contribution of between 13 and 16.5 per cent payable by employers/employees). The first IR£1,040 of your annual 'reckonable income' is exempt from PRSI (reckonable income includes interest from investments or savings, dividends, rent from Irish property, etc., as well as earned income) and you'll pay 5 per cent on all income above that amount up to IR£24,200 per year.

The minimum PRSI contribution, however, is IR£215, so in practice if you earn between IR£2,500 and IR£5,340 you'll be making the minimum contribution (IR£5,340 – IR£1,040 = IR£4,300 X 5 per cent = IR£215). Earnings above IR£24,200 are exempt from PRSI, so there's effectively a maximum contribution of IR£1,158 (IR£24,200 – IR£1,040 = IR£23,160 X 5 per cent = IR£1,158). In addition, if your annual reckonable income exceeds IR£10,750, you'll be charged a 1.25 per cent health contribution and a 1 per cent employment and training levy on your *whole* income (the exemption on the first IR£1,040 and the ceiling of IR£24,200 don't apply). So, for example, on an annual reckonable income of IR£25,000, you must pay a total of IR£1,720.50 in PRSI and levies.

If you're a company director and your share holding is 50 per cent or more, you'll be classed as self-employed with regard to PRSI contributions. If your share holding is less than 50 per cent, your social insurance position will need to be individually assessed.

Social Welfare

Social welfare in Ireland isn't just for those who are unemployed. You may be entitled to welfare for a number of reasons (e.g. simply because you have children) and it's worth finding out in advance the benefits for which you qualify. It's also important to keep records of any welfare you receive in your country of residence. Many benefits cannot be backdated, so you should make a claim as early as possible.

Since 1994, anyone who's claiming social welfare benefits in an EU or EEA country is entitled under EU regulations to claim the same benefits in any other member country and to be treated exactly as a national of that country. If you're going to work in Ireland from another EU/EEA country, you should take with you a record of your previous social welfare contributions on forms E301 and E304. There are also special bilateral agreements between Ireland and Australia, Canada, New Zealand and the USA. If you're moving from any non-EU country (including these four), you should contact the International Operations section of Social Welfare Services (☎ 01-874 8444).

The Irish Social Welfare system is operated by the Department of Family, Social and Community Affairs (☎ 01-874 8444). The benefits available include child benefit; maternity benefit; one parent family payment (formerly called the lone parent's allowance); free travel; disability benefit; accident at work or occupational injury benefit; invalidity pension; survivors' and orphans' pensions; death grant; treatment benefit (dental, optical and aural); and unemployment benefit. These benefits fall into three categories: contributory (social insurance) payments such as maternity benefit, unemployment benefit, disability benefit, treatment benefit and contributory pensions, which are made against PRSI contributions (or the equivalent in the country from which you're moving); non-contributory (social assistance) payments such as the one parent family payment, and non-contributory pensions, which are made according to need (and subject to a means test); and universal services such as child benefit and free travel, which are unrelated to PRSI contributions or means. Note that even if you don't qualify for unemployment or disability benefit, you may be entitled to non-contributory unemployment or disability assistance.

Payments in respect of contributory benefits are calculated on the basis of your earnings and payments in the year *before* the period of claim. For example, if you're claiming disability benefit for the period January to December 1999, your claim will be based on your earnings and payments in the tax year 1997/98. Payments are usually made weekly and you can choose from four payment methods.

Child benefit: Child benefit can be claimed by all parents with children up to 16 years old (in some cases 18) and is paid monthly. The benefit is IR£31.50 per month for each of the first two children and IR£42 per month for each of the next two. Note that these payments are separate from the child allowances against income tax.

Maternity benefit: Maternity benefit is available to employed women who meet the PRSI contribution requirements, in which case they receive 70 per cent of their weekly earnings (up to a maximum of IR£250). If they're already receiving another benefit (e.g. a one parent family payment), the percentage will be reduced. Claims should be made around ten weeks before a baby is due, although payments won't start until around four weeks before the birth. Further details are obtainable from the Maternity Benefit Section of the Social Welfare Office (☎ 043-45211).

One parent family payment: The one parent family payment is a means-tested benefit available to those who are bringing up a child or children without a partner's financial support. It's separate from the single parent tax allowance. To claim the full weekly benefit of IR£70.50 plus IR£15.20 per child, you must be earning less than IR£115 per week. If you earn between IR£115 and IR£230 per week, you can claim reduced benefit.

Survivor's pension: The survivor's pension, which used to be called the widow's pension, is based on the PRSI record of the claimant (or of the claimant's deceased partner). Contributory benefits are IR£76.10 per week if you're over 66 and IR£74.10 if you're under 66. Non-contributory benefits are IR£72.50 (over 66) a week and IR£70.50 (under 66). If you're aged over 66, you're also entitled to free travel (subject to certain conditions) and possibly additional allowances for electricity, and TV and telephone rentals (etc.).

Details of the one parent family payment and all pension allowances can be obtained from the Pension Services Offices (☎ 071-69800).

Secondary benefits: If you're receiving certain types of social welfare payments (e.g. a pension or one parent family payment), you may be entitled to secondary benefits. These include: rent/mortgage interest supplement; fuel allowance (to help with heating costs during the winter months); smokeless fuel allowance (applicable in certain areas of Dublin and Cork where bituminous fuel is banned); butter vouchers; and back to school clothing and footwear allowance. Secondary benefits aren't paid immediately and you may have to wait for a 'qualifying period' of up to 15 months.

Tax Calculation

You should begin by listing all your income. This may include self-employment earnings; consultancy income (net of expenses); trading profits (net of expenses); employment income (including benefits-in-kind); investment income (including net profits from rented property, dividends and deposit interest excluding interest from special savings accounts); and any miscellaneous income such as pensions. From this you should deduct any capital allowances to give you your 'aggregate income'. Make your tax deductions (i.e. covenants, non-mortgage interest and pension contributions) to arrive at your 'total income'. Calculate your tax at 24 or 46 per cent and your PRSI and levies at the appropriate rate (see page 117). From your total tax deduct any tax credits and reliefs (on PAYE paid, dividends, mortgage interest, medical insurance and local authority service charges) to arrive at your net tax liability. Finally, deduct any preliminary tax already paid.

Married Couples: If you're married, you should list your and your spouse's income separately. Income which arises in joint names should be split equally between you. In the year of marriage, a couple are taxed as two single people unless the tax paid as such is greater than the tax payable by a married couple, in which case a refund can be claimed, but only from the date of your marriage. In subsequent years married couples have a choice of joint assessment, separate assessment or single person assessment. Unless you specify that you would like separate or single person assessment, you're automatically given joint assessment (also known as joint aggregation), which in any case is the only option when one partner isn't earning and is usually also the best arrangement in other cases.

Joint Assessment: Under joint assessment, you must decide which partner is the 'assessable spouse' (usually the higher earner), who's responsible for making the tax return and paying the tax. You'll both qualify for tax allowances as if you were single, but you're entitled to transfer allowances between you. If one of you is employed and the other self-employed, for example, there could be a cash flow advantage transferring all the allowances to the employed partner. As tax isn't payable under self-assessment until ten months after the end of the tax year, you would effectively be delaying payment of the bulk of your combined tax. If one partner earns less than your combined total tax allowances, you can transfer 'unused allowances' to the other. Similarly, if one partner earns less than IR£10,000 (the maximum income taxed at the lower rate of 24 per cent), you can transfer the 'unused rate band' to the other partner. For example, if one partner earns IR£8,000 and the other IR£12,000, you can effectively both be taxed at 24 per cent on all your earnings.

Separate Assessment: Under separate assessment you're still entitled to transfer allowances between spouses, but each partner's tax affairs are treated separately, so that you must each submit a tax return and pay your share of tax. Separate assessment may be chosen by couples who prefer to be financially independent yet don't want to lose out on the tax benefits available to married couples.

Single Person Assessment: Single person assessment (or separate treatment) is similar to separate assessment in that each partner is treated separately for tax purposes. The difference is that allowances aren't transferable between partners, so you can lose out on unused allowances and rate bands. This method of assessment is really only suited to couples who are both paying tax at the higher rate of 46 per cent.

Income Tax for Property Owners

Residents: Property income earned by residents should be included in their annual income tax declaration and tax is payable at their standard income tax rate. You're eligible for deductions such as repairs and maintenance, security, cleaning costs, management and letting expenses (e.g. advertising) and insurance, but can no longer (as of 23rd April 1998) claim a deduction for mortgage interest on a let property. You should seek professional advice to ensure that you're claiming everything to which you're entitled.

Non-Residents: Non-resident property owners in Ireland are liable for income tax on any income arising in Ireland, including income from letting a property (whether long-term or holiday letting). Because they aren't part of the self-assessment system, the tax must be deducted at source. This means that where rent is paid directly to a non-resident, income tax at the standard rate (24 per cent) should be deducted by the tenant. The non-resident can reclaim tax if the amount deducted is greater than his Irish tax liability on the net profit from the rent. If you appoint an agent to collect the rent on your behalf, the agent will be responsible for paying the tax rather than the tenant.

Declarations & Tax Returns

Tax returns must be submitted by both residents and non-residents with income in Ireland, unless they're on PAYE and have no other source of income. The tax year in Ireland runs from 6th April to 5th April, as in the UK. Since most taxes in Ireland are based on self-assessment, individual taxpayers are liable to report, calculate and pay any tax due within prescribed time limits. These are as follows:

- 5th July is the last date for claiming separate assessment (see below);

- 1st November is the deadline for preliminary payment of tax for the year ended 5th April last (you may pay either 100 per cent of your previous year's tax bill or 90 per cent of the current year's bill) and for payment of at least 90 per cent of your capital gains tax liability for the previous tax year;

- 31st January is the last date for submitting your tax return for the previous tax year (i.e. the year ended the previous 5th April), for payment of any retirement pension premium which you wish to claim against tax for the previous year, and for payment of the remaining 10 per cent of your capital gains tax liability;

- 1st March is the deadline for applying to pay next year's tax bill (i.e. the year starting 6th April next) by direct debit;

- 5th April is the last date for availing of tax deductible investments (e.g. film schemes and BES).

You can pay your preliminary tax by direct debit, in which case the cost is spread over the year. Note that with effect from 1999, preliminary tax will be due by 30th November following the start of the tax year and the deadline for submitting your tax return will be 30th November following the end of the tax year.

If you set up a business part way through the tax year (e.g. on 1st October), your first tax return should cover the period from 1st October to 5th April. Your second tax return will then be for the period from 6th April to 30th September, and thereafter you'll be taxed on your full accounting year (i.e. from 1st October to 30th September).

Companies liable to corporation tax must pay income tax and advance corporation tax (ACT), as well as preliminary tax on their profits, within six months of their accounting year end and make a final tax return within nine months. Close companies must account for distribution of profits within 18 months of their year end in order to avoid a close company surcharge. Claims for excess capital allowances, trading and rental losses, and group or consortium relief must be submitted within two years of the end of the relevant accounting year. Final ACT adjustments must also be made by then.

Tax forms can only be obtained from tax offices in Ireland. If you're self-employed or a company director, you should use form 11; PAYE employees and pensioners should complete form 12 and first-time workers form 12A. Form 1 is for partnerships and Form CT1 for companies.

There are penalties for being late with either your tax return or your payments. If you submit your tax return up to two months late, you'll be liable for a surcharge of 5 per cent of the tax payable or IR£10,000, whichever is lower. If your return is more than two months late, the surcharge is 10 per cent or IR£50,000, whichever is less. If you fail to pay your preliminary tax by the due date, you'll be surcharged at 1 per cent per month. You can be fined up to IR£1,200 if you fail to produce the required documents or (either negligently or fraudulently) make a false declaration of your income. If you falsify your tax return in order to reduce your tax liability, you can be imprisoned for up to 12 months and will be fined up to twice the amount owing. If you fail to pay the fine, you can be imprisoned for up to eight years. The Revenue Commissioners can publish a list of names of people who have been fined or imprisoned for tax evasion. They also carry out regular checks (called 'revenue audits') to ensure that everyone is paying the correct amount of tax. A cross-section of returns is selected as well as a certain number at random. From time to time particular trades or professions are targeted for audit.

If you need any help in completing your tax return, you can contact the central information office of the Revenue Commissioners (☎ 01-878 0000) or your tax office (there are 13 provincial tax offices, listed in the green pages of the phone book). Note, however, that this won't necessarily be the office in the area where you live. If you're an employee of a company whose headquarters is in another part of the country, for example, your tax office will be the one in that area. If you wish to see an inspector, you should make an appointment, but general assistance is always available (staff will even help you complete your tax form!). When you go to the tax office, you should take along some form of identification (if you're a non-resident), your PRSI number, your P45 (if appropriate) and any forms you have received from the Revenue Commissioners. It isn't necessary to take other documentation (such as rent books) unless requested to do so.

Before submitting your tax return, you should check that you've completed all the sections (where you have no income in a particular category, you should write 'none' rather than leave it blank). If you're claiming mortgage interest relief, you should enter the loan account number of your lender and attach you mortgage interest certificate stating the amount paid during the last tax year, as well as an estimate of the interest payable in the following year. Tax forms include customised pay slips showing your PRSI number, tax type, etc., which must be returned with the tax form, even if you're making a nil return. You should also include copies of the following documents:

- form P60;
- form P45 if you have ceased employment;
- details of any benefit-in-kind (especially a company car);
- if you're receiving any social welfare income, a statement from the Department of Social, Community and Family Affairs confirming the kind of income, the date payment began and the weekly amount;
- details of any rent paid (which should be entered on form 'Rent 1');
- if you're receiving rental income, a detailed account of gross rent and expenses such as furniture on which you may be entitled to a wear and tear allowance;
- details of any acquisitions and disposals of assets during the tax year which may be liable for capital gains tax;
- documentation relating to government stocks, rents and other income;
- the relevant claim form if you're claiming a dependent relative allowance for the first time;
- details of any allowable medical and dental expenses (which should be entered on forms 'Med 1' and 'Med 2' respectively);
- confirmation of any private health insurance subscriptions paid during the *previous* tax year;
- form RICT for any BES or film scheme investments;
- receipts for private tuition if appropriate;
- certificates of private pension contributions.

If you're a company or a sole trader, you'll also need to submit:

- a trading account showing details of sales and profit/loss for the tax year;
- a profit and loss account;
- a capital account;
- a balance sheet showing business assets and liabilities.

N. B. Finally, make sure that you sign the form!

There are three ways of paying your income tax in Ireland. You can post your payment to the Collector-General's Office using the pre-paid envelope provided with your tax form; you can pay it in person at the Collector-General's Office (at Apollo

House, Tara Street, Dublin 2 or Sarsfield House, Francis Street, Limerick); or you can pay by bank Giro. The last method is obligatory for payments of preliminary tax, VAT and employer's PAYE/PRSI.

Unless your tax affairs are simple, it's prudent to employ an accountant or tax consultant to complete your tax return and ensure that you're correctly assessed.

VALUE ADDED TAX (VAT)

You're obliged to register for value added tax (VAT) if your taxable supplies are likely to exceed IR£40,000 (in the case of goods) or IR£20,000 (in the case of services). You may register voluntarily before your turnover reaches those limits (e.g. if you're supplying goods or services to other VAT registered traders or if you're supplying zero-rated goods), but it's worth taking advice first. The standard rate of VAT in Ireland is 21 per cent. A reduced rate of 12.5 per cent applies to new buildings and building services; certain types of fuel; electricity; repairs and maintenance of cars; hotel and restaurant meals; cinema, theatre and concert tickets; sporting activities; waste disposal; veterinary services; agricultural services; newspapers and periodicals; tour guide services; short-term car hire; works of art and antiques; hairdressing; photographic prints and services; truck driving lessons; and non-basic foods. Livestock is taxable at 2.8 per cent. Basic foods; seeds for producing food; animal feed; fertilisers; oral medicine; books and booklets; children's clothing; education and training; insurance and banking services; passenger transport; and medical equipment are zero rated, as are items for export outside the EU or to VAT registered companies within the EU. Various financial, medical and educational services are exempt from VAT.

The difference between zero-rated and exempt supplies is that you can claim a VAT refund on your taxable business expenses if you make zero-rated supplies, but not if you make exempt supplies. VAT is usually payable (or redeemable) every two months, but it's possible to set up a monthly direct debit and submit a VAT return once a year only. There's a new form BP1 (Business Profile) on which you can present simplified accounts for revenue inspection. All records relating to VAT calculation must be kept for a minimum of six years.

Commercial property transactions may be subject to VAT at 12.5 per cent unless the property was developed before 31st October 1972 and hasn't since been extended, altered or adapted. The rules concerning VAT on property are complicated and you should take expert advice before completing any commercial property transaction, particularly as there can be serious implications if you make a mistake. Two leaflets, *VAT on Property Transactions* and *VAT on Property* are available from the Revenue Commissioners (☎ 01-874 6821).

PROPERTY TAX

There's no longer a residential property tax, 'rates' or 'poll tax' in Ireland, although a charge of around IR£50 a year is made for refuse collection. Note, however, that when selling a property you may be required to provide evidence that any property tax due before its abolition has been paid (e.g. by obtaining a clearance certificate). **There's no wealth tax in Ireland.**

CAPITAL GAINS TAX (CGT)

Capital gains tax (CGT) is levied on the profit realised on the sale of certain assets. Gains made on the sale of your principal residence (and up to one acre of land) are exempt. If there's more than one acre of land or the land has development value, there's only partial exemption and the gain must be calculated separately for the house and the land. In the case of a secondary residence, allowances are made for inflation and capital expenditure, so it's important to keep records of everything you've spent on the property. Note that if you let your family home in Ireland before leaving the country, you must reoccupy it on your return in order to preserve the 'principal private residence exemption' from CGT on any future sale of the property. You're also entitled to an annual CGT exemption of IR£1,000 which you should take advantage of by, for example, selling any shares which have risen in value. It's no longer possible to transfer your CGT exemption to your spouse and disposals between spouses or relatives (known as 'connected persons') are treated as if they were made at the open market value, with CGT payable in the usual way.

In December 1997, the rate of CGT was halved from 40 to 20 per cent on all disposals except development land valued at over IR£15,000, which remains subject to CGT at 40 per cent. The aim of the reduction was to encourage investors who had tied up large amounts in stocks and shares for the last 20 or 30 years to dispose of them and re-invest. Early indications are that the plan is working and many investors are doing just that (a side effect of all this re-investment is that Irish share prices are rising, in some cases to record levels). To qualify for the reduced rate of CGT, serviced land valued at less than IR£15,000 must be released for development before 2002, after which it will be subject to CGT at 60 per cent.

If you're resident and domiciled in Ireland, you'll be subject to CGT on the disposal of assets anywhere in the world. If you're a non-resident, your CGT liability is confined to certain Irish assets (mainly land and buildings). If you've been absent from Ireland for a period which includes three consecutive tax years, you may dispose of certain Irish assets free of CGT before your return, but you may incur tax in your present country of residence. If you elect to be resident in the year of your entry into Ireland, you'll be liable to CGT on gains in the whole tax year, even if you took up residence at the end of the year (although you'll be eligible for relief on any foreign tax paid on disposals of assets).

When calculating the gain that's subject to CGT, you may deduct the incidental costs of buying a property; any expenditure which enhances its value; costs incurred in establishing, preserving or defending title to or rights to a property; and the incidental costs of disposing of a property (e.g. legal and professional costs, advertising and stamp duty). Note that all these expenses can be 'indexed' (i.e. increased to current values to compensate for inflation) except in the case of development land.

You cannot claim interest against CGT except where a company borrows money to build a property (but not to enhance an existing property) and capitalises the interest. In the case of leasehold property, rent from the grant of a lease is liable to income tax, but if you receive a lump sum on granting the lease this is liable to CGT (providing that the lease is for more than 50 years – if it's for less than 50 years the lump sum is liable partly to income tax and partly to CGT).

If you sell a property for more than IR£150,000, you must obtain a clearance certificate from the Revenue Commissioners that CGT has been paid; otherwise the buyer is obliged to withhold 15 per cent of the purchase price against the possibility of CGT being unpaid.

A capital gain (or loss) on property must be declared by 31st January following the end of the tax year in which the disposal takes place. Preliminary CGT is payable on 1st November after the end of the tax year. Note that the period of ownership (for capital gains tax purposes) starts when 'beneficial ownership' of a property is acquired.

CAPITAL ACQUISITION TAX & PROBATE TAX

Ireland imposes a tax on gifts and inheritances called capital acquisition tax (CAT), which ranges from 20 to 40 per cent. For CAT to be payable, either the donor of the gift or inheritance must be 'domiciled' in Ireland or the gift itself (e.g. a property or bank balance) must be situated there. Note that 'domiciled' doesn't mean residing permanently or habitually or even at all, but having the intention to become resident in Ireland, so the Revenue Commissioners must prove intent if they want to collect taxes!

CAT (often loosely referred to as gift tax) is payable if you receive a gift or inheritance above a certain value unless it's a transfer between spouses, which is exempt. If you're the parent or child (or, in some cases where there are no children, a nephew or niece) of the donor, you may receive gifts or inheritance up to the value of IR£188,400 free of CAT. If you're a brother or sister, a niece or nephew, or a lineal ancestor or descendant, you're allowed to receive up to IR£25,120 free of CAT. Any other person may receive up to IR£12,560. Note that, in the case of inheritance from someone who has died, these amounts *include* all gifts received during the lifetime of the deceased! Above these thresholds, CAT is payable at 20 per cent on the first IR£10,000 (this rate was halved on 3rd December 1997), 30 per cent on the next IR£30,000 and 40 per cent above this amount.

For example, if you aren't related to the donor and you inherit a gift worth IR£60,000, you'll be liable to pay CAT of IR£12,976 (IR£60,000 – IR£12,560 = IR£47,440; IR£10,000 X 10 per cent = IR£1,000, IR£30,000 X 30 per cent = IR£9,000, IR£7,440 X 40 per cent = IR£2,976; IR£1,000 + IR£9,000 + IR£2,976 = IR£12,976). If you inherit a home from a brother or sister, its taxable value is reduced by 80 per cent or IR£150,000, whichever is lower. Note also that if the donor has previously paid CGT on a gift (e.g. a property), the amount of CGT paid may be deductible from the CAT liability of the recipient.

There are various (legal) ways of avoiding or reducing your liability to CAT. To begin with, you're entitled to receive gifts valued up to IR£500 annually from any person free of CAT, so large donations can be 'broken down' into smaller annual gifts to escape CAT. If a gift or inheritance is a business asset, you're entitled to business relief, which reduces the taxable value of the asset by 90 per cent. The asset must have been held by the donor for at least five years in the case of a gift and for at least two years in the case of an inheritance. The recipient must in turn retain the asset for a minimum of ten years or the tax relief may need to be 're-paid'. Agricultural property (including land, machinery, livestock and buildings) is also reduced in value by 90 per cent for CAT purposes. Items of cultural, scientific or artistic interest, such as paintings, books or historic buildings, may be exempt from CAT, providing the recipient allows reasonable public access to them for at least six years after the transfer. The proceeds of certain life assurance policies may also be exempt from CAT if they're used to pay taxes due on the insured person's death. So, for example, if the beneficiary is liable for inheritance taxes of IR£10,000 and the policy is worth IR£15,000, he will have to pay CAT only on the balance of IR£5,000 after other taxes have been paid.

If you want to spare your beneficiaries from CAT, there are certain measures you can take. For example, if your spouse is of pension age and you have no children, you should think about putting your property into a company, in which case no inheritance taxes applies on your death. If you have children, you can set up a trust by which you and they jointly own the property (a trust is a concept of the common law system which may be unfamiliar to mainland Europeans). There are certain charges involved in setting up and maintaining a trust, but these are negligible if your net worth is less than IR£500,000. If a transfer is a 'lifetime gift' (i.e. given while you're alive rather than inherited after you're dead), the amount of CAT due is reduced by 25 per cent and the first IR£500 is exempt. However, if you die within two years of making such a gift, the remaining 25 per cent of the tax becomes due. Note that the same taxes apply to intestacy (i.e. if you have no will) as to disposition by will. The rules of succession on intestacy state that, where there's no child or other descendant, the spouse takes all; where there's a spouse and descendants, the spouse takes two-thirds, the children one third; where there's no spouse, the children take all.

As in most countries, dying in Ireland doesn't free you (or more correctly your beneficiaries) from the clutches of the tax man. In addition to CAT, the beneficiary of an estate is liable to probate tax (or death tax) at 2 per cent of its value when it's over IR£10,000. Providing that the deceased was domiciled in Ireland at the time of his death, all his assets are liable to tax, even if some are located abroad. As with CAT, transfers between spouses are exempt, as is the permanent home of the deceased. Any debts owed by the deceased as well as funeral expenses (etc.) can be deducted from the taxable value of the estate. In the case of agricultural property, only 70 per cent of its value is taxable. Probate tax itself is an allowable deduction in calculating the taxable value of a gift or inheritance for CAT purposes. Note that probate tax can be avoided by transferring assets before death.

It's important for both residents and non-residents with property in Ireland to decide in advance how they wish to dispose of their Irish property. Ideally this should be decided even before buying property. Property can be registered in a single name; both names of a couple or joint buyers' names; the names of children, giving the parents sole use during their lifetime; or in the name of an Irish or foreign company or trust. You should obtain professional advice regarding the registration of an Irish property. It's advisable for a couple not only to register joint ownership of a property, but to share their other assets and have separate bank accounts, which will help reduce their dependants' liability for inheritance tax. Note that Irish law doesn't recognise the rights to inheritance of a non-married partner, although there are a number of solutions to this problem, e.g. an insurance policy used to fund payment of tax.

One way to reduce your liability for inheritance tax is to transfer legal ownership of property to a relative as a gift during your lifetime (see above). However, this is treated as a sale (at the current market price) and therefore incurs capital gains tax as well as any fees involved in the sale, which need to be compared with your anticipated inheritance tax liability. Whether you should will or 'sell' a property to someone depends on the value of the property and the relationship, and it may be cheaper for a beneficiary to pay CAT. Take, for example, a couple jointly owning a property in Ireland who wish to leave it to a child. When one of the parents dies the child inherits half of the property and pays CAT on its value above IR£188,400. Inheritance tax on the other half of the property is paid when the other parent dies. In this way no tax is paid on a property with a value of less than IR£376,800.

Inheritance law is a complicated subject and professional advice should be sought from an experienced solicitor who understands both Irish inheritance law and the law of any other countries involved. Your will is also a vital component in reducing Irish inheritance tax to the minimum or deferring its payment.

COST OF LIVING

No doubt you would like to try to estimate how far your punts will stretch and how much money (if any) you'll have left after paying your bills. Unfortunately, the cost of living in Ireland is high, particularly in relation to salaries, which are particularly low in rural areas, i.e. the majority of the country. Cars, books, alcohol, tobacco and luxury items are particularly expensive. The standard rate of VAT is also high at 21 per cent, although there are reduced rates for certain goods (see page 124). However, there's some compensation in the form of benefits to pensioners, which include free travel, healthcare, TV licences, telephone rental (plus a number of free calls), plus allowances for clothing, fuel, electricity and gas. This makes Ireland an attractive place for retirement as an increasing number of foreigners have discovered.

It's difficult to calculate an average cost of living in Ireland as it depends on each individual's circumstances and lifestyle. Your food bill, for example, will depend on what sort of food you're used to eating. A list of the approximate minimum monthly major expenses for an average single person, couple, and couple with two children are shown in the table below, although many live on less (most people will argue that the figures are either too high or too low). When comparing costs of living, remember to allow for differences in income tax and PRSI contributions (see pages 104 and 117 respectively). The numbers in brackets refer to the notes following the table.

ITEM	MONTHLY COST (IR£)		
	Single	Couple	Couple with 2 Children
Housing (1)	200	300	450
Food (2)	100	200	300
Utilities (3)	75	100	125
Leisure (4)	100	150	200
Transport (5)	75	90	100
Insurance (6)	60	100	125
Clothing (7)	40	60	100
TOTAL	650	1,000	1,400

1. Rent or mortgage payments for a modern or modernised apartment or house in an average small town or suburb, excluding Dublin and other high-cost areas. The properties envisaged are a studio or one bedroom apartment for a single person, a two bedroom property for a couple, and a three bedroom property for a couple with two children.

2. Doesn't include luxuries or alcoholic drinks.

3. Includes electricity, gas, telephone and cable or satellite TV.

4. Includes entertainment, dining out, sports and holiday expenses, plus newspapers and magazines.

5. Includes running costs for an average family car (i.e. third-party insurance, annual taxes, petrol, servicing and repairs), but excludes depreciation and credit costs.

6. Includes 'voluntary' insurance such as health, household (building and contents), third-party liability, travel, vehicle breakdown and life insurance. **Expensive private health insurance isn't included.**

7. Includes 'essential' clothing for work and play, but not extravagant shopping sprees.

4.

FINDING YOUR DREAM HOME

After having decided to buy a home in Ireland, your first tasks will be to choose the region and what sort of home to buy. If you're unsure where and what to buy, the best decision is usually to rent for a period. The secret of successfully buying a home in Ireland (or anywhere else for that matter) is research, research and more research, preferably before you even set foot there. You may be fortunate and buy the first property you see without doing any homework and live happily ever after. However, a successful purchase is much more likely if you thoroughly investigate the areas you're interested in; compare the range and prices of properties and their relative values; and study the procedure for buying property. It's a lucky person who gets his choice absolutely right first time, but there's a much better chance if you do your homework thoroughly.

For centuries Ireland's principal export was people, with the result that millions of people the world over can claim Irish ancestry. Now the tables are turning and many of these, as well as others without a drop of Irish blood in their veins, are being attracted to Ireland by its new-found prosperity. Whereas a few years ago the only foreign property buyers in Ireland were American 'showbiz' stars and business tycoons, Europeans now predominate, accounting for some 80 per cent of purchases in the early '90s. At first the Germans and Dutch were the keenest buyers, but the recent decline of the Irish punt against sterling as well as easier and cheaper travel has brought the British back in force. They currently account for about 60 per cent of property buyers, other Europeans 15 per cent, Americans around 10 per cent and the Irish themselves some 15 per cent. (After centuries of British occupation, the Irish take it as a compliment that so many Britons are 'returning' to Ireland now that they no longer own it!) In particular Ireland is attracting artists (musicians, painters and writers) due to its liberal tax regime (some 2,600 artists were granted tax exemption in 1995 alone). Tourism is also on the increase and the number of visitors to Ireland rose by over 10 per cent in 1996 compared with a European average of around 3 per cent. In fact, Ireland is very much the place to be, whether temporarily or permanently.

This chapter is designed to help you decide what sort of home to buy and, most importantly, its location. It will also help you avoid problems and contains information about the different regions of Ireland; the importance of research; the choice of location; renting as a prelude to buying; the cost of property and the fees involved in house purchase; buying new and resale; leasehold properties; timesharing (and other part-ownership schemes); estate agents (known as auctioneers in Ireland); inspections and surveys; conveyance, purchase contracts and completion; renovation and restoration; moving house; security; utilities and heating; property income; and selling a home.

REGIONS

Ireland is comprised of 26 counties divided between four provinces (or regions), Connacht, Leinster, Munster and Ulster, each of which has its own distinct identity forged in history and proclaimed in local laws, customs and values. The regions and provinces are described below and shown on the map in **Appendix D**.

Connacht

In the north-west of Ireland is the province of Connacht (or Connaught), encompassing 21 per cent of the Republic and comprising Counties Galway, Leitrim, Mayo, Roscommon and Sligo. Once regarded as a wilderness and the scene of the worst suffering during the potato famine of the 1840s, the west of Connacht is a get-away-from-it-all wilderness of rugged mountains, craggy cliffs, lakes and valleys, where little seems to have changed in centuries. The inland part of the province, bounded by the ubiquitous Shannon, is less striking, consisting of tidy fields and stone walls.

Galway: County Galway, the second-largest county in Ireland, is full of contrasts – flat in the south, alternately mountainous and boggy in the north. Irish Nationalists have traditionally referred to this area as the 'real Ireland' because its population is the least anglicised (half of its inhabitants still speak Gaelic as their first language). Galway is the centre of the *Gaeltachta* (Irish-speaking districts), where people are encouraged by government grants to go and live. The IDA (Industrial Development Authority) has even managed to attract industrial businesses to the area. Efforts to preserve the language are supported by Galway-based *Radio na Gaeltachta* and the new national Irish-language newspaper, *Foinse*, as well as by summer colleges where students from all parts of Ireland come to study Gaelic and learn traditional *ceili* dancing.

Connacht's capital, Galway City, is a busy place that has benefited from tourism and EU subsidies to such an extent that it's now one of Europe's fastest growing cities. Ireland's third largest city, with a population of some 50,000, Galway has its origins in the 13th Century. In mediaeval times the city had strong commercial ties with Spain (the so-called Spanish Arch remains to this day) and tradition has it that Christopher Columbus said a prayer at St Nicholas's Collegiate Church before setting out to discover America. In the 16th and 17th centuries the city's 'fat cats' traded skins for Spanish wine. Today its young population combined with 10,000 or more students from University College and Galway's many other educational establishments, make the city a lively, cosmopolitan place. It's famous for its festivals, notably the Galway Races and Oyster Festival, and manages to retain a friendly, intimate atmosphere. Galway City is the business capital of the west, offering some of the best conference facilities in Ireland.

The city is also the gateway to the strikingly beautiful Connemara, a wonderland of lakes and mountains now converted into a national park. Ferries provide a year-round link to the Aran islands, as does the world's shortest scheduled air service, Aer Árann's daily six-minute flights from Galway Airport. Surprisingly, there are airfields on all three main islands, the smallest of which, Inisheer (*Inis Oírr* in Gaelic), measures just 3km by 4km (2 by 3mi). Irish Gaelic is the first language on the islands, where ancient traditions co-exist with a more modern lifestyle. The largest island, Inishmore (*Inis Mór*), 12km (7mi) long and has a population of 900, while the middle island of Inisheer (*Inis Meáin*) is said to be one of the most unspoilt places in the world. Apart from one of Europe's most important pre-historic monuments (the cliff fort at Dun Aengus), you'll find only one pub and no bank – except once a month, when the bank pays the island a flying visit!

Mayo: Even wilder than Galway, although no longer remote since the opening of Knock (or Horan) International Airport in 1986, is the neighbouring County of Mayo, where towering cliffs alternate with sandy inlets and the countryside is littered with ancient monuments. It's one of Ireland's loveliest counties and today earns most of its income from tourism, although foreign companies have been encouraged to set up factories there. The so-called Barony of Erris (Mayo's *Gaeltacht* area) incorporates Europe's largest area of bogland, barely inhabited but teeming with wildlife. Mayo also boasts the earliest known land enclosure in the world, known as Ceide Fields. The county is an angler's paradise, with some of the best salmon, brown trout and sea angling in Europe, and it also boasts excellent climbing, hill-walking and golf. Ten of Mayo's beaches have been awarded EU 'Blue Flags' for cleanliness, four of which can be found on the island of Achill (Ireland's largest), joined to the Corraun Peninsula by a bridge. Achill is 22km (14mi) long and 19km (12mi) wide with a population of 3,000, while Clare Island (just to the south) is home to just 150 people and can be reached only by ferry.

The coastal town of Westport, one of Ireland's most popular resorts, is unusual in that it's a 'planned' town. The nearby Croagh Patrick mountain (known locally as The Reek) isn't just a famous landmark but a place of pilgrimage (Saint Patrick is reputed to have spent 40 days and nights praying and fasting on its slopes in 441 AD). The Marion Shrine in the town of Knock, where 15 people saw a vision of the Virgin Mary, St. Joseph and St. John, attracts over 1.5 million pilgrims from throughout the world each year and has been visited by the late Mother Teresa and Pope John Paul. Ireland's largest church, the Basilica of Our Lady, Queen of Ireland, was built in 1976 to accommodate 12,000 people and in 1986 Knock International Airport was opened to handle the vast influx of visitors (there are daily scheduled flights to and from the UK as well as charter flights from Switzerland and Germany during the summer). In contrast the resident population is sparse, with little over 100,000 in the whole county.

The people of Mayo are considered by some to be the 'purest' Irish and the county can lay claim to some celebrated inhabitants such as Michael Davitt (founder of the Land League in 1879, the biggest mass movement in modern Irish history), Mary Robinson (the first female President of Ireland) and Captain Charles Boycott, whose name has passed into the English language. Mayo's administrative capital is Castlebar, a market town of 6,000 people, which is in every way the centre of the county. Its largest town is Ballina in the north, with just 7,000 inhabitants. Property is less hard to come by in Mayo than in some other areas of Ireland, although prices aren't as low as may be expected. A three-bedroom house costs in the region of IR£65,000 and a half-acre plot as much as IR£25,000.

Leitrim: Leitrim ('lee-trim') is a quiet county which seems to have been forgotten by the rest of Ireland. It stretches from the sea to the island's centre, with all the varied landscapes that implies. Carrick-on-Shannon in the south-west of the county claims to be the loveliest town on the Shannon and is the principal base for cruising Ireland's most famous river. It's also an attractive and lively place with plenty of visitor attractions. Lough Allen is the first great lake on the Shannon and has recently been linked to the Shannon Navigation by the restoration of the Lough Allen Canal. Along with neighbouring County Cavan, Leitrim is an angler's paradise with literally dozens of lakes offering unrestricted access. Both new and resale properties are available in Leitrim and prices are reasonable.

Roscommon: Inland is County Roscommon, the only county in Connacht without a coastline. Rich farmland in the centre gives way to bog at its edges, while lakes and rivers abound. Lough Key Forest Park near Carrick-on-Shannon is Ireland's largest public forest, where herds of deer are among the abundant wildlife. The population of just 50,000 is almost entirely rural and the small town of Roscommon is the largest in the county. Property is readily available for those who are drawn to this part of Ireland and prices are modest, with a three-bedroom house costing from as little as IR£20,000.

Sligo: The gentle, civilised landscape of County Sligo (pronounced 'sly-go'), to the north-west, is broken spectacularly by the Ben Bulben and Knocknarea mountains. Sligo is noted for its archaeological remains and its music, traditionally played on the violin or 'fiddle'. It's also W. B. Yeats' county and most of the places which inspired his poetry are still intact. Colourful Sligo Town, the largest town in north-west Ireland and its unofficial capital, is a busy and prosperous place famous for its Yeats summer school. There's considerable demand for property in County Sligo, although both new and resale homes are available at reasonable prices.

Leinster

The province of Leinster covers the eastern and south-eastern parts of Ireland. Although it includes the greatest number of counties (Carlow, Dublin, Kildare, Kilkenny, Laois, Longford, Louth, Meath, Offaly, Westmeath, Wexford and Wicklow), it's the third largest province comprising some 23 per cent of the Republic. With slightly more sunshine and less rain than the rest of Ireland, although just as green, Leinster is a pleasant place to live. It's an area of tranquil rivers and soft hills contrasting with boglands and mountains. Outside County Dublin (with its one million inhabitants) the province is largely rural and has many attractions. The coastline boasts long, sandy beaches and picturesque towns such as Wexford and Kilkenny. Leinster also has more than its fair share of castles, monasteries, mansions and ancient monuments, and has always enjoyed a reputation for wealth thanks to its fertile soil.

Carlow: Carlow is the second-smallest county in Ireland and is mostly flat, although it borders mountains to the south-east and north-east. It's particularly unspoilt, being far enough from Dublin to escape the notice of commuters and having also managed to avoid the indiscriminate construction of bungalows ('bungalow bliss'), which are so often a blot on the landscape of the western counties. The rivers Barrow and Slaney are excellent angling waters and the county is a good place for pony trekking and golf. Carlow is known as the Celtic Centre of Ireland and contains many Druid and early Christian as well as Celtic relics. Most of its few inhabitants are farmers or workers at the sugar-beet factory in historic Carlow Town.

Dublin: County Dublin is completely dominated by the City of Dublin, whose rapid growth over the last 20 years or so has affected the whole county. It's divided into four regions: Fingal to the north of the city, Dun Laoghaire Rathdown to the south-east, South Dublin to the south-west and Dublin City itself.

Covering an area of 448km² (173sq mi), Fingal is the fastest growing region in Dublin County (it experienced a population increase of almost 10 per cent in the period 1991–1996) and includes several burgeoning city suburbs as well as Dublin Airport and the industrial area of Balbriggan. On the other hand, County Dublin boasts some magnificent coastline with picturesque seaside villages such as Loughshinny, Rush and Skerries, Finghal's 'jewel'. Inland there are tranquil river valleys and unspoilt rural villages such as Ballyboughal, Naul, Oldtown and Garristown, as well as some 30 golf courses. The Howth peninsula (just a few minutes from the capital) is a popular centre for sailing and other watersports, and provides spectacular views of Dublin Bay. Just to the north are the two-mile long 'Velvet Strand' of Portmarnock and the heritage town of Malahide with its marina and 14ᵗʰ century castle. One of the newest and largest shopping centres in the Dublin region is located at Blanchardstown, just to the west of the city.

On the opposite side of Dublin City, Dun Laoghaire Rathdown also has a beautiful stretch of coastline and some attractive seaside resorts. One of these is Dun Laoghaire itself (pronounced 'dun leary'), one of the main ports for ferries from Britain and the site of a vast new shopping centre. Nearby Blackrock is known for its traditional weekend market. Dalkey and Killiney, just south of Dun Laoghaire, have become favourite locations for the rich and famous, reputedly including such luminaries as Chris de Burgh, Nigel Mansell, Damon Hill, Lisa Stansfield, Gloria Hunniford, Neil Jordan and Enya – so much so that the area has recently earned the nickname "Bel Eire". Inland among the foothills of the Wicklow Mountains (also referred to as the Dublin Mountains) are several scenic areas such as Marlay Park, the starting point for walks along the Wicklow Way. Ireland's highest pub, Johnnie Fox's, is also here and is renowned for its seafood and unique atmosphere.

South Dublin also boasts fine parks (some 1,400 hectares), where there are facilities for golf, riding, angling and watersports. King John's Bridge in Lucan's Griffeen Valley Park is claimed to be Ireland's oldest. The Griffeen River is a tributary of the better known Liffey, which holds a special place in the hearts of Dubliners. The Liffey Valley, which separates South Dublin from Finghal, has recently been developed into an 'amenity' offering a variety of recreational facilities. South Dublin also has a vast, modern shopping centre (The Square in Tallaght) as well as a wealth of more traditional shops in villages such as Clondalkin, Lucan, Rathfarnham, Saggart, Rathcoole, Newcastle and Tallaght itself. South Dublin's position, on the main road and rail routes westward out of the capital and equidistant from Dublin Airport and the sea ports of Dun Laoghaire and Dublin itself, has made it an important centre for conferences and business meetings. The number of hotels in the area, particularly at the cheaper end of the market, is constantly increasing.

Property prices rose by as much as 40 per cent in just 12 months during 1997/98 in South Dublin, where apartments start at around IR£150,000 for one bedroom and can reach IR£500,000 for a penthouse. Two bedroom apartments selling for between IR£200,000 and IR£250,000 are particularly popular among what are called MBUs (marriage break-uppers), who want a spare room for visiting children. Farmland is understandably hard to come by but good value (as little as IR£3,000 per acre) when it can be found.

Ireland's capital, Dublin City is over twice the size of any other city in the country and is generally regarded as a separate province in itself. Sometimes referred to as 'dear dirty Dublin' by the Irish themselves, the city is certainly no Paris or Prague and suffered particularly in the '70s from careless town planning. Its Millennium Celebrations (not to be confused with those for the year 2000) in 1988 prompted a good deal of renovation, as did its selection as European City of Culture three years later. Unfortunately there are still thoughtless developments such as the recent construction of a 'virtual' motorway through the city centre. However, Dublin isn't about architecture but atmosphere and there's no shortage of that, although the relaxed reputation of the many bars is somewhat tempered by the conspicuous presence of bouncers on every door.

House prices in Dublin rose by around 35 per cent in 1997 and increases of 30 per cent were reported in the first quarter of 1998 alone! In fact the trend in recent years has been for most annual growth to take place in the first three months of the year, with a levelling off during the spring and summer. One-bedroom houses in the city centre now start at around IR£100,000, while extraordinary prices are being paid for houses in smart suburbs such as Donnybrook, Ballsbridge and Sandymount. More than IR£2 million has been achieved and IR£1 million or more is now almost routine in some particularly desirable areas.

The building industry in Dublin is booming and the number of new houses increased by around 30 per cent in 1997 alone. The city is bristling with cranes and new apartments, which comprised one in three homes constructed in Dublin in 1996, are springing from every available site. Older three-bedroom apartments in Dublin are fetching IR£350,000 and one-bedroom apartments in the city centre are hitting the IR£100,000 mark. In the late '80s, the Government looked for a way of renewing Dublin's city centre, which was racked with dereliction, particularly on the Quays and in the north inner city. Tax incentives were offered to builders and owner-occupiers and the latest Docklands Development is set to revitalise the last undeveloped part of Dublin. IR£1.6 billion will be spent over 15 years, a large part of which will be ploughed into apartment developments. Some 16-storey blocks have already been built and an estimated 10,500 homes are to be created by the year 2012.

Louth & Meath: The most northerly counties of Louth and Meath are predominantly farmland, but Louth, Ireland's smallest county, has a wild side, and in the Cooley Peninsula near the border with Northern Ireland it's one of the most beautiful and unspoilt places in the whole country. The coastal town of Dundalk is the county capital and contains a number of fine 15th century buildings, while nearby Carlingford has even earlier remains including a castle and mint. Ancient relics are concealed in the rich pastures of Meath (the seat of the ancient kings of Ireland is said to be on Tara Hill, from where you can see seven counties), but the county also boasts the popular seaside resorts of Clogherhead, Laytown and Bettystown, all part of a 'coastal resort' scheme. Meath's principal town, Drogheda, is a colourful place with medieval origins. Both counties have experienced a huge increase in population in recent years as more and more people working in Dublin have settled there and commute to the capital.

Kildare: County Kildare is one of the most densely populated counties (relatively speaking), being within easy commuting distance of Dublin. Towns such as Naas and Kilcullen tend to be clogged with traffic at peak times and villages such as Celbridge and Leixlip have been all but swallowed by the rapidly expanding capital. In fact Collinstown Industrial Park near Leixlip, where in 1990 there were stud farms and potato fields, is now Ireland's answer to 'silicon valley', home to Intel Ireland (the European subsidiary of one of America's largest microchip producers), Rank Xerox and IBM, among other giant corporations. None the less, there's still plenty of countryside to be enjoyed in County Kildare. The river Barrow, for example, provides good fishing and attractive cruising, and there are lovely drives and walks (and even barge trips) along the Grand and Royal Canals, which meet near Robertstown on their way to Dublin and the sea. Even the rather unattractive town of Kildare lies on the edge of the famous Curragh, a 2,000 hectare plain where some of the world's best race horses are bred and trained. The National Stud and Horse Museum is at Tully, adjacent to the famous Japanese Gardens.

Kilkenny: To the west of Carlow is Kilkenny, one of the most 'English' counties of Ireland, with its neat villages and well-tilled fields. It's a prosperous agricultural area noted for its craftsmen, particularly in Kilkenny City, Ireland's mediaeval capital and one of its architecturally most interesting towns. If Carlow is the Celtic Centre of Ireland, Kilkenny claims to be its 'hospitable heart': an abundance of hotels, restaurants, pubs, festivals and warm-hearted people make Kilkenny an excellent place for relaxation and enjoyment (but then the same could be said for most of Ireland!).

Laois: On the other side of the Slieve Bloom range and furthest south of this group of counties is Laois, a rural area divided by the N7 Dublin-Limerick road. Its only proper town, Portlaoise, has been bypassed by one of the few stretches of motorway outside the capital. The major employer in this part of Ireland is the Irish turf development authority (*Bord na Mona*), which provides work for some 5,000 people.

Longford: The counties of Longford, Westmeath, Offaly, and Laois, in the centre of Ireland, are flat and wet, being covered with lakes and bogland. They tend to be ignored by visitors passing through on their way from Dublin to the south and west, and as a result have their own unique, quiet beauty. Longford is a peaceful and picturesque county bordering Lough Ree, one of the great lakes on the Shannon. It has many pretty villages including Ardagh, Newtowncashel and Lanesborough.

Offaly: Offaly to the south, boasts the internationally famous monastic site at Clonmacnoise (one of Ireland's holiest places), the Slieve Bloom mountains with their cascading streams and waterfalls, the restored 18th century town of Birr (with the world's tallest box hedges!), and one of the Shannon river's main boating centres at Banagher. The principal town of Tullamore is another cruising base, but on the Grand Canal rather than the River Shannon (it's also home to a famous Irish whiskey).

Westmeath: Westmeath is similarly tranquil, although watersports enthusiasts are attracted to its chain of smaller lakes (Ennel, Owel, Derravaragh and Lene). Westmeath is particularly rich in places of interest such as Edgeworthstown House, seventeenth century Fore Abbey and Tullynally Castle (one of the 'Seven Wonders of Fore'), Delvin Castle and Castlepollard, the largest castellated house in Ireland. Glasson, known as the 'village of the roses', is in the heart of 'Goldsmith Country', where Oliver Goldsmith, one of Ireland's most famous poets, lived in the 18th century. Kinnegad, in the extreme east of the county, lies at the junction of the main roads from Galway and Sligo to Dublin, and is the centre of 'An Boreen Bradach' (a walker's paradise). The historic town of Athlone, once one of the few crossing points of the Shannon, is now the largest town on the river, a busy and prosperous place and a popular base for pleasure cruisers, while the county town of Mullingar ('capital of the lakes') is a thriving business and industrial centre on the Royal Canal.

Wexford: At the south-eastern tip of Ireland is County Wexford, the warmest and driest place in the country. In fact many Irish families spend their summer holidays there in preference to Spain! Wexford has some 200km (124mi) of coastline and numerous unspoiled sandy beaches, including the magnificent Curracloe Beach (which doubled as the scene of the Normandy landings in Steven Spielberg's film *Saving Private Ryan*). Wexford is one of the world's most important wild bird sanctuaries, visited by flocks migrating to and from the Arctic. Known as the 'model county', Wexford also offers heritage parks and museums, golf courses and race tracks (greyhounds as well as horses). The Blackstairs Mountains in the north-west of the county are a popular hiking area. Wexford is the closest point to Wales and in the past has been the landing place of many a foreign invasion, while Rosslare Harbour is a major ferry port for modern 'invaders' travelling to and from Britain and France. Nearby Wexford Town is among the most atmospheric and historically interesting places in Ireland and is internationally famous for its annual Opera Festival in October. Both new and resale property is readily available and prices are around average for the country as a whole.

Wicklow: County Wicklow, to the south, is another quintessentially Irish county, yet it's within half an hour's drive of Dublin. City dwellers call it the 'garden of Ireland', although it may be more accurately described as the 'playground of Dublin'. Many of the growing population of 100,000 work in the capital and commute from towns such as Greystones and Blessington, where the Liffey Valley was flooded in 1940 to create the Blessington Lakes. Further south, on the other hand, farming is widespread and the Wicklow Mountains are among the most impressive in Ireland (the film 'Braveheart', supposedly set in Scotland, was filmed here). The 6th century monastic complex at Glendalough, one of Ireland's greatest national monuments, nestles in the heart of the mountains at the spectacular Wicklow Gap, and there are other fascinating places nearby such as the Devil's Glen Forest Park, wild and beautiful Glenmalure, the 'meeting of the waters' at Avoca (location for the popular British TV series 'Ballykissangel'), Baltinglass Abbey and Roundwood (Ireland's highest village).

The county town of Wicklow is situated on the slopes of Ballyguile Hill, overlooking a wide curve of coastline. On the coast, the fishing port of Arklow is renowned for its pottery, Brittas Bay boasts 5km (3mi) of safe sandy beach and Bray, on the border with County Dublin, is one of Ireland's principal resorts. Wicklow contains no fewer than five of Ireland's finest Heritage Gardens and also claims to be one of the best golfing counties in Ireland, with over 20 courses including the country's oldest at Woodenbridge.

Munster

Munster is Ireland's largest province, covering some 29 per cent of the country and taking in the counties of Clare, Cork, Kerry, Limerick, Tipperary and Waterford. It's

Ireland's most southerly region and the most popular with both holidaymakers and foreign homebuyers. The counties of Cork, Kerry and Waterford are particularly sought-after – indeed Bantry Bay in West Cork has become something of a magnet for the international jet-set (e.g. American and British film and pop stars) and a few once parochial fishing villages now have a cosmopolitan feel. Geographically, Munster has everything that's considered typically Irish: brooding mountains, a craggy coastline with sandy bays between rocky cliffs, alternately fertile and barren plains. Cut off from the rest of Ireland by mountains, bogs and the River Shannon, Munster has become a land of myth and legend with strong musical and poetic traditions. Its people are also traditionalists: warm and relaxed but with an argumentative streak.

Cork: Munster's principal town is Cork City, the second-largest city in Ireland and capital of its biggest and most southerly county of the same name. Cork is the unofficial capital of the south of Ireland, although its citizens (who Dubliners dismiss as *culchies* or country folk) think their city should be the capital of the country. Sophisticated and cosmopolitan with its own University, Cork is much smaller than Dublin (its population is just 420,000) and has managed to retain a friendly, small-town atmosphere. It's nevertheless a lively place full of young people and bustling with traffic. Cork County has some of the richest farming land in Ireland as well as some of the most spectacular coastal and mountain scenery, combined with gentle bays and hills and numerous marshes (Cork comes from the Gaelic Corcaigh, meaning 'marshy place'). Nearby is the port of Cobh (pronounced 'cove'), from where some two and a half million people have emigrated to America since 1848. It's also home to the famous Blarney Stone, which it's said will bestow the 'gift of the gab' upon whoever kisses it (unless your Irish, in which case you're born with it)! Ringaskiddy and Little Island near Cork city are among the few industrial areas in Ireland (the largest being at Leixlip near Dublin), where a number of large pharmaceutical companies are based.

Property prices in and around Cork city are the highest in the country after Dublin and Galway, and are rising at between 10 to 15 per cent annually. Increases of up to 20 per cent have been reported in the last two or three years. As demand exceeds supply and most buyers are retirees who aren't concerned with rises in interest rates or the availability of employment, property prices are expected to remain high. Two-bedroom apartments start at around IR£50,000 and can cost as much as IR£105,000 in desirable areas. A three-bedroom townhouse costs in the region of IR£65,000 to 75,000 and a four or five-bedroom detached house up to IR£250,000.

Clare: County Clare is one of the most barren parts of Ireland and is almost untouched by tourism despite the nearby presence of Shannon Airport. Covering an area of 160 km² (62sq mi), the area known as the Burren is particularly desolate and has a unique landscape (with no bogs and few pastures) strewn with limestone slabs and boulders. Legend has it that one of Oliver Cromwell's soldiers described it as 'a savage land, yielding neither water enough to drown a man, nor tree to hang him, nor soil enough to bury him'. Nevertheless, the Burren is also famous for its variety of plant and animal life, including the rarely seen pine marten and 26 of the country's 33 species of butterfly, one of which, the Burren Green, is peculiar to the area. The Burren's wild beauty is under threat, however, from the proposed siting of a Public Works Interpretative Centre (whatever that is?) in its very centre. Ireland's largest hydro-electric plant, the Shannon Scheme, is also situated in County Clare. With three-quarters of its border on the sea, County Clare is one of Ireland's premier holiday centres. Traditional seaside resorts such as Spanish Point, Lahinch and Kilkee, and the spectacular Cliffs of Moher plunging over 200 metres into the Atlantic, make it popular with both foreign and Irish holidaymakers. Clare also has its fair share of historical interest, like the ancient town of Ennis and the Poulnabrone Dolmen (or Portal Tomb), one of Ireland's most photographed monuments. Ennis is also of interest for another reason: in a national competition sponsored by Telecom Éireann in 1997 it was selected as Ireland's 'Information Age' town, where IR£15M is being invested in cutting-edge IT development for both businesses and the local community.

As a result, land and property prices are soaring. In the 12 months between mid-1997 and mid-1998 the average cost of an acre of land increased by 40 per cent and the price of a new three bedroom, semi-detached house jumped by 30 per cent. Nearby Shannon is Ireland's only new town to have been built for centuries, having developed as recently as the '60s to accommodate workers at the Shannon Industrial Tax Free Zone, created by act of parliament in 1947. Today it's a thriving small town of 10,000 inhabitants. As elsewhere in the west, property in Clare is scarce despite extensive new building. Prices, however, compare favourably with other parts of the country, with a three-bedroom cottage costing as little as IR£25,000.

Kerry: The archetypal Ireland is to be found in County Kerry, which contains three of the country's most visited places: the rather commercialised town of Killarney with its magnificent lake, the Iveragh Peninsula (better known as the 'Ring of Kerry') and the Dingle Peninsula (not to mention its grandest and highest range of mountains, MacGillycuddy's Reeks). Ballybunion is one of Ireland's premier seaside resorts and Kinsale is popular for yachting as well as a claim to be Ireland's gourmet capital (it has hosted the International Gourmet Festival in October since 1987). Tralee is home to the internationally famous Festival of Kerry and Rose of Tralee Festival, which was established in 1939 in an attempt to attract visitors away from Killarney, plus Ireland's biggest selection of all-weather visitor attractions. Kerry is also said to be where you'll find Ireland's friendliest, most flamboyant and humorous people – as well as its wettest weather! In fact the Gulf Stream keeps the climate fairly mild and snow and frost are rare.

The recent property boom has centred on Kerry, which boasts easy access (direct flights to Dublin as well as Luton and Manchester in the UK), some of the cleanest water and air in Europe, and 25,000 acres of National Park for golf, fishing and walking. Not surprisingly, resale property is scarce, particularly in coastal areas. Most of what's available is newly built, but even that's snapped up almost as soon as the mortar is dry – or even before. However, prices aren't as high as in nearby Cork, where demand from Irish buyers wishing to live close to the city has inflated property values. In parts of Kerry it's possible to buy a three-bedroom house for as little as IR£55,000, although a half-acre plot with planning permission for a new home can cost as much as IR£20,000.

Limerick: Limerick was a county long before it became the name for a 'nonsense' verse, although the tradition of inventing five-line stanzas is said to have originated in the 18th century in the drinking games of a group of would-be poets from the town of Croom. County Limerick itself is a peaceful farming area with some of the country's finest dairy cattle (it's also famous for its horses). The fertile pastures are dotted with the ruins of hundreds of castles and surrounded by hills and mountains and, to the north, the River Shannon, which unofficially divides the south-west from the west. Where the Shannon meets the Atlantic lies the ancient city of Limerick, the country's fourth largest city (after Dublin, Cork and Galway). Once felt to be rather drab, the city has recently had a substantial facelift and boasts particularly smart clothes shops as well as a thriving arts centre and lively nightlife. Limerick is also the home of one of the most important collections of mediaeval artefacts in the world, the Hunt Collection. There's still high unemployment, but new industries have been established in and around the city. Colourful market towns are scattered throughout the county, notably Castleconnell, Kilfinane, Kilmallock and Newcastle West. Adare, with its old-world, thatched cottages and mediaeval churches, recalls a bygone way of life and claims to be Ireland's prettiest village.

Tipperary: "It's a long way to Tipperary" goes the song, but that rather depends on where you set out from. Tipperary is the most southerly of the inland counties of Ireland (Carlow, Cavan, Kildare, Kilkenny, Longford, Laois, Monaghan, Offaly, Roscommon and Westmeath also lack a coastline) and one of the most beautiful. Tipperary is rich in contrast with flat, fertile farmland (known as the Golden Vale) interspersed by low but spectacular mountains: the Silvermines and Devil's Bit in the north and the Galtee in the south. The River Suir is noted for its trout and Lough Derg on the river Shannon is Ireland's largest lake, while hunting is a popular pastime in other parts of Tipperary. Clonmel (in the south) means 'honeyed meadows' and has a prosperous air deriving from the abundance of food produced in the county.

Waterford: County Waterford is a fertile area watered by three rivers, that come together at Waterford City, and is also noted for its mountains, tiny lakes and pine forests, as well as an abundance of ruins. West Waterford's mountain passes are among the most beautiful scenery in Ireland, while the south-east coast is one of the sunniest parts of the country, offering 'miles' of safe, sandy beaches. The capital, Waterford City, is most famous for its glass factory, which has been producing Waterford Crystal for over 200 years. It's also a bustling maritime centre with regular visits from cruise ships, yachts and other vessels, not to mention its own sizeable fishing fleet.

Ulster

Ulster is Ireland's most northerly province, most of which, with the exception of the counties of Cavan, Donegal and Monaghan, is part of the United Kingdom. The counties of Antrim, Armagh, Down, Fermanagh, Londonderry and Tyrone form the region known today as Northern Ireland, which remained part of the UK when the Irish state was established in 1921.

Cavan: With a population of just 4,000, landlocked Cavan is another peaceful, unspoilt county (it's said to be Ireland's 'Garden of Eden'), although the recent re-opening of the Ballinamore-Ballyconnell canal (originally constructed in 1860 but only operational for nine years) between the Shannon and Erne waterways is attracting a good deal of tourist traffic. Cavan is a favourite of fishermen due to the abundance of fish in its many beautiful lakes and rivers, winding between wooded hills. Ireland's largest river, the Shannon, has its source here, on the slopes of Cuilcagh in a pool known as the Shannon Pot.

Donegal: The most northerly county in Ireland and one of its largest, Donegal, is virtually cut off from the rest of the country by the Northern Irish county of

Fermanagh. It has changed less during the 20th century than almost anywhere else in
Ireland and has the largest Gaelic-speaking population of any county. The Ulster
dialect though has more in common with Scottish Gaelic than 'official' Leinster Irish
and the county maintains strong links with Scotland: the buses even go to Glasgow
(but not by road)! Donegal has a bit of everything to be found in the rest of the
country: cliffs, mountains, heather-clad moors, bogs and fertile pastures. It differs in
being one of the few parts of Ireland with a growing population, having been
particularly affected by the post-war baby boom. The coastal town of Killybegs,
where the *Gaeltacht* begins, is untypical of the area, having developed into one of
Europe's principal fishing ports, complete with fishmeal factory whose smell
pervades nearby Donegal Town. They say that the best fish and chips in Ireland are
to be had at Melly's opposite the harbour!

Monaghan: Neighbouring Monaghan is an undulating county where lakes
alternate with gentle hills. Market towns, farms and quiet waterways make up the
quintessentially Irish landscape, which is dotted with ancient monuments and ruined
castles. Renowned as an angling centre, Monaghan also offers watersports, golf,
riding and other outdoor pursuits, although it has no coastline. Monaghan is a
peaceful place, yet it's just an hour's drive from Dublin in one direction and Belfast
in the other, thus offering the best of several worlds.

RESEARCH

There's plenty of choice of property for sale in Ireland, but it's a sellers' market in
most areas and likely to remain that way for some years. As when buying property
anywhere, it's never advisable to be in too much of a hurry. It's a wise or lucky
person who gets his choice absolutely right first time, which is why most experts
recommend that you rent before buying unless you're absolutely sure what you want,
how much you wish to pay and where you want to live. Have a good look around in
your chosen area(s) and obtain an accurate picture of the kind of properties available,
their relative prices and what you can expect to receive for your money. However,
before doing this, you should make a comprehensive list of what you want (and don't
want) from a home, so that you can narrow the field and save time on wild goose

chases. In most areas, properties for sale include derelict farmhouses, unmodernised village homes, modern townhouses and apartments with all modern conveniences, as well as more grand residences. You can also buy a plot of land and have an individual architect-designed house built to your own specifications. If, however, after discussing it at length with your partner one of you insists on a new luxury apartment in Dublin and the other an 18th century farmhouse in the Connemara, the easiest solution may be to get a divorce!

To reduce the chances of making an expensive error when buying in an unfamiliar region, it's often prudent to rent a house for a period (see **Renting** on page 151), taking in the worst part of the year (weather-wise). This allows you to become familiar with the region and the weather, and gives you time to look around for a home at your leisure. There's no shortage of properties for sale in Ireland and whatever you're looking for, you should have plenty to choose from. Wait until you find something you fall head over heels in love with and then think about it for another week or two before rushing headlong to the altar! One of the advantages of buying property in Ireland is that there's usually another 'dream' home around the next corner – and the second or third dream home is often even better than the first. Better to miss the 'opportunity of a lifetime' than end up with an expensive pile of stones around your neck. However, don't dally too long as good properties at the right price don't remain on the market for ever!

If you're looking for a holiday home, you may wish to investigate mobile homes or a scheme that restricts your occupancy of a property to a number of weeks each year. These include shared ownership, leaseback, time-sharing and a holiday property bond (see page 171). Don't rush into any of these schemes without fully researching the market and before you're absolutely clear about what you want and what you can realistically expect to get for your money. The more research you do before buying a property in Ireland the better, which should (if possible) include advice from those who already own a home there, from who you can usually obtain invaluable information (often based on their own mistakes). Many people set themselves impossible deadlines for buying a property or business (e.g. a few days or a week) and often end up bitterly regretting their impulsive decision. Although it's a common practice, mixing a holiday with property purchase isn't advisable as most people are inclined to make poor decisions when their mind is set on play, rather than business.

Publications & Exhibitions: Outbound Publishing (1 Commercial Road, Eastbourne, East Sussex BN21 3XQ, UK, ☎ 01323-412001) publish *World of Property*, a quarterly publication containing many properties for sale in Ireland (and other countries) and organise property exhibitions in the south and north of England. Other international property exhibitions that include Ireland are organised by Homebuyer Events Ltd. (Mantle House, Broomhill Road, London SW18 4JQ, UK, ☎ 0181-877 3636. Property is also advertised for sale in many newspapers and magazines in Ireland and abroad (see **Appendix A**) and on the Internet.

AVOIDING PROBLEMS

The problems associated with buying property abroad have been highlighted in the last decade or so, during which the property market in many countries has gone from boom to bust and back. However, although the pitfalls must never be ignored, buying property in Ireland needn't be a gamble. There are hundreds of thousands of Irish homeowners – in fact a higher percentage of Irish people own their own homes than the inhabitants of any other European Union (EU) country – and the vast majority are happy with their purchases and encountered few or no problems when buying their homes. This should be borne in mind when you hear or read horror stories concerning foreign buyers in Ireland (not that you will hear many). The possible dangers have been highlighted not in order to discourage you, but simply to ensure that you go into a purchase with your eyes open and to help you avoid problems ('forewarned is forearmed').

Legal Advice: It cannot be emphasised too strongly that anyone planning to buy property in Ireland must take expert, independent legal advice. Never sign anything, or pay any money, until you have sought legal advice from a solicitor who's experienced in Irish property law. If you aren't prepared to do this, you shouldn't even think about buying property in Ireland! Most people purchasing property in Ireland take legal advice only after having paid a deposit and some take none at all. Trying to cut corners to save on legal costs is foolhardy in the extreme when tens (or even hundreds) of thousands of pounds are at stake. You will find that the relatively small price (in comparison with the cost of a home) of obtaining legal advice is excellent value, if only for the peace of mind it affords. However, be careful who you engage, as some solicitors are part of the problem rather than the solution! Don't pick a solicitor at random, but hire one who has been highly recommended by someone you can trust.

Employing Professionals: There are professionals in all areas of Ireland, and many expatriate professionals (e.g. architects and surveyors) also practise there. However, don't assume that because you're dealing with a fellow countryman that he'll offer you a better deal or do a better job than an Irishman (the contrary is often true). It's always wise to check the credentials of all professionals you employ, whatever their nationality. Note that it's *never* wise to rely solely on advice proffered by those with a financial interest in selling you a property, such as a developer or real estate agent, although their advice may be excellent and totally unbiased. You should also avoid 'cowboy' agents and anyone who does property deals on the side (such as someone you meet in a bar or restaurant), as dealing with them often leads to heartache.

Problems: Among the myriad problems which can be experienced by buyers are properties bought without a legal title; properties built illegally without planning permission; properties sold that are subject to embargoes; properties sold with forged deeds; properties with missing infrastructure; builders or developers going bust; developers' loans being undischarged after completion; undischarged mortgages from the previous owner; intermediaries disappearing with the seller's proceeds; overcharging by vendors (particularly when selling to foreigners); properties sold to more than one buyer; and even properties sold that don't exist! On the other hand, buyers must also accept their share of the blame. It's not uncommon for buyers to 'leave their brains behind at the airport' and some do incredibly irresponsible things, such as literally handing over bags full of cash to agents or owners without any security. It's hardly surprising that they're sometimes defrauded! **However, it should be noted that Ireland is one of the safest countries in Europe in which to buy property.**

Mistakes: Common mistakes made by buyers in Ireland include buying in the wrong area (rent first!); buying a home that's unsaleable; buying a property for renovation and grossly underestimating the restoration costs; not having a full survey done on an old property; not taking legal advice; buying a property for business (e.g. to convert to self-catering accommodation) and being too optimistic about the income; and taking on too large a mortgage. It's possible when buying a property directly from the vendor that he will suggest you pay part of the price with an 'under the table' cash payment, thus lowering the price declared to the tax authorities and reducing the vendor's capital gains tax liability. You will also save money on taxes and fees, but will have a higher capital gains tax bill when you sell. If you're selling a property and the buyer refuses to make the 'illicit' payment after the contract has been signed, you'll have no legal redress! You should steer well clear of this practice, which is of course strictly illegal. Checks must be carried out both before signing a contract and before signing the deed of sale. Note that if you get into a dispute over a property deal it can take years to have it resolved in the Irish courts and even then there's no guarantee that you'll receive satisfaction.

Subrogation: One of the Irish laws that property buyers should be aware of is the law of subrogation, whereby property debts, including mortgages, service and management charges, remain with a property and are inherited by the buyer. This is an open invitation to dishonest sellers to 'cut and run'. It is of course possible to check whether there are any outstanding debts on a property and this should be done by your solicitor a few days before completion (see page 183). If annual bills for services or management charges have already been paid, they are usually divided between the vendor and buyer according to how much of the year is left.

Buying Off Plan: Many problems can arise when buying off plan, i.e. unbuilt properties, or a property on an unfinished development. A 'finished' property is a property where the building is complete in every detail (as confirmed by an architect), all communal services have been completed, and all infrastructure is in place such as roads, parking areas, external lighting, landscaping, water, sewerage, electricity and telephone services. A builder is supposed to provide buyers purchasing off plan in stage payments with an insurance policy or banker's 'termination' guarantee, which protects them against the builder going broke before construction is completed. Make sure that your builder offers such a guarantee.

Take Your Time: Many people have had their fingers burnt by rushing into property deals without proper care and consideration. It's all too easy to fall in love with the attractions of a home in Ireland and to sign a contract without giving it sufficient thought. If you aren't absolutely certain, don't allow yourself to be rushed into making a hasty decision, e.g. by fears of an imminent price rise or of losing the property to another buyer who has 'made an offer'. Although many people dream of buying a holiday or retirement home in Ireland, it's vital to do your homework thoroughly and avoid the 'dream sellers' (often fellow countrymen) who will happily prey on your ignorance and tell you anything in order to sell you a home.

CHOOSING THE LOCATION

The most important consideration when buying a home in Ireland is usually its location – or, as the old adage goes, the *three* most important points are location, location and location! A property in a reasonable condition in a popular area is likely to be a better investment than an exceptional property in a less attractive location. There's usually no point in buying a dream property in a terrible location.

Where you buy a property in Ireland will depend on a range of factors including your personal preferences, your financial resources and, not least, whether you plan to work or not. If you have a job in Ireland, the location of your home will probably be determined by the proximity to your place of employment. However, if you intend to look for employment or start a business, you must live in an area that allows you the maximum scope. Unless you have good reason to believe otherwise, it would be foolish to rely on finding employment in a particular area. If, on the other hand, you're looking for a holiday or retirement home, the whole of Ireland is your oyster. The most popular areas are the south and west coasts, particularly counties Waterford, Cork, Kerry and Galway. When seeking a permanent home, don't be too influenced by where you have spent an enjoyable holiday or two. A town or area that was adequate for a few weeks' holiday may be totally unsuitable for a permanent home, particularly regarding the proximity to shops, medical services, and sports and leisure facilities.

If you have little idea about where you wish to live, read as much as you can about the different regions of Ireland (see **Regions** on page 132) and spend some time looking around your areas of interest. Note that the life-style and cost of living can vary considerably from region to region (and even within a particular region). Before looking at properties it's important to have a good idea of the kind of property you want and the price you wish to pay, and to draw up a shortlist of the areas and towns of interest. Most importantly make a list of what you want and don't want in a property, as if you don't do this, you're likely to be overwhelmed by the number of properties to be viewed.

The 'best' area in which to live depends on a range of considerations including proximity to your place of work as well as to schools, shops, public transport, entertainment and sports facilities, places of worship, pubs, etc. There are beautiful areas to choose from throughout Ireland, most within easy travelling distance of a town or city. Don't, however, always believe the travelling times and distances stated in adverts and quoted by estate agents, but check for yourself. When looking for a home, bear in mind travelling times and costs to your place of work, shops and schools (and the local pub/restaurant). If you buy a remote country property, the distance to local amenities and services could become a problem, particularly if you plan to retire to Ireland. If you live in a remote rural area you'll need to be much more self-sufficient than if you live in a town.

If possible, you should visit an area a number of times over a period of a few weeks, both on weekdays and at weekends, in order to get a feel for the neighbourhood (it's better to walk rather than drive around). A property seen on a balmy summer's day after a delicious lunch and a few pints of Guinness may not be nearly so attractive on a subsequent visit without sunshine and the warm inner glow. Ideally you should also visit an area at different times of the year, e.g. in both summer and winter, as somewhere that's wonderful in summer can be forbidding and inhospitable in winter. In any case, you should view a property a number of times before deciding to buy it. If you're unfamiliar with an area, most experts recommend that you rent for a period before deciding to buy (see **Renting** on page 151). This is particularly important if you're planning to buy a permanent or retirement home in an unfamiliar area. Many people change their minds after a period and it isn't unusual for buyers to move once or twice before settling down permanently.

If you'll be working in Ireland, obtain a map of the area and decide the maximum distance you'll consider travelling to work, e.g. by drawing a circle with your work place in the middle. Obtain a large scale map of the area and mark the places that you've seen, at the same time making a list of the plus and minus points of each property. If you use an estate agent, he will usually drive you around and you can then return later to the properties that you like best at your leisure (providing that you have marked them on your map!). Note, however, that agents may be reluctant to give you the keys to visit a property on your own.

There are many points to consider regarding the location of a home. These can roughly be divided into the local vicinity, i.e. the immediate surroundings and neighbourhood, and the general area or region. Take into account the present and future needs of all members of your family, including the following:

- The climate. You won't have chosen Ireland for its year-round sunshine record. Nevertheless, some areas are drier than others and you may prefer to give yourself the best chance of avoiding a wet summer holiday. Bear in mind both the winter and summer climate, position of the sun, and the average daily sunshine and rainfall (see **Climate** on page 58). The orientation or aspect of a building is vital and if you want morning or afternoon sun (or both) you must ensure that balconies, terraces and gardens are facing the right direction.

- Check whether the area you're interested in is liable to natural disasters such as floods or storms. The north-west coast, for example, is subject to particularly high winds, and low lying areas near the coast or the River Shannon can become flooded. Properties in such areas may be expensive to insure.

- Noise isn't usually a problem in Ireland, which is one of the quietest countries in Europe. Nevertheless, it's a consideration, particularly in urban areas. Although you cannot choose your neighbours, you can at least ensure that a property isn't located next to a busy road, industrial plant, commercial area, building site, discotheque, night club, bar or restaurant (where revelries may continue into the early hours). Look out for objectionable neighbouring properties which may be too close to the one you're considering and check whether nearby vacant land has been zoned for commercial activities. In 'communal' developments (e.g. apartment blocks) some properties may be second homes that are let short term, which means you may have to tolerate boisterous holiday-makers as neighbours throughout the year (or at least during the summer months). In towns, traffic noise may continue all night!

- Bear in mind that if you live in a popular tourist area, i.e. almost anywhere on the south-west coast, you'll be inundated with tourists in the summer. They won't only jam the roads and pack the beaches and shops, but also occupy your favourite table at your local bar or restaurant! Bear in mind that while a 'front-line' property on the beach sounds attractive and may be ideal for short holidays, it isn't always the best solution for permanent residence. Many beaches are crowded in the peak season, parking may be impossible, services stretched to breaking point, and the constant coming and going of tourists may drive you crazy. Some people prefer to move inland where it's generally less busy, you're isolated from the tourists and can also enjoy the beautiful scenery. On the other hand, getting to and from isolated properties can be a slow business and minor roads can become virtually impassable in winter.

- Do you wish to live in an area with many other expatriates or as far away from them as possible (which may not in fact be very far on parts of the south-west coast)? If you wish to integrate with the local community, avoid the foreign 'ghettos' and choose an Irish village or an area or development with mainly local inhabitants. However, bear in mind that it may take time for you to become accepted in small communities, although residents in rural areas who make an effort to integrate into the local community are invariably warmly welcomed. If you're buying a permanent home, it's important to check on your prospective neighbours, particularly when buying an apartment. For example, are they noisy, sociable or absent for long periods? Do you think you'll get on with them? Good neighbours are invaluable, particularly when buying a second home in a village. On the other hand, if you wish to mix only with your compatriots, then living in a predominantly foreign community, or at least a cosmopolitan city such as Dublin or Galway may be your ideal.

- Do you wish to be in a town or do you prefer the country? Inland or by the sea? How about living on an island? Life on an island is more restricted and remote, e.g. you cannot jump into your car and drive to Cork or Galway or 'pop' over to Northern Ireland or the rest of the UK. Bear in mind that if you buy a property in the country you may have to tolerate poor public transport, long travelling distances to a town of any size, solitude and remoteness, and the high cost and amount of work involved in the upkeep of a country house and garden. You won't be able to pop into the local shops for fresh bread and milk, drop into the local bar for a glass of your favourite tipple with the locals, or have a choice of restaurants on your doorstep. In a town or large village the weekly market will be just around the corner, the doctor and pharmacy close at hand, and if you need help or run into any problems, your neighbours will be nearby.

  On the other hand, in the country you'll be closer to nature, will have more freedom (e.g. to make as much noise as you wish) and possibly complete privacy. Living in a remote area in the country will suit those looking for peace and quiet who don't want to involve themselves in the 'hustle and bustle' of town life (not that there's a lot of this in Irish rural towns). If you're after peace and quiet, make sure that there isn't a busy road or railway line nearby or a local church within 'donging' distance! Note, however, that many people who buy a remote country home find that the peace of the countryside palls after a time and they yearn for the more exciting city life. If you have never lived in the country, it's advisable to rent before buying. Note also that while it's cheaper to buy in a remote or unpopular location, it's usually much more difficult to find a buyer when you want to sell.

- If you're planning to buy a country property with a large garden or plot of land, bear in mind the high cost and amount of work involved in its upkeep. If it's to be a second home, who will look after the house and garden when you're away? Do you want to spend your holidays mowing the lawn and cutting back the undergrowth? Do you want a home with a lot of outbuildings? What are you going to do with them? Can you afford to convert them into extra rooms or guest accommodation?

- How secure is your job or business and are you likely to move to another area in the near future? Can you find other work in the same area, if necessary? If there's a possibility that you may need to move in a few years' time, you should rent or at least buy a property that will be relatively easy to sell and recoup the cost.

- What about your partner's and children's jobs or your children's present and future schooling? What is the quality of local schools? Note that even if your family has no need or plans to use local schools, the value of a home is often influenced by the quality and location of schools.

- What local health and social services are provided? How far is the nearest hospital with an emergency department? Are there doctors and dentists in the area?

- What shopping facilities are provided in the neighbourhood? How far is it to the nearest sizeable town with good shopping facilities? How would you get there if your car was out of commission?

- What is the range and quality of local leisure, sports, community and cultural facilities? What is the proximity to sports facilities such as a beach, golf course or waterway? Bear in mind that properties in or close to coastal resorts are more expensive, although they also have the best letting potential. '

- Is the proximity to public transport, e.g. an international airport, port or railway station, or access to a main road important? Don't believe all you're told about the distance or travelling times to the nearest airport, railway station, beach or town, but check it for yourself.

- If you're planning to buy in a town or city, is there adequate private or free on-street parking for your family and visitors? Is it safe to park in the street? Note that in Dublin it's important to have secure off-street parking if you value your car. Traffic congestion is fast becoming a problem in the major cities and towns in Ireland. Bear in mind that an apartment or townhouse in a town may be some distance from the nearest road or car park. How do you feel about carrying heavy shopping hundreds of metres to your home and possibly up several flights of stairs? If you're planning to buy an apartment above the ground floor, you may wish to ensure that the building has a lift.

- What is the local crime rate? The incidence of housebreaking and burglary is higher in some areas than others, which also means more expensive home insurance. Check the crime rate in the local area, e.g. burglaries, housebreaking, stolen cars and violent crime. Is crime increasing or decreasing? Note that professional crooks like isolated houses, particularly those full of expensive furniture and other belongings that they can strip bare at their leisure. You're much less likely to be the victim of crime if you live in a village, where crime is virtually unknown (strangers stand out like sore thumbs in villages, where their every move is monitored by the local populace).

- Is the local council well run? What are the views of other residents? If the municipality is efficiently run you can usually rely on good local social and sports services and facilities.

- **Radon:** A final consideration when choosing the location of your property is the likelihood of its being affected by radon. Radon is a naturally occurring radioactive gas formed underground by the radioactive decay of uranium, which is present in small quantities in rocks and soils and is particularly prevalent in Ireland. It's estimated that over half of the radiation dose received by the average person in Ireland is due to radon. For the majority of people the radiation dose received from radon isn't high enough to be a cause for concern. Radon surfacing in the open air is quickly diluted to harmless concentrations. However, when it enters an enclosed space, such as a house, it can sometimes build up to potentially dangerous concentrations. The acceptable limit for radon concentration (known as the 'reference level') is 200 becquerels per cubic metre of air ($200Bq/m^3$). It has been shown that prolonged exposure to concentrations of radon above this level increases the chance of contracting lung cancer, and in a minority of homes and other buildings in Ireland with very high radon levels, there's a significant health risk for occupants. To put this risk into perspective: whereas the average person in Ireland has a 3 per cent risk of contracting fatal lung cancer, someone living in a building which is above the reference level may have a 4 or 5 per cent risk of the same fate.

Recognising the possible dangers of radon, the government has recently undertaken a survey of the whole country which identifies the areas of greatest risk. There are high risk areas in most parts of the country, but Counties Carlow and Sligo appear to have more such areas than other parts of the country. A copy of the survey and a leaflet entitled 'Radon Radiation in Homes' can be obtained free of charge from the Radiological Protection Institute of Ireland (☎ 01-269 7766). Note also that building regulations introduced in December 1997 require all new houses to have a radon 'sump' and those in high risk areas a radon 'barrier'. There are three important points to bear in mind when considering the possible effects of radon gas on your choice of property:

- The health danger of high radon levels is small, particularly if you're only spending short periods in your Irish home.

- Radon cannot be seen or smelt but it can easily be detected by special equipment. The necessary equipment can be hired from the Radiological Protection Institute for IR£15. However, readings should be spread over at least three months, so it may not be possible to obtain a reliable measurement before you buy a property.

- Even if a property is found to contain a high level of radon gas, there are ways of reducing it to a safer level. Various measures that can be taken are outlined in a guide, *Radon in Buildings* (price IR£5), published by the Environmental Information Service, 17 St, Andrew Street, Dublin 2 (☎ 01-679 3144).

RENTING

If you're uncertain about exactly what sort of home you want and where you wish to live, it's advisable to rent for a period in order to reduce the chances of making a costly error. Renting long term before buying is particularly prudent for anyone planning to live in Ireland permanently. If possible, you should rent a similar property to the one you're planning to buy, during the time of year when you plan to occupy it. Renting allows you to become familiar with the weather, the amenities and the local people; to meet other foreigners who have made their homes in Ireland and share their experiences; and not least, to discover the cost of living at first hand. Providing you still find Ireland alluring, renting 'buys' you time to find your dream home. You may even wish to consider renting a home long term (or even 'permanently') as an alternative to buying, as it saves tying up your capital and can be surprisingly inexpensive in many regions. People who are relocating to Ireland for up to five years often prefer to rent rather than buy. Some let their family homes abroad and rent one in Ireland, when it's even possible to make a profit!

If you're looking for a long-term rental, e.g. three to six months, it's best not to rent unseen, but to rent a holiday apartment for a week or two to allow yourself time to look around for a longer term rental. Properties for rent are advertised in local newspapers and can also be found through property publications in many countries (see **Appendix A** for a list). Many estate agents in Ireland offer a long-term rental service and a number of agencies (listed under 'Auctioneers, Estate Agents & Valuers' in the Golden Pages) deal in short and long-term rentals (see below).

Some accommodation agencies charge a registration fee, while others take a percentage of the rental fee from the landlord so that their service is effectively free (although you may find yourself paying a higher rent as a result). In general you should try to obtain a reference before signing up with an agency and, particularly if you're being asked to pay a registration fee, find out how likely the agency is to find you suitable accommodation, i.e. what sort of accommodation it has to offer and how frequently its lists are updated. You should also ask whether the agency is licensed (estate agents are required by law to be licensed and bonded, but the legal position regarding accommodation agencies is less clear), what services are provided in return for the fee, and whether you're entitled to a refund if the agency fails to find you accommodation within a reasonable period. Also ensure that you receive a receipt for any money you pay.

Rental prices have been adversely affected by the spiralling property market and have increased by as much as 50 per cent in the last four or five years. The recent abolition of mortgage interest relief on residential investment property, which came into effect in April 1998, is expected to lead to even sharper rises in rental charges, which could double by the year 2000. Also bear in mind that demand for rented accommodation has increased as a result of growth in employment opportunities and the number of university students in Ireland, and there's a shortage of property for rent in many urban areas. It's estimated that some 11,000 new rental properties are required each year (3,000 in Dublin) to meet the current demand. In particularly short supply are luxury properties and suburban houses close to public transport, as most properties available for rent are apartments. (Note that in Ireland there's a distinction between 'flats' and 'apartments': a flat may be above a shop or office or in a converted old house, whereas an apartment is usually purpose-built.) September and October are particularly busy times for renting in Ireland, particularly in university towns when students return from their summer holidays.

Most rental properties, whether long or short-term, are let furnished and long-term unfurnished properties are particularly difficult to find. Standards of rented accommodation in Ireland are generally good. The Housing (Standards for Rented Houses) Regulations 1993 specified certain minimum requirements with regard to structural condition; the provision of sinks, toilets, baths/showers, cooking and food storage facilities; the safety of electrical and gas installations; the adequacy of heating, lighting and ventilation; and the maintenance of communal areas, so you shouldn't be offered anything less than habitable.

A rental contract is necessary when renting any property in Ireland, whether long or short-term (except for holiday lettings), and must contain certain information. This includes the address of the accommodation; the names and addresses of the landlord and letting agent; the tenant's name; the length of the tenancy; the amount of rent and when and how it's to be paid; details of other charges that aren't included in the rental fee (e.g. telephone, electricity); the deposit to be paid and the conditions under which it may be returned; the basic rights of the tenant and the landlord; and an inventory of items included with the accommodation. In accordance with the Housing (Rent Books) Regulations 1993, your landlord must provide you with a rent book or written lease which specifies the above and all rental or other payments must be recorded in the rent book or provided in writing.

With all rental agreements it's important to establish under what circumstances your landlord may have access to the accommodation and what maintenance or repair costs you're liable for. Also ensure that you have an emergency contact number for your landlord. If you require more information about rented accommodation in Ireland or experience a problem with a landlord, you should contact a Threshold Advice Centre in Cork, Galway or Dublin (☎ 01-872 6311). Threshold, a voluntary body funded by the Department of the Environment and local government, also publishes various information leaflets to help you find suitable accommodation and avoid the less reputable accommodation agencies.

Rent is usually payable monthly, in advance, and an initial deposit of one or two months' rent (one or two weeks' rent for a weekly tenancy) is also required as security. Landlords can legally raise the rent by as much and as often as they like, unless there's a specific agreement to the contrary (e.g. in your lease), but you must be given sufficient notice of any increases. This is at least a week for weekly tenancies and at least a month for monthly tenancies.

Long-Term Rentals: The usual minimum 'long-term' rental period in Ireland is six months, although three month lets can be found, and the maximum three years. Most rental contracts, however, are for nine or twelve months. Rental costs vary considerably depending on the size (number of bedrooms) and quality of a property, its age and the facilities provided. However, the most significant factor influencing rents is the region, the city and the neighbourhood. A small, one or two bedroom apartment (e.g. 50 to 75m²) which rents for between IR£450 and IR£800 per month in Dublin can cost as little as IR£200 a month in a rural area (outside the main tourist season). A three or four bedroom house in Cork can be rented for between IR£350 and IR£550 per month, while a five bedroom suburban house can rent for anything between IR£1,900 and IR£5,000 a month, depending on the location.

Note that if you sign a lease, you're committing yourself to renting for that period, so don't sign one unless you're happy with all the terms and conditions. If you want to leave before the lease expires, you'll usually be held liable for the rent for the remaining period. However, if you can arrange for another tenant to take over the lease, the landlord may waive any charges.

Agencies which deal mostly in long-term rentals include Accommodation Lettings in Dublin (☎ 01-496 2866), who offer a free list of accommodation for rent; Home Locators (☎ 01-679 5233) produce a list of available accommodation in Dublin, but you pay a IR£45 registration fee to view as many properties as you like within one month; for a fee of IR£40, Express Accommodation (☎ 01-878 2100) will keep looking until they find something suitable. In Cork City, Apartmentfinders (☎ 021-277718) offer a free service for long-term rentals, as do Marian Rose Properties (☎ 021-293333), who offer both short and long-term accommodation.

Short-Term Rentals: There's an abundance of properties for rent short term in Ireland including apartments, cottages, farmhouses, townhouses, bungalows, mansions, castles and even mobile homes. The best source of short-term rental accommodation in Ireland is the Tourist Board (*Bord Failte*), which publishes an annual Self-Catering Accommodation Guide. This can be obtained from the Irish Tourist Board in many countries for a small fee (e.g. the UK price is GB£4). The guide lists some 3,000 premises nation-wide, classified by a star rating. Individual regions, e.g. Cork/Kerry, also publish holiday guides which include lists of self-catering accommodation. Agencies offering short-term urban rentals include Home Bureau in Dublin (☎ 01-679 2222) and Marian Rose Properties in Cork (see above). Many hotels also offer lower rates for long stays during the low season (see below).

Rents for short term lets are usually higher pro rata than for longer lets, particularly in popular holiday areas where many properties are let as self-catering holiday accommodation. However, many agents let self-catering properties in holiday areas at a considerable reduction during the 'low season', which may extend from September to June. In some cases the rental year is divided into as many as four seasons, e.g. November to March, April and October, June and September, and July/August, but in most cases there are three periods: July/August; May/June and September, and the rest of the year. Only a few owners charge the same rate all year round.

For an average two-bedroom holiday cottage in a popular area such as Kerry, you may pay between IR£120 and IR£160 per week in the low season, compared with up to IR£350 in mid-summer. In less popular areas, although the low season rate would be similar, you usually pay 'only' IR£200 to IR£250 in July or August. The price of urban accommodation varies even less with the time of year; for an ordinary two-bedroom apartment in Dublin or Cork you could expect to pay around IR£200 per week in low season and around IR£250 in the summer months. Rental fees usually include linen but exclude electricity and gas.

Hotels & Guest Houses: Hotel rates in Ireland vary according to the time of year, the standard of the establishment and its location. In hotel terms there are usually only two seasons: high (July/August) and low (the rest of the year). Prices are generally between 30 and 40 per cent less in the low season than in the high season, although quite a few establishments close between November and March. Many hotels offer special deals for weekend stays (two nights), three nights mid-week (one night free) and seven nights 'partial board' including dinner and breakfast. Like self-catering accommodation, hotels and guest houses are graded by the Irish Tourist Board using a star rating system. One star indicates basic facilities but also in many cases includes 'luxuries' such as a TV and shower room. The highest rating for hotels is five stars; the maximum for guesthouses (which tend to be smaller, family-run establishments) four stars.

Hotels and guest houses in large towns and cities and popular coastal areas tend to be more expensive than comparable establishments in other parts of Ireland, and rates in cities such as Dublin and Cork are similar to those in other major European cities. However, inexpensive hotels can be found in most towns, where a single room can be had for IR£25 or less and a double around IR£40 (usually without en suite bath/shower room) in low season. Elsewhere room rates start at around IR£20 and rarely rise above IR£80 per person, per night. Hotels obviously aren't a cost-effective, long-term solution for home hunters, although there's usually little alternative if you need accommodation for a short period only.

Hostels and B&Bs: There are hostels in most main towns in Ireland (there are 18 in Dublin, for example, and nine in Cork) which have no age restrictions. Dormitory accommodation costs around IR£10 per night and double rooms are available for around IR£20. Bed and breakfast accommodation is also widely available in Ireland. In fact in some areas it seems as if every other house is offering 'B&B'. Rates start at around IR£15 per person, per night, the average being between IR£17 and IR£20.

Home Exchange: An alternative to renting is to exchange your home abroad with one in Ireland for a period. This way you can experience home living in Ireland for a relatively small cost and may save yourself the expense of a long-term rental. Although there's an element of risk involved in exchanging your home with another family (depending on whether your swap is made in heaven or hell!), most agencies thoroughly vet clients and have a track record of successful swaps. There are home exchange agencies in most countries, many of which are members of the International Home Exchange Association (IHEA).

There are many home exchange companies in the USA including HomeLink International (16,500 members in around 50 countries), Box 650, Key West, FL 33041, USA (☎ 305-294 7766 or 800-638 3841). Two long-established home exchange companies in Britain are HomeLink International, Linfield House, Gorse Hill Road, Virginia Water, Surrey GU25 4AS, UK (☎ 01344-842642), who publish a Directory of homes and holiday homes for exchange, and Home Base Holidays, 7 Park Avenue, London N13 5PG, UK (☎ 0181-886 8752), who market a book, *Trading Places*, written by Bill and Mary Barbour (Rutledge Hill Press) containing invaluable information for novice house swappers.

COST

Property prices started soaring throughout Ireland in the late '80s. In the decade from March 1988 to March 1998 new house prices increased by 123 per cent compared with average wage increases of 32 per cent and a 27.5 per cent rise in the consumer price index. In the last two or three years of this period, property values rose on average an astonishing 25 per cent a year in some areas, while inflation was running at no more than 3 per cent. Price rises were particularly steep in Dublin and Galway cities, County Kerry and throughout Munster, where annual increases of up to 30 per cent were reported. As a result there was a rush to buy property as an investment and substantial profits were made. In 1997, as many as a quarter of all new properties were purchased by investors. This in turn made things difficult for homebuyers (particularly first-time buyers), who were faced not only with sharply rising prices but with a shortage of available houses. It wasn't unusual for people to queue overnight in order to be first in line for new properties being released onto the market.

From the mid-'90s there was also been a marked swing in Ireland towards the European practice of apartment living: over 20 per cent of all new properties built in the first half of 1997 were apartments. This meant that the cost of apartments rose even more steeply than that of houses, particularly in Dublin and Galway, where prices increased by almost 25 per cent in 12 months between 1997 and 1998. The average price of a new apartment in these cities is now higher than that of a comparable new house. Note that a garage is rarely provided with apartments or townhouses in Ireland, although there may be a private parking space in an underground or surface car park. However, these are usually sold separately and can cost as much as IR£15,000 in Dublin!

Fears that the Irish property market would spiral out of control before crashing spectacularly (as it did in the UK in the early '90s) have been partially allayed by recent government measures to penalise investors. The principal changes in legislation were to stamp duty, capital gains tax and tax relief on rental property, all of which were substantially reduced in April 1998 as a result of the government-commissioned Bacon Report. These measures have to some extent discouraged investment with the result that price rises have begun to slow, although they're still way ahead of inflation. Most experts believe that there won't be a crash for several reasons: Ireland's sound economic situation; the large owner-occupier base; the reasonably tight controls which banks and building societies still impose on lending; and for demographic reasons. The baby boom of the '60s and '70s means that some 110,000 Irish men and women aged between 28 and 34 (the average house-buying age) will enter the property market between 1999 and 2004.

But despite the current popularity of Ireland and the recent rise in property prices, a slice of the quiet life still needn't cost the earth, although the idyllic dream of a traditional thatched cottage on a bit of land overlooking the sea for IR£15,000 is very much a thing of the past. Small rural properties start at around IR£20,000, semi-detached, three-bedroom houses from around IR£45,000 and detached three-bedroom houses from IR£55,000. However, if you're after a property in one of the fashionable regions (such as the south-west) where there's strong demand from foreign buyers, you can expect to pay a premium of up to 50 per cent (depending on the area).

If you're looking for an urban property, demographic statistics show that towns of over 10,000 people are growing fastest. Since the early 1950s these larger towns have increased their share of Ireland's population from 3.5 to 10.5 per cent. Galway is the fastest growing city in Ireland, having increased its population by over 10 per cent in the last eight years, where it's estimated a quarter of all homes have been built since 1960. In comparison, Dublin has grown by just 1 per cent in the same period, although its satellite towns have expanded rapidly. After Dublin, Galway has also experienced the greatest house price rises in recent years.

There are other positive aspects of buying a home in Ireland: purchase fees are relatively low, particularly for new houses; there are no rates or community charges and mains water is free; and the cost of maintaining a property is small compared with many other European countries.

Average property prices aren't necessarily an accurate indication of the relative values of specific kinds of property in different areas (there may be a greater number of cheaper or more expensive houses in one area than another), but they give some idea of the variation in values across the country. Average property prices (in IR£) in Ireland in June 1998 were as follows:

Type of Property	Whole Country	Region Dublin	Galway	Cork	Limerick	Waterford	Other Areas
New House	91,600	112,400	93,300	84,000	78,600	72,500	86,200
Resale House	91,900	118,300	91,900	81,200	74,200	69,000	77,800
New Apartment	94,200	110,700	96,800	80,800	82,600	72,000	78,300
Resale Apartment	95,800	112,200	86,300	74,600	69,800	79,400	77,800

For those with the financial resources the sky's the limit, with luxury Dublin apartments and country estates costing many hundreds of thousands of punts, although only a handful of properties sell for over IR£1 million.

Apart from obvious factors such as size, quality and land area, the most important consideration influencing the price of a house is its location. Properties in the cities, particularly in and around Dublin and in Galway and Cork, can cost up to five or six times as much as equivalent properties in rural parts. There's also a considerable price variation between sought-after west coast areas such as County Kerry and less popular inland counties. Approximate prices outside Dublin are shown below:

Property	Price range (IR£'000)
1-bedroom apartment	10 to 60
2-bedroom apartment	15 to 75
3-bedroom apartment	30 to 90
2-bedroom cottage	20 to 70
3-bedroom cottage	30 to 85
2-bedroom townhouse	45 to 60
3-bedroom townhouse	60 to 80
4-bedroom townhouse	60 to 120
2-bedroom country house	20 to 90
3-bedroom country house	30 to 120
4/5-bedroom country house	40 to 250

The quality of properties obviously varies considerably in respect of materials, fixtures and fittings, and workmanship. You should therefore compare at least half a dozen properties in order to get a good idea of their relative values.

When property is advertised in Ireland the number of rooms is usually stated but the floor area isn't, although the size of the plot or garden is generally specified. The dimensions of individual rooms are only given in the agent's details. If you're in any doubt about the size of rooms you should measure them yourself, rather than rely on the measurements provided by the vendor or agent, who may 'cheat' by measuring into alcoves and doorways.

FEES

Various fees are payable when you buy a property in Ireland, which usually add a minimum of 5 per cent to the purchase price. Fees are considerably lower on new compared with resale properties, on which stamp duty must be paid. The fees payable when buying a property in Ireland include some or all of the following:

- stamp duty (except for first-time buyers and new properties);

- legal fees;

- deed registration fee;

- survey or valuation fee;

- ground rent (leasehold properties only);

- management fee (apartments only);

- VAT (certain commercial properties only);

- utility connection fees (new properties only);

- selling agent's fees;

- mortgage costs, e.g. application fee, mortgage indemnity fee (on loans above a certain percentage of the purchase price), and life insurance or a mortgage protection policy.

Always ensure that you know exactly what the total fees will be before signing a contract.

Stamp Duty: Stamp duty is the main fee involved when buying a home in Ireland. It's the tax on the purchase deed payable by the buyer when the sale is closed. The rates and criteria for stamp duty were changed on 23rd April 1988. New houses and apartments with a floor area of less than 125m^2 are still exempt from stamp duty. However, the duty will usually become payable if a property is let within five years of the date of purchase, which means that if you purchase a new property as a holiday home with the intention of letting it for the rest of the year, you'll no longer escape paying stamp duty.

In the case of new houses or apartments of 125m^2 or more, the stamp duty is calculated on the basis of the site value or 25 per cent of the combined value of the site and the building, whichever is greater; for example, if the total cost of the site and building is IR£200,000 (x 25 per cent = IR£50,000) and the site is worth IR£60,000, stamp duty will be payable on IR£60,000. In the case of resale properties, stamp duty is payable on the full value of site and building.

The rates of stamp duty on residential property have been reduced and are as follows:

Purchase Price (IR£)	Stamp Duty (%)
up to 60,000	0
60,001 to 100,000	3
100,001 to 170,000	4
170,001 to 250,000	5
250,001 to 500,000	7
over 500,000	9

These rates apply only to residential property or to the value of the residential component of a mixed-use property (e.g. an apartment above a shop). On non-residential property and on the non-residential component of mixed-use property, the rates of stamp duty remain as follows:

Purchase Price (IR£)	Stamp Duty (%)
up to 5,000	0
5,001 to 10,000	1
10,001 to 15,000	2
15,001 to 25,000	3
25,001 to 50,000	4
50,001 to 60,000	5
over 60,000	6

Note that the cost of any fixtures and fittings (e.g. carpets and curtains) included in a purchase is taken into account when determining the stamp duty 'band'; for example, if you purchased a house for IR£168,000 with fixtures and fittings worth an extra IR£3,000, you would be liable for 5 per cent stamp duty instead of 4 per cent (which would mean that you were effectively paying nearly IR£1,700 more for the fixtures and fittings!). You can, of course, buy the fixtures and fittings separately.

There's a 50 per cent stamp duty relief on conveyances between certain classes of relatives; for example, if you give a property worth IR£200,000 to your son or daughter, the stamp duty chargeable is 2.5 per cent of IR£200,000 instead of the usual 5 per cent. There's also a small stamp duty (0.1 per cent up to a maximum of IR£500) payable on mortgages above IR£20,000.

Legal Fees: Since the Competition Act, solicitors' fees for conveyance (see page 179) are no longer subject to a fixed scale of charges and you must agree them in writing with a solicitor in advance. Under section 68 of the Solicitors Act 1994 a solicitor is bound to notify a client in writing of the fee to be charged for a particular transaction or of the basis on which the fee will be calculated. The actual amount depends upon the work involved, although according to the Incorporated Law Society of Ireland you should expect to pay between 1 and 1.5 per cent of the property price. Note that Irish solicitors won't usually agree to undertake only part of the conveyance (e.g. checking the sales contract). Although engaging a solicitor and paying legal fees is optional, it's highly recommended. Legal fees are exclusive of disbursements and are subject to VAT (at 21 per cent). Fees are usually paid on closing but before registration. This can take a year for a new house and even longer for a very old, unregistered property. If there are problems with registration, you may be liable for additional fees.

Deed Registration Fee: Your solicitor will pass onto you the charges relating to registration of the title deed to your property. There are two kinds of title in Ireland: registered and unregistered. Registered land was introduced by the local Registration of Title (Ireland) Act 1891 and means that a record of the land is kept with the land registry. Registration, which is compulsory in all counties of Ireland, provides proof of ownership. When a property is sold, a Deed of Transfer is lodged with the Land Registry and the Registrar simply deletes the vendor's name and substitutes the buyer's.

In the case of unregistered land, all title documents must be inspected by your solicitor to establish ownership. Copies of these documents are lodged with the Registry of Deeds in accordance with the Registration of Deeds Act 1707 in case there's a conflict of interest, e.g. if two people try to take out mortgages on the same piece of land simultaneously. A deed of conveyance is used to transfer freehold unregistered land, a deed of assignment for leasehold unregistered land (see below). There's roughly an equal amount of registered and unregistered land in Ireland, although in rural areas land is more likely to be registered.

The fee for registration with the Land Registry is currently IR£250 (for properties costing over IR£30,000). In addition, you'll be charged for Land Registry searches (around IR£50), commissioners' fees (IR£10.50) and a copy folio and map (IR£9). In the case of registration with the Registry of Deeds, the fees will include searches (IR£50 to IR£80), commissioners' fees (IR£10.50), and memorials (copies) of the purchase deed and mortgage deed (IR£52).

Survey or Valuation Fee: If you employ a surveyor to inspect a building or plot of land before you offer to buy it (which is strongly advised), the fee will depend on the kind of survey, any special requirements and the value of the property. The cost of a valuation report (which is usually a minimum requirement of your mortgage lender) is usually between IR£1.30 and IR£1.50 per IR£1,000 of a property's value. So, for example, for a property valued at IR£100,000 you'll pay between IR£130 and IR£150. Some lending institutions make a fixed charge on a sliding scale according to the value of the property, which may be as little as IR£75 for a property worth up to IR£50,000 rising to IR£120 or more for a property worth over IR£100,000. The valuer's travelling expenses are sometimes added to the bill. If the mortgage is refused, the valuation fee is refunded.

The cost of a full structural survey is generally around IR£150 in addition to the valuation report fee, but if you use the same firm for both you may well be able to negotiate a reduced rate. Note that your mortgage lender may insist on a structural report if a property is over 100 years old.

Ground Rent: Title may be freehold, where the property is theoretically held forever free of rent, or leasehold, where it's held for anything from 250 to 9,999 years. In the case of leasehold property, it's normal for a nominal ground rent to be paid to a superior title holder, i.e. landlord. This is usually around IR£10 per year, but may be as little as a penny. There are even cases where the property is held free of rent.

Management Fee: If you're buying an apartment (or, in some cases, a house on an up-market estate), you'll usually be liable for annual management fees. Each apartment owner automatically becomes a member of the management company responsible for the insurance and upkeep of the common elements of the property, e.g. grounds, entrances, hallways, lifts and stairs (see below). To cover the costs involved there's usually be a fund to which each owner must contribute. The amount payable depends on a number of factors (e.g. the extent of the grounds and age and condition of the property), but you should expect to pay in the region of IR£400 per year.

VAT: Under the Finance Act 1997, VAT is now included in the price of new properties and doesn't apply to resale properties. However, commercial property transactions may be subject to VAT at 12.5 per cent unless the property was developed before 31st October 1972 and hasn't been extended, altered or adapted since. The rules regarding VAT on property are complicated and you should take expert advice before completing any commercial property transactions, particularly as there can be serious implications if you make a mistake (see page 124).

Utility Connection Fees: If you buy a new property, you may need to pay for connection to electricity, gas and mains water supplies, as well as for the installation of meters. Your builder will usually provide electricity and gas connections and meters, and the cost of these should be included in your quotation. Providing a property is within 15 metres of a gas main, there should be no charge for connection. If it's more than 15 metres from the nearest main, the charge should be IR£3.50 per foot (*Bord Gáis* have only partially gone metric!).

On the other hand, in the case of electricity there's a fixed connection charge of IR£650 (plus VAT at 12.5 per cent) if the property is within a certain distance from the medium voltage network. If the property is further than the specified distance from the network, an additional charge will be made according to the work necessary and in some cases there's an extra charge even if the property is within the specified distance (see page 191).

You usually need to arrange your own water main connection, which can be expensive. Connection charges vary considerably from county to county; they may be as little as IR£80 or as much as IR£500 or more if major work needs to be done (e.g. roads dug up). You should make enquiries at your local city, county or borough council concerning how much to budget for.

Selling Agent's Fees: Estate agents' fees are usually paid by the vendor. They are, however, usually allowed for in the asking price, so in effect are paid by the buyer. As a buyer you would only be responsible for a separate fee if you retained an auctioneer to purchase a property on your behalf, in which case you should agree a fee in advance and confirm it in writing. The auctioneer's fee can vary between 1 and 3.5 per cent of the selling price, depending on the cost of the property and the type of contract, but it's usually around 2.5 per cent and is subject to VAT (at 21 per cent).

Mortgage Application Fee (also called an 'acceptance' or 'arrangement' fee): Most banks and building societies charge a fee of around IR£50 or 0.5 per cent of the value of the loan when they grant a mortgage. When shopping around for a mortgage, however, you should ask if the lending institution is prepared to waive the fee, which with increasing competition for mortgages is quite likely. Note that mortgage lenders shouldn't ask you to pay any legal costs as they usually use your solicitor for their legal work. Check this with them before confirming your mortgage.

Mortgage Indemnity Fee (also called a 'mortgage indemnity bond'): If you borrow over 70 or 80 per cent (depending on the lending institution) of the purchase price, you must pay a fee of around 3 per cent of the difference between the specified percentage of the purchase price and the amount borrowed, plus a 2 per cent government levy (see page 97). Some lenders spread the cost of the indemnity over the term of the mortgage, while others don't charge an indemnity fee but charge a higher rate of interest for loans above 80 per cent. If you're buying a property for investment, the indemnity fee is at 4 per cent.

Mortgage Life Insurance (or 'mortgage protection policy'): You will need to obtain life insurance cover before your lender will agree to advance your mortgage; a mortgage protection policy is usually the minimum cover required. There are various plans available, costing around IR£4.50 per IR£100 of your monthly repayment.

Running Costs: In addition to the fees associated with buying a property, you should also take into account the running costs. These include management fees (for apartments); garden maintenance (if necessary); and building and contents insurance (see page 70). There are no local authority charges, 'rates' or 'poll taxes' for residential property in Ireland, but you will incur standing charges for utilities (electricity, gas and telephone). Water is free (unless you run a business from home) and the cost of refuse collection varies from between IR£30 and IR£100 or more per year depending on the county and the property. If you're letting a property, you should also allow for property management fees, income tax on rental income and possibly a tax consultant's fees.

BUYING A NEW HOME

According to UN figures, Ireland has the highest rate of house building in Europe at 9.5 units per thousand people compared, for example, with 3.5 units per thousand in the UK and an EU average of 5 units per thousand. Despite this high rate of construction, new properties can barely keep pace with demand and many people are purchasing plots of land and having their own homes built to order (see page 164). Most new properties in the main cities are apartments, whereas in rural areas the majority are detached bungalows, which are springing up almost everywhere you look. Prices of new properties vary considerably depending on their location (see page 146) and quality, but it's often cheaper to buy a new home than an old property requiring modernisation as the price is fixed, unlike the cost of renovation which can soar way beyond original estimates (as many people have discovered to their cost). If required, a new property can usually be let immediately and modern homes have good resale potential. On the other hand, new homes may be smaller than older properties and have less land.

A major advantage of buying new is that you don't have to pay stamp duty, although you'll incur connection charges for electricity, water and sometimes gas. It's even possible to obtain a grant of IR£3,000 from the Department of the Environment towards the cost of a new house. However, a number of conditions must be met, which are principally as follows:

1. The total floor area must be between 38 and 125 square metres (except in the case of houses specially adapted for the disabled);

2. Applicants mustn't have previously built or purchased another house in Ireland for their own occupation;
3. The house must be built in accordance with certain standards and practices;
4. The house must be built by a VAT registered contractor with a tax clearance certificate or, in the case of 'self-build' houses, at least IR£15,000 worth of VAT registered work must be carried out;
5. The house must be the applicant's principal residence.

Applications should be made well before any work begins in order to ensure that the plans comply with the appropriate requirements. Plans must be accompanied by various documents including a tax certificate, purchase contract, specifications, planning permission and a fire safety certificate. No payment will be made until all work has been satisfactorily completed and you're actually occupying the property. You will then be given a certificate of provisional approval (by the Department of the Environment) which you should take to your lending institution. The grant will be paid on completion of your mortgage arrangements. You can give your builder or lending institution power of attorney to receive the grant on your behalf (in which case the DoE should send you a 'letter of undertaking' to confirm that they will pay the third party). Further details of New House Grants can be obtained from the Department of the Environment (Housing Grants Section), Government Offices, Ballina, Co. Mayo (☎ 096-70677).

Note that new properties are also covered by a 10-year warranty called a 'Homebond' (see page 167) and it's against the law to sell a new house without one. The warranty is transferable to a new owner if a property is sold within the warranty period.

If you're considering buying a property in a large development, there will often be a 'show house' that will give you a good idea of how the finished building will look (although not everything in the show house will be included in the price!). If you're buying 'off plan' (i.e. before a house has been built), you can usually choose your bathroom suite, kitchen, fireplace, wallpaper and paint, wall and floor tiles, some or all of which may be included in the price. You may even be able to alter the interior room layout, although this will increase the price. Note that it's advisable to make any changes or additions to a property during the design stage, such as including a more luxurious kitchen, a chimney or an additional shower room, which will cost much more to install later.

When a building is purchased off plan, payment is made in stages as building work progresses over a period of one to two years (see below). Note that it's imperative to ensure that each stage is completed satisfactorily before making payments. If you're unable to do this yourself, you should engage an independent representative (e.g. an architect) to do it for you.

The quality of new property in Ireland is variable, although all builders must conform to certain standards. The quality of a building and the materials used will be reflected in the price, so when comparing prices ensure that you're comparing similar quality. Cheaper properties aren't usually the best built, although there are exceptions. If you want a permanent rather than a holiday home, you're better off opting for quality. Average prices for new properties are around IR£27,000 for a small (75m^2) three-bedroom bungalow, IR£31,000 to IR£35,000 for a medium size

(95m^2) three-bedroom bungalow and IR£36,000 to IR£40,000 for a 125m^2 four-bedroom house, plus the cost of land.

Most builders include a standard bathroom suite and kitchen sink unit, a back boiler and radiators, twin sockets in each room, floor and wall insulation in the basic price. Some will also include fitted wardrobes, an electric shower, ventilation units for bathroom and kitchen, and a fire alarm. Optional extras may include double glazing, oil or gas central heating and exterior paving. Items such as carpets, kitchen units, light fittings, etc. need to be installed separately by specialist contractors.

Resale 'New' Homes: Buying 'new' doesn't necessarily mean buying a brand new home of which you're the first occupant. There are many advantages in buying a modern resale home which may include better value for money; an established development with a range of local services and facilities in operation; more individual design and style; the eradication of 'teething troubles'; fixtures and fittings and other extras included in the price; a mature garden and trees; and possibly a larger plot of land. With a resale property you can see exactly what you will get for your money (unlike when buying off plan), most problems will have been resolved, and the previous owners may have made improvements or added extras such as a roof conversion or conservatory, which may not be fully reflected in the asking price. See also **Buying a Resale Home** on page 169.

Retirement Homes: Purpose-built retirement properties (or sheltered housing) are becoming more common in Ireland, although developments are still few and far between. Some large older properties have been converted into retirement homes, but large purpose-built developments are rare. It's more usual for individual buyers to have properties specially built, taking into consideration the requirements of older people (e.g. access ramps, stair lifts and emergency systems).

Building Your Own Home

If you want to be far from the madding crowd, you can buy a plot of land and have a house built to your own design and specifications or to a standard design provided by a builder. Note, however, that building permission is quite difficult to obtain, particularly in the south-west where it's strictly controlled by the local authorities. In general, building a home in Ireland, or anywhere else for that matter, isn't recommended for the timid. However, there are many excellent builders in Ireland who will build an individually designed house on your plot of land or will sell you a plot and build a house chosen from a range of standard designs.

The Cost: The cost of land in Ireland varies considerably depending on the area, e.g. from between around IR£5,000 to IR£25,000 or more for a standard half-acre plot. Prices have escalated sharply in recent years in some areas, fuelled by the demand for new homes. Land can represent up to half the cost of building a home, although it's still possible in many areas to buy a plot of land and build a bigger and better home for less than the cost of a resale property. And the more land you buy, the cheaper it is: for example, a 50-acre farm in county Kerry could cost as little as IR£150,000. But when putting in your bid, don't forget the old Irish adage: "The wrath of God has nothing on the wrath of an Irishman outbid for land"!

Building your own home allows you not only to design it yourself, but ensure that the quality of materials and workmanship are first class. Building costs are around IR£300 to IR£550 per square metre, depending on the quality and the area. There's no VAT on land purchased for building a home, but VAT at 12.5 per cent is payable on the building itself (it's should be included in the prices quoted by builders).

Some builders offer 'package deals' which include the land and the cost of building a home. However, it isn't always wise to buy the building plot from the builder who's going to build your home, and you should shop around and compare separate land and building costs. If you do decide to buy a package deal from a builder, you should insist on separate contracts for the land and the building, and obtain the title deed for the land before signing a building contract (see below). In most cases a plot of land is purchased and then a builder is contracted to build a house on it.

Buying a Building Plot: You must take the same care when buying land as you would when buying a home. The most important point when buying land is to ensure that it has been approved for building and that the plot is large enough and suitable for the house you plan to build. You must check with the planning authority of the local county, borough or urban district council that's responsible for preparing and updating the development plan for the area. According to the development plan, land is 'zoned' for particular use: residential, amenity, commercial or industrial. Some areas may be zoned for mixed use, but any development must be in accordance with the zoning. These plans are revised every five years and many are under review (particularly around Dublin, where strategic planning guidelines for the next 12 years are expected to be finalised by January 1999, on which the local development plans will be based). Development plans may be consulted at the planning authority's office or at the local library.

You should also check with the planning officer whether there are restrictions on the type of building which may be constructed. In scenic areas, for example, there may be limits on a building's height. Some plots are unsuitable for building as they're too steep or require prohibitively expensive foundations. Also check that there aren't any obstructions such as high-tension electricity lines, water pipes or rights of way which may restrict building. Note that the cost of providing services to a property in a remote rural area can be prohibitive and it must have a reliable water supply. It's also worth checking whether a plot is in an area where there are high levels of radon gas (see page 150).

It may be possible to build on agricultural land, but it will depend on whether or not you're an EU citizen and whether the land has been zoned for house building. Although there are theoretically no restrictions on EU citizens purchasing land in Ireland, the authorities may insist that farm land is retained as such and not purchased for conversion into residential or commercial property. If you're a non-EU citizen, you may need written consent from the Land Commission to buy agricultural land, although obtaining such consent is more or less a formality and it's rarely, if ever, withheld. You will need to obtain Form NQ1 from the Department of Agriculture and Food. The minimum plot that can be built on is usually $2,000m^2$ (half an acre) with a frontage of at least 60m (200ft).

Before buying land for building, you should obtain a land registry map to certify that the plot has been properly registered. Note that if you're buying an odd corner of land, it's possible that it won't be registered, in which case ownership is usually established by extended ownership. Ensure also that the purchase contract is dependent on obtaining the necessary planning permission and check for yourself that the correct planning permission is obtained (don't simply leave it to the builder).

If planning permission is flawed, you may have to pay extra to improve the local infrastructure or the property may even need to be demolished!

Planning Permission: Planning permission is required for building a house or an extension of over 23m^2 (including conservatories), as well as for erecting a fence or wall over 2m high or a path or pond over 1m above the surrounding ground level. Certain internal constructions may also require planning permission. There's a set procedure for making a planning application. First you must place an advertisement in the local newspaper indicating your intentions and your planning application must be submitted within two weeks of the appearance of the advertisement. The application must include two copies of the newspaper advertisement as well as a site location map (four copies), detailed drawings/elevations (four copies), a site layout plan (four copies), a site notice (two copies) and the application fee of IR£47. Obviously the cost of preparing drawings and plans will be far greater than the application fee itself.

You need to decide in advance whether or not to apply for outline planning permission first. This is a sort of agreement in principle, a way of 'testing the water' if you're unsure whether permission will be granted. The costs involved are less, but you cannot start building until full approval has been granted. Once outline planning permission has been given, you can submit detailed plans for approval. Alternatively, you can make a full application for planning permission from the start. This will save you time but, if it's refused, you'll have wasted money on producing plans and drawings. As they say, "you pays your money and you takes your choice", although by taking expert advice you can minimise the risk involved.

Once you've submitted your application for planning permission, the local authority has two months in which to make a decision, although they may ask for more details. There are three possible outcomes: permission is granted, permission is refused or permission is granted under certain conditions. If permission is granted, you have five years in which to complete the construction (note that the planning authorities are under no obligation to renew the permission after this period). However, it's important not to start building work until at least a month after the planning authority's decision to grant permission. During this time it's possible for other people to object to your planning application or to appeal against the planning authority's decision. The official 'grant of permission' is therefore not issued until one month after the initial decision. Even then you may need to obtain other approvals before building can start, such as permission to connect to a public water main or sewer. Finally, building control regulations require the service of a commencement notice on the building control authority (which is generally the planning authority itself).

If planning permission is refused or you're dissatisfied with the authority's decision, you can appeal to *An Bord Pleanála*, a sort of planning appeal court, whose decision is final. Your appeal must be lodged within one month of the planning authority's decision. The penalties for carrying out work without the necessary planning permission are severe and include fines of up to IR£1M and prison sentences of up to two years.

Bye-Law Approval: Even if you don't need planning permission (e.g. for an extension of less than 23m^2), you may (depending on the area) need bye-law approval from the 'building control' section of your local authority. You must obtain the appropriate application form and pay a small fee (around IR£30). The authorities are particularly concerned about safety standards (particularly in Cork City and parts of Dublin County), e.g. that a kitchen extension doesn't cover a main sewer, that an attic or loft conversion has adequate ventilation, and that extra toilets and bathrooms have proper plumbing and drainage. Note that even garden sheds must be constructed in accordance with the bye-laws relating to open spaces.

The authorities have two months to consider bye-law applications. Once you have obtained approval, you must notify them in writing when you intend to start work and when you've finished. It may seem a lot of bother for what may be only a minor alteration, but it's obviously in your interest to ensure that any work meets the required standards so that you're adding value to a property rather than subtracting it. In fact you may not be able to sell the property at all if you haven't obtained the necessary approval. Prospective buyers may be unable to secure a loan if the planning documents aren't in order (they can apply for a retention order, i.e. permission to retain an unauthorised structure, but this can take a long time and there's no guarantee that it will be granted). Note also that it isn't possible to obtain retrospective bye-law approval. When buying, you should therefore ensure that your solicitor checks that the necessary approvals for alterations or extensions have been received (see below).

Finding an Architect & Builder: When looking for an architect and builder it's advisable to obtain recommendations from local people you can trust, e.g. an estate agent, neighbours or friends. Note, however, that estate agents or other professionals aren't always the best people to ask as they may receive a commission. You can also obtain valuable information from expatriates in local bars and from owners of properties in an area that you particularly like. Architects' fees are usually calculated as a percentage of the total costs of the work (usually around 10 per cent), which doesn't encourage them to cut costs. You're advised to use an architect who's a member of The Royal Institute of the Architects of Ireland (RIAI), which requires a high standard of qualification and competence. The RIAI can supply you with a copy of their Conditions of Appointment for Domestic Work, which cover all aspects of the services offered by their members (☎ 01-676 1703).

A good architect should be able to recommend a number of reliable builders, but you should also do your own research, as the most important consideration when building a home is the reputation (and financial standing) of the builder. However, you should be wary of an architect with his 'own' builder (or a builder with his own architect), as it's the architect's job to ensure that the builder does his work according to the plans and specifications (so you don't want their relationship to be too cosy). Inspect other homes a builder has built and check with the owners what problems they have had and whether they're satisfied. Bear in mind that building standards vary and you shouldn't assume that the lowest offer is the best. Your best insurance when building a property is the reputation of the builder and his liquidity. Note that it's imperative that the builder has an insurance policy (or 'termination' guarantee) to cover you in the event that he goes bust before completing the property and its infrastructure, which must be specified in the contract.

There are few large national building companies in Ireland, where most builders are more or less 'one man bands'. When choosing a builder, make sure that he's registered with Homebond, the scheme set up by the Construction Industry Federation and operated by the National House Building Guarantee Company Ltd. If a builder is a member of the Irish Home Builders' Association (IHBA), he'll automatically be Homebond registered. Homebond provides three types of guarantee: against loss of deposit in the event of the builder going bust; against water and smoke damage for two years after completion; and against major structural defects for ten years after completion. Note that banks and building societies require Homebond registration on new houses, which is certified by Homebond Certificate HB47. When you enter into an agreement with a builder, you should immediately receive the Homebond Form HB10 incorporating the guarantee protection, and you should ensure that your solicitor receives this document at the earliest possible stage. According to the IHBA, a significant number of houses are still being built without certification, particularly in the west and north-west, therefore if you're buying without finance through an Irish bank or building society, make sure you obtain the necessary Homebond certification. Queries relating to Homebond should be addressed to: Homebond, Construction House, Canal Road, Dublin 6 (☎ 01-491 0210).

If you want a house built exactly to your specifications, you'll need to personally supervise it every step of the way or employ an architect to do it for you. Without close supervision it's highly likely that your instructions *won't* be followed to the letter.

Contracts: You should obtain written quotations from a number of builders before signing a contract. Once you've chosen a builder, your architect will prepare the contract documents, which will include a 'form of contract' and a set of drawings and specifications. These will be sent to the builder for completion. The builder will then provide you with a programme for the job indicating the projected start and finish dates, and evidence that he holds the insurance required under the contract. The contract should include a detailed building description and a list of the materials to be used (with references to the architect's plans); the exact location of the building on the plot; the building and payment schedule, which must be made in stages according to building progress; a penalty clause for late completion; the retention of a percentage (typically 10 per cent for domestic work) of the building costs for up to 12 months as a guarantee against defects; and how disputes will be settled.

Ensure that the contract includes all costs including the architect's fees (unless contracted separately); landscaping (if applicable); all permits and licences; and the connection of utilities (electricity, gas, etc.) to the house, not just to the building site. The only extra is usually the cost of the mains water connection.

Before accepting a quotation, it's advisable to have it checked by a building consultant to confirm that it's a fair deal. You should check whether the quotation (which should include VAT at 12.5 per cent) is an estimate or a fixed price, as sometimes the cost can escalate wildly due to contract clauses and changes made during building work. A fixed price contract isn't usual in one-off projects because the scope of the work required frequently changes during the project. It is, however, possible to have a fixed rate contract whereby the unit cost of each element in the project is fixed against inflation. It's vital to have a contract checked by a solicitor, as they are often heavily biased in the builder's favour.

Payment: You're usually expected to pay an initial deposit of up to 10 per cent of the agreed price. How the remainder of the cost is paid varies from one part of the country to another. In Dublin, for example, you usually pay the balance on completion, whereas in Cork you'll usually pay in instalments. Instalment payments may be made at fixed stages in the construction process, e.g. on completion of the external walls, the roof and the wiring. More often, however, the work is valued and paid for at fixed intervals, perhaps monthly. In either case, your architect will value the work as it proceeds and advise you by way of 'architect's certificates of payment due' the money owed to the builder. Make sure you have all work inspected by your architect before making any stage payments. In any case, Homebond's own inspectors will be required to see the work at certain stages (typically when the foundations have been opened, when the drains are available and on completion).

When building work is nearing completion, your architect will carry out particular inspections and have the builder attend to any defective or outstanding work before 'practical completion' of the work is certified, half of the retention money released and the job handed over to you. At this stage you will need to ensure continuity of insurance cover from the builder to yourself. After practical completion there's a 'defects liability period', during which the builder will remedy defects without charge. This usually lasts for between 6 and 12 months and, ideally, extends through a winter. At the end of the defects liability period and after the builder has made good any defects that have become apparent, the balance of the retention money is released; this constitutes 'final completion'.

Note that it's important to ensure that payments are made on time, otherwise you could lose all previous payments and the property could be sold to another buyer. See also **Avoiding Problems** on page 144, which particularly applies to buying off plan or buying unfinished properties.

Warranties: On completion of the work you'll require an 'opinion on compliance' with Planning and Building Regulations to be completed by your architect. This document is necessary to sell a property and banks and building societies also usually require it as a condition of lending you money for a mortgage.

A useful booklet entitled *A Home of Your Own Making* is published by AIB Bank in association with The Royal Institute of the Architects of Ireland.

BUYING A RESALE HOME

Resale (or second-hand) properties represent good value for money in Ireland and are often more attractive and interesting than new buildings. Another advantage of buying a resale property is that you can see exactly what you'll get for your money and will save on the cost of installing such things as telephone lines and connections to main services. When buying a resale property in a development, it's advisable to ask the neighbours about any problems, planned developments and anything else that may affect your enjoyment of the property. Most residents are usually happy to tell you (unless of course they're trying to sell you their own property!)

If you want a property with abundant charm and character, a building for renovation or conversion, outbuildings or a large plot of land, you must usually buy an old property. Note, however, that old country homes such as farmhouses may be harder to find and you'll need to go to small local auctioneers rather than large national companies. Some old homes lack basic services such as electricity, a reliable water supply and sanitation. Because purchase prices are often low, many foreign buyers are deceived into believing that they're getting a wonderful bargain, without fully investigating renovation and modernisation costs (see page 185).

Occasionally owners advertise their properties directly in the local paper or by simply putting a 'for sale' sign in the window. But although you can save money by buying direct from an owner, particularly when he's forced to sell, you should *always* employ a solicitor to carry out the necessary checks (see **Conveyance** on page 179). If you're unsure of the value of a property, you should obtain a professional valuation.

Leasehold Properties

In Ireland, as in the UK, properties with common elements (whether buildings, amenities or land) shared with other properties are usually sold on a leasehold rather than freehold basis. Owners of leasehold properties not only own their homes, but also own a share of the common elements of a building or development including foyers, hallways, passages, lifts, patios, gardens, roads, and leisure and sports facilities (such as gyms and tennis courts). This means that you'll become part of a management company responsible for the insurance and upkeep of the common elements of the property. Note that being part of a management company is usually to your advantage, in that you at least have some control over expenditure on the property rather than it being determined ad hoc by some absentee landlord. When buying a leasehold property, however, you should check whether the company has a healthy reserve or 'sink' fund and whether any major expenditure (e.g. a new roof) is imminent. Otherwise you could find yourself being asked for several thousand pounds shortly after moving in. When you come to sell your apartment, you hand over a share transfer form that transfers your membership of the management company to the buyer.

When considering buying a leasehold property, the first thing you should do is ascertain the length of the lease, i.e. how many years it has left to run. If it's a new apartment this may be as many as 9,999 years, in which case you needn't worry too much about outliving your lease! However, if there are only, say, 80 years left you should take into account that if you come to re-sell the property in 10 or 20 years, it may be difficult to find a buyer (note that a lease cannot be extended). On the other hand, once the lease expires the lessee acquires the right to purchase the freehold, in which case a short lease may be attractive (although this right applies only to owner-occupiers, not to investors).

Note that Landlord and Tenant legislation introduced in 1978 made it illegal to purchase a freehold property and resell part of it on a leasehold basis.

Advantages: The advantages of owning a leasehold property may include increased security (all new apartments must be fitted with full fire alarm systems and most have individual intercom-controlled access); a range of communal facilities; community living with frequent social contacts and the companionship of close neighbours; no garden maintenance; and fewer of the responsibilities of home ownership.

Disadvantages: The disadvantages of leasehold properties can include excessively high management fees (owners may have no control over increases); restrictive rules and regulations; a confining living and social environment and possible lack of privacy; noisy neighbours (particularly if neighbouring properties are rented to holiday-makers); limited living and storage space; expensive parking (or insufficient off-road parking); and acrimonious management company meetings.

Research: Before buying a leasehold property it's advisable to ask current owners a few questions. For example, do they like living there; what are the fees and restrictions; how noisy are other residents; are the recreational facilities easy to access; would they buy there again (why or why not); and, most importantly, is the management company solvent and well run. You may also wish to check on your prospective neighbours and if you're planning to buy an apartment above the ground floor you may want to make sure that the building has a lift. Upper floor apartments may offer more security than ground floor apartments, and apartments that have other apartments above and below them are generally more noisy than ground or top floor apartments.

Cost: The recent fashion for apartment living in Ireland has caused prices to soar, so that some apartments now cost more than similar sized houses with extensive grounds (see page 155).

Management Fees: Owners of leasehold properties usually need to pay management fees for the upkeep of communal areas and for communal services. Charges are calculated according to each owner's share of the development or apartment building and *not* whether they're temporary or permanent residents. Shares may be calculated according to the size of properties, e.g. ten properties of equal size would each pay 10 per cent of management fees. Fees vary enormously depending on the quality of the development, the extent of the grounds, and the age and condition of the property. You may pay as little as IR£200 per year, but the average annual management fee is around IR£400. If the fee is very low, you should check whether it actually includes all management costs or whether you're liable to be stung for extra charges for any major repairs that need to be done. Fees are usually billed annually. If you're buying an apartment from a previous owner, always ask to see a copy of the management charges for previous years.

TIMESHARE & PART-OWNERSHIP SCHEMES

If you're looking for a holiday home, you may wish to investigate a scheme that provides sole occupancy of a property for a number of weeks each year. These include co-ownership, leaseback, timesharing and a holiday property bond. Don't rush into any of these schemes without fully researching the market and before you're absolutely clear what you want and what you can realistically expect to receive for your money.

Co-Ownership: Two or more people buying a property together are called co-owners. There are two kinds of co-ownership in Ireland: joint tenancy and tenancy in common. In a joint tenancy, all the co-owners own the property as one legal entity and on the death of one co-owner his interest accrues to the others by 'right of survivorship' (*jus accrescendi*). This kind of ownership is most usual with married couples but could be used by any group of people. In tenancy in common, each co-owner owns an undivided share of the property, so that if he dies his interest devolves to his estate (as specified in his will). This is generally the better option for business or commercial purchases.

Co-ownership allows you to recoup your investment in savings on holiday costs and still retain equity in the property. A common arrangement is a four-owner scheme (which many consider to be the optimum number of co-owners), where you buy a quarter of a property and can occupy it for up to three months a year. However, there's no reason why there cannot be as many as 12 co-owners, with a month's occupancy each per year (usually divided between high, mid and low seasons).

Co-ownership provides access to a size and quality of property that may otherwise be unaffordable, and it's even possible to have a share in a substantial mansion, where a number of families could live together simultaneously and hardly ever see each other if they didn't want to! Co-ownership can be a good choice for a family seeking a holiday home for a few weeks or months a year and has the added advantage that (because of the lower cost) a mortgage may be unnecessary. Co-ownership is usually much better value than a timeshare (see below) and needn't cost much more. Note, however, that a water-tight contract must be drawn up by an experienced solicitor to protect the co-owners' interests.

One of the best ways to get into co-ownership, if you can afford it, is to buy a property yourself and offer shares to others. This overcomes the problem of getting together a consortium of would-be owners and trying to agree on a purchase in advance, which is difficult unless it's just a few friends or family members. Many people form an Irish company to buy and manage the property, which can in turn be owned by a company in the co-owners' home country, thus allowing any disputes to be dealt with under local law. Each co-owner receives a number of shares depending on how much he has paid, which entitle him to so many weeks' occupancy a year. Owners don't need to have equal shares and can all be made direct title holders. If a co-owner wishes to sell his shares he must usually offer first refusal to the other co-owners, although if they don't wish to buy them and a new co-owner cannot be found, the property will need to be sold.

Leaseback: Leaseback or sale-and-leaseback schemes are designed for those seeking a holiday home for a limited number of weeks each year. Properties sold under a leaseback scheme are usually located in the most popular areas, e.g. near golf courses or coastal resorts, where self-catering accommodation is in high demand. Buying a property through a leaseback scheme allows a buyer to buy a new property at less than its true cost, e.g. 30 per cent less than the list price. In return for the discount the property must be leased back to the developer, usually for 9 to 11 years, so that he can let it as self-catering holiday accommodation. The buyer owns the freehold of the property and the full price is shown in the title deed. The buyer is also given the right to occupy the property for a period each year, usually six or eight weeks, spread over high, mid and low seasons. These weeks can usually be let to provide income or can possibly be exchanged with accommodation in another resort (as with a timeshare scheme). The developer furnishes and manages the property and pays all the maintenance and bills (e.g. for utilities) during the term of the lease, even when the owner occupies the property. Note that it's important to have a contract checked by a solicitor to ensure that you receive vacant possession at the end of the leaseback period *without* having to pay an indemnity charge, otherwise you could end up paying more than the property is worth.

Timesharing: Timesharing, also called 'holiday ownership', 'vacation ownership' and 'holidays for life', has earned a poor reputation in recent years, but things are slowly improving. The Timeshare Council (UK), in particular (and its new Irish counterpart, the Timeshare Council of Ireland), as members of the Organisation for Timeshare in Europe (OTE), is working to restore respectability to the concept of timeshare. Its members are bound by a code of conduct which includes a requirement that buyers have secure occupancy rights and that their money is properly protected prior to the completion of a new property. Further details can be obtained from the OTE/Timeshare Council (☎ UK 0171-821 8845).

Since April 1997, an EU Directive has required timeshare companies to disclose information about the vendor and the property, and, at least in the UK, to allow prospective buyers a 14-day 'cooling off period' during which they may cancel any sales agreement they have signed without penalty. Elsewhere in the EU, although timeshare companies are technically bound by the directive, if they flout it you'll need to seek redress from the government of the country, which may not be something you want or can afford to do.

There are only three recognised timeshare resorts in Ireland: Fitzpatrick Castle near Dublin, Connemara Cottages west of Galway and Knocktopher Abbey in County Kilkenny. Only the last of these is officially 'approved' by the OTE and it's managed by Seasons Holidays (sales ☎ 01994-427332). If you buy a timeshare at Knocktopher Abbey you automatically earn the right to use Seasons Holidays' other resorts in Wales, Cornwall and Portugal. If you want a wider choice of alternative resorts, you can join Resort Condominium International (☎ UK 01536-310101) or Interval International (☎ UK 0181-336 9300). RCI has timeshares in Counties Dublin, Galway, Kilkenny and Cork; Interval's are in Kerry and Cork.

Most experts believe that there's little or no advantage in a timeshare compared with a normal holiday rental and that it's simply an expensive way to pay for your holidays in advance. It doesn't make any sense to tie up your money for what amounts to a long-term reservation on an annual holiday (usually you don't actually 'own' anything). An average timeshare in Ireland cost around IR£4,000 for one week per year, to which must be added annual management fees. You should also bear in mind that timeshare owners can be hit by hefty levies which can run into IR£thousands per owner.

Most financial advisers believe you're better off putting your money into a long-term investment, where you retain your capital and may even earn sufficient interest to pay for a few weeks holiday each year. For example, IR£10,000 invested at just 5 per cent yields IR£500 a year, which, when added to the saving on management fees, is sufficient to pay for a week's holiday in a self-catering apartment almost anywhere!

Often timeshares are difficult or impossible to sell at any price and 'pledges' from timeshare companies to sell them for you or buy them back at the market price are just a sales ploy, as timeshare companies aren't interested once they've made a sale. Note that there's no real resale market for timeshares and if you need to sell, you're highly unlikely to get your money back. If you want to buy a timeshare, it's best to buy a resale privately from an existing owner or a timeshare resale broker, when they sell for a fraction of their original cost. When buying privately you can usually drive a hard bargain and may even get a timeshare 'free' simply by assuming the current owner's maintenance contract.

Holiday Property Bond: A Holiday Property Bond is a good alternative to timesharing for those with a minimum of GB£2,000 to invest. Holiday Property Bond (operated by HPB Management Ltd., HPB House, Newmarket, Suffolk CB8 8EH, UK, ☎ 01638-660066) owns more than 700 Bond properties in over a dozen countries as well as 'tenancy' properties in a dozen more, including Ireland. The Bond is a life assurance bond investing in holiday properties and in securities producing income for management charges. Each GB£1 invested is equal to one point and each week's stay in each property is assigned a points rating depending on its size, location and the time of year. There are no extra fees apart from a 'user' charge to cover cleaning and utility costs. Furthermore, there's a buy-back guarantee after two years, when an investment can be sold at the current market value. Whereas bond properties are owned by HPB Management, tenancy properties are privately-owned and leased by HPB for the exclusive use of bondholders, who pay fewer points but a slightly higher user charge for these tenancy properties than for bond properties. HPB has three tenancy properties in the Republic of Ireland, located in counties Cork and Waterford and in Connemara.

BUYING FOR INVESTMENT

In recent years Irish property has been an excellent investment, although changes to tax legislation in early 1998 have made it somewhat less attractive to investors. There are various kinds of property investment. Your own home is an investment of sorts in that it gives you rent-free accommodation. It may also yield a return in terms of increased value (a capital gain), although that gain may be difficult to realise unless you trade down or move to another area or country where similar property is less expensive. Of course, if you buy property other than for your own regular use (i.e. a property which isn't your principal home), you'll be in a position to benefit from a more tangible return on your investment. There are essentially four main categories of investment property:

- A holiday home, which can provide a return in a number of ways. It can give you and your family and friends rent-free accommodation while (you hope) maintaining its value, or you may be able to let it to generate supplementary income. It may also produce a capital gain if property values rise faster than inflation (as they have in Ireland in many areas in recent years).

- A home for your children, which may also realise a capital gain.

- A business property, which could be anything from bed and breakfast accommodation to a car park. Particularly attractive are properties which qualify for tax relief (e.g. under the Seaside Resort scheme – see page 110).

- A property purchased for pure investment.

Any property investment needs to be considered over the medium to long term. For example, over the 25 years from 1972 to 1996 an Irish property would have yielded an average pre-tax return of 15 per cent per annum compared with average inflation at 9 per cent. But the divergence was not a constant one and there were short periods during this time when the increase in property values failed to keep pace with inflation (i.e. 1974–1976, 1981–1986 and 1991–1992). You also need to take into account the various tax implications in owning and selling property, particularly capital gains tax (see page 125). Before deciding to invest in any property, you should ask yourself the following questions:

- Can I afford to tie up capital in the medium to long term, i.e. at least five years?

- How likely is it that the value of the property will rise during this period?

- Will I be relying on a regular income from my investment? If so, how easy will it be to generate that income, e.g. to find tenants for a property?

- Am I aware of all the risks involved and how comfortable am I with taking those risks?
- Do I have enough information to make a rational decision?

Note that capital gains tax (CGT) can take a large slice out of any profit made on the sale of a second home, although the rate has recently been reduced (see page 125).

BUYING AT AUCTION

Although sales by auction tend to make the headlines in Ireland's property pages, only some 6 per cent of properties in Ireland are sold by public auction and these tend to be of the more prestigious kind. Nevertheless, buying at auction is becoming more popular and the number of properties sold at auction is increasing by around 10 per cent a year. There were over 250 auctions in the first quarter of 1998, although the majority take place in spring and summer. They're usually advertised three or four weeks in advance so that there's sufficient time for prospective buyers to make the necessary preparations.

Before bidding at an auction, you must make sure you have the legal title of the property approved by your solicitor; obtain a structural survey of the property by a qualified architect, engineer or building surveyor (if necessary); secure formal written loan approval (if required), which will necessitate a mortgage valuation report by a qualified valuer; and have sufficient cash to pay a deposit (usually 10 per cent) on the day of the auction, with the balance payable on completion of the sale (usually five to eight weeks after the auction).

Bear in mind that when bidding at auction, you bid unconditionally. If you're successful, your deposit is at risk if you cannot complete the purchase for any reason. Note also that guideline prices given by agents prior to the auction tend to be deliberately conservative (in order to attract more prospective buyers). Although the IAVI (Irish Auctioneers & Valuers Institute) recommends that guidelines should be within 15 per cent of the anticipated reserve price, the actual selling price is often so much higher than the reserve figure that the guidelines are virtually meaningless. In any case, reserve prices aren't disclosed in advance of the auction. The auctioneer's fee is usually the same as for a private treaty sale (see below), but may vary depending on the value of the property and in some cases may be subject to negotiation.

BUYING BY PRIVATE TREATY

Most property in Ireland is sold by private treaty. Under this method a price is put on a property by the vendor which is usually subject to negotiation between the seller and prospective buyers. A fair number of sales occur outside the normal system of auctions and estate agents, and you won't find out about these unless you know where to look or have a well-connected 'agent' in Ireland. However, by far the majority of sales are conducted through estate agents (see below) and it's rare for developers to sell directly as in some other countries.

If there are several buyers interested, the selling agent may suggest a closed or private tender, whereby written or oral bids must be submitted by a set time on a 'best and final offer' basis. Normally in such cases the highest bidder secures the property, but not always. If, for example, an offer is subject to the sale of another property, a lower offer from a first-time buyer or someone who's in a position to buy unconditionally may be accepted instead. In a private treaty sale you must bear in mind that the purchase isn't secure until all the formal documentation has been signed and exchanged between the buyer and seller. Up to that point the seller may still accept a higher offer, in which case the original buyer is said to have been 'gazumped'. It is in fact the agent's duty to inform the seller of all offers received at any time during the selling process. Gazumping isn't as common in Ireland as it is in the UK (the Irish blame the British for 'exporting' this unethical practice), but it's happening more frequently nowadays.

'Starter' homes targeted at first-time buyers often sell within two weeks of coming on the market. Estate agents will usually be offered the asking price on the first viewing, but will then invite bids from other would-be buyers in order to increase the price. In such circumstances your deposit will be returned, but there's nothing you can do to oblige the vendor to honour the agreement. You simply have to start looking for another property and try to put all thoughts of the one you thought you were buying out of your mind!

ESTATE AGENTS

The vast majority of property sales in Ireland, particularly those where overseas buyers are involved, are handled by estate agents, who are usually referred to as auctioneers. It's common for foreigners in many countries, particularly Britain and Germany, to use an agent in their own country who works in conjunction with an Irish agent. Many Irish agents also advertise abroad, particularly in the publications listed in **Appendix A**, and in expatriate magazines and newspapers in Ireland. If you want to find an agent in a particular town or area, you can look under 'Auctioneers' in the local Irish Golden Pages (available at main libraries in many countries).

Qualifications: Irish estate agents are regulated by law and must be professionally qualified and licensed. You should choose an agent who's a member of a professional association such as the Irish Auctioneers & Valuers Institute (IAVI), which is by far the largest professional body in Ireland, or the Institute of Professional Auctioneers and Valuers (IPAV). You should ensure that an agent has a current auctioneer's licence. IAVI members are obliged to display their licences prominently in their offices. Licensed auctioneers are 'bonded' (i.e. provide security against claims) to the sum of IR£10,000 in the high court. To become an individual member of the IAVI, auctioneers must have undertaken relevant studies or passed the Institute's own exams. IAVI 'member firm status' is granted only to practices in which the majority of equity is held by qualified IAVI individual members. Member firms are also subject to a disciplinary code and must have professional indemnity insurance, and the IAVI compensation fund (a deposit protection fund) applies only to IAVI members and (in the case of residential and land sales) associate member firms.

When you pay a deposit to an agent, it must (by law) be deposited in a separate client or current account so that the agent derives no interest from the money. Note that the rules for Irish estate agents also apply to foreigners, who cannot sell property in Ireland without an Irish auctioneer's licence.

Fees: There are no government controls on agents' fees in Ireland, but the commission charged by most Irish agents is between 2 and 2.5 per cent. This fee is included in the sale price and effectively paid by the buyer. Foreign agents located abroad often work with Irish agents and share the standard commission, so vendors usually pay no more by using them. When buying, check whether you need to pay commission or any extras in addition to the sale price (apart from the normal fees and taxes associated with buying a property).

Viewing: If possible, you should decide where you want to live, what sort of property you want and your budget *before* visiting Ireland. Obtain details of as many properties as possible in your chosen area and price range, and make a shortlist of those you wish to view. The details provided by Irish estate agents can be sparse. Often there's no photograph and even when there is, it usually doesn't do a property justice. Note that there are no national property listings in Ireland, where each agent has his own list of properties for sale and it's unusual for the same property to be listed with more than two agents. Irish agents who advertise in foreign journals or who work closely with overseas agents may provide coloured photographs and a full description, particularly for the more expensive properties. The best agents provide an abundance of information. Agents vary in their efficiency and enthusiasm as well as in the number and variety of properties they have to offer. If an agent shows little interest in finding out exactly what you want, you should look elsewhere. If you're using a foreign agent, confirm (and reconfirm) that a particular property is still for sale and the price, before travelling to Ireland to view it.

Note that Irish estate agents don't usually require you to sign an agreement before showing you properties, although they may do so if you're buying at auction. In Ireland you're usually shown properties personally by agents and won't be given the keys (particularly to furnished properties) or be expected to deal with tenants or vendors directly. You should make an appointment to see properties as agents don't usually like people turning up 'on spec'. If you cannot keep an appointment, you should always call and cancel it. If you happen to be on holiday, it's okay to drop in unannounced to have a look at what's on offer, but don't expect an agent to show you properties without an appointment. If you view properties during a holiday, it's advisable to do so at the beginning so that you can return later to inspect any you particularly like a second or third time. Irish estate agents are usually open during lunch hours and on Saturdays.

You should try to view as many properties as possible during the time available, but allow sufficient time to view each property thoroughly, to travel between properties and for breaks for sustenance. Make sure you also allow plenty of talking time, which is always necessary in Ireland! Although it's important to see sufficient properties to form an accurate opinion of price and quality, don't see too many properties in one day (around six to eight is usually a manageable number), as it's easy to become confused over the merits of each property. If you're shown properties that don't meet your specifications, tell the agent immediately. You can also help an agent narrow the field by telling him exactly what's wrong with the properties you reject. It's advisable to make notes of both the good *and* bad features and take lots of photographs of the properties you like, so that you're able to compare them later at your leisure (but keep a record of which photos are of which house!). It's also wise to mark properties on a map so that should you wish to return later on your own, you can find them without getting lost (too often). The more a property appeals to you, the more you should look for faults and negative points; if you still like it after stressing all the negative points, it must have special appeal.

Most agents offer after sales services and will help you arrange legal advice, insurance, utilities, interior decorators and builders, and many offer a full management and rental service on behalf of non-resident owners. Note, however, that agents may receive commissions for referrals and therefore you may not always receive independent advice.

INSPECTIONS, VALUATIONS & SURVEYS

When you've found a property that you like, you should make a close inspection of its condition. Obviously this will depend on whether it's an old house in need of complete restoration, a property that has been partly or totally modernised, or a modern home. One of the problems with a property that has been restored is that you don't know how well the job has been done, particularly if the owner did it himself, although he may have had to obtain local bye-law approval (see above), in which case certain standards will have been met. If work has been carried out by local builders, you should ask to see the bills.

Some simple checks that you can do yourself include testing the electrical system, plumbing, mains water, hot water boiler and central heating. Don't take someone's word that these are functional, but check them for yourself. If a property doesn't have electricity or mains water, check the nearest connection point and the cost of extending the service to the property, as it can be *very* expensive in remote rural areas. If a property has a well or septic tank, you should have it tested. An old property may show visible signs of damage and decay, such as bulging or cracked walls, rising damp, missing roof slates (you can check with binoculars) and rotten woodwork. Common problems also include rusting water pipes and leaky plumbing; inadequate sewage disposal; poor wiring; humidity and rising damp (no damp course); uneven flooring or no concrete base; subsidence; and cracked internal and external walls. Some of these problems are even evident in relatively new properties. In areas that are liable to flooding, storms or subsidence, it's advisable to check an old property after a heavy rainfall, when any leaks should come to light. If you find or suspect problems, you should have a property checked by a builder or have a full structural survey carried out by a surveyor.

You should never make an offer on an old property before at least having it checked by a builder, who will also be able to tell you whether the price is too high, given any work that needs to be done. It's important to check who was the developer or builder of a relatively new property, as a builder with a good reputation is unlikely to have cut corners. Note that a property over ten years old is no longer be covered by a builder's warranty (see page 167). If you require a mortgage to buy a property, the lending institution (e.g. bank or building society) will require at least a valuation report, which, as well as verifying the value of the property, will usually reveal any major defects. However, a valuation report won't necessarily tell you whether there are (or are likely to be) any minor problems, such as unsafe wiring, leaking roofs, etc. Therefore it's prudent to obtain a full structural survey, which will reveal any major or minor defects in a property and indicate the likely cost of any repairs or renovations required. If serious problems are discovered that would be expensive to rectify, you may decide to look for another property or renegotiate a reduction in the price with the vendor. Note that your mortgage lender may insist on a structural report if a property is over 100 years old.

You could ask the vendor to have a survey done at his expense, which, providing it gives the property a clean bill of health, will help him sell it even if you decide not to buy. However, it's unlikely that he will agree to this as buying property in Ireland is very much a case of 'caveat emptor' (buyer beware)! You can employ a foreign (e.g. British) surveyor practising in Ireland. However, an Irish surveyor may have a more intimate knowledge of local properties and building methods. If you employ a foreign surveyor, you must ensure that he's experienced in the idiosyncrasies of Irish properties and that he has professional indemnity insurance covering Ireland (which means you can happily sue him if he does a bad job!).

Always discuss with a surveyor exactly what will be included, and most importantly, excluded from a survey (you may need to pay extra to include certain checks and tests). A full structural survey should include the condition of all buildings, particularly the foundations, roofs, walls and woodwork; plumbing, electrical and heating systems. A survey can be limited to a few items or even a single system only, such as the wiring or plumbing in an old house. You should receive a written report on the structural condition of a property, including anything that could become a problem in the future. Some surveyors allow you to accompany them and provide a video film of their findings in addition to a written report. The IR£300 or so fee for a full structural survey on an average size home is a small price to pay for the peace of mind it affords.

Buying Land: Before buying a home on its own plot of land you should walk the boundaries and look for fences, driveways, roads, and the overhanging eaves of buildings that may be encroaching upon the property. If you're uncertain about the boundaries you should have the land surveyed, which is advisable in any case when buying a property with a large plot of land. When buying a rural property in Ireland, you may be able to negotiate the amount of land you want included in the purchase. If a property is part of a larger plot of land owned by the vendor or the boundaries must be redrawn, you'll need to hire a surveyor to measure the land and draw up a new cadastral plan. You should also ask your solicitor to check the local municipal plans to find out what the land can be used for and whether there are any existing rights of way.

CONVEYANCE

Conveyance (often improperly referred to as conveyancing) is the legal term for processing the paperwork involved in buying and selling a property and transferring the deeds of ownership. As this can be a complicated process, it's virtually essential to use a solicitor. Essentially the procedure is as follows. Once the selling price has been agreed between the vendor and the buyer, the vendor's solicitor prepares a contract and sends it to the buyer's solicitor, who checks the title and asks the buyer to sign the contract and pay a deposit to secure the property. If the buyer is obtaining a loan (mortgage), the contract will be subject to the loan being granted, which in turn will be subject to a satisfactory valuation report. Some selling agents insist that the valuation is carried out before negotiations are concluded, and provisional loan approval can now be secured quickly (within 72 hours) therefore the vendor's solicitor will generally refuse a contract that's subject to provisional loan approval.

The buyer's solicitor will then draft the purchase deed and raise his queries (requisitions) on title before sending the deposit, draft deed and any objections with regard to title back to the vendor's solicitor. Note that at this stage the buyer has committed himself to buying (subject to satisfactory title) whereas the vendor isn't yet committed to selling. The requisitions (commonly referred to as 'searches') carried out usually include:

- A planning search, with the local planning office, to reveal whether there are plans to construct anything which would adversely affect the value, enjoyment or use of the property such as roads, railway lines, airports, shops or factories, and whether applications for planning permission in respect of the property have been lodged or refused;

- A compulsory purchase order search with the local authority to find out whether the land is subject to a compulsory purchase order, e.g. for road building or widening;

- A licensing search (in the case of a hotel or pub).

    The solicitor will also check:

- That the property belongs to the vendor or that he has legal authority to sell it. If the property is registered with the land registry this is a simple matter. If it's with the registry of deeds, 30 years' title is usually regarded as 'sufficient' (note that the vendor's solicitor is now obliged by law to disclose any relevant legal matters, although not physical matters, relating to the title of a property);

- That the property was built in accordance with the appropriate regulations, e.g. bye-laws, building standards, etc.

- That there are no encumbrances (e.g. mortgages or loans) against the property or any outstanding debts such as gas, electricity or telephone bills and management fees (in the case of a leasehold property). Note that you *must* ensure that any debts against a property are cleared before you sign the deed of sale, as all unpaid debts on a property in Ireland are inherited by the buyer.

- Whether there are any remaining guarantees from which you can benefit, such as the Homebond 10-year warranty for new homes.

- That all the agreed fixtures and fittings included in the price you have negotiated are actually included in the legal documentation.

When he has received satisfactory replies to these queries, the buyer's solicitor will draft a deed transferring title in the property to the buyer and give the lending institution a certificate of title. If the vendor is happy with the contract, he will also sign it. The draft deed is then approved by the vendor's solicitor and returned for 'typing up' (engrossment) by the buyer's solicitor before being returned again to the vendor's solicitor for signing by the vendor (no wonder solicitors' fees are so high!).

    The buyer's solicitor will also need to check whether capital gains tax has been paid by the vendor (if applicable). If the purchase price is over IR£150,000, he will need to obtain a CGT clearance certificate, otherwise the buyer is obliged to submit 15 per cent of the purchase price to the Revenue Commissioners against the possibility of CGT being unpaid (the vendor will then have to obtain a refund of the same amount once the clearance certificate has been produced).

Warning: Anyone buying (or selling) property in Ireland shouldn't even think about doing it without taking expert, independent legal advice. You should certainly never sign anything or pay any money before doing so. Before hiring a solicitor, compare the fees charged by a number of practises and get quotations in writing. Always check what's included in the fee and whether it's 'full and binding' or just an estimate (a low basic rate may be supplemented by more expensive 'extras'). Note that it isn't advisable to use the vendor's solicitor, even if this would save you money, as he's primarily concerned with protecting the interests of the vendor and not the buyer. See also **Avoiding Problems** on page 144.

PURCHASE CONTRACTS

Your solicitor should draw up the purchase contract and ensure that it includes everything required, particularly any necessary conditional clauses. The basis of all house purchase contracts in Ireland is the 'Standard Incorporated Law Society' contract (copies are obtainable from the Law Society of Ireland), which is revised from time to time (the one in use dates from 1995). The particulars of the purchase (i.e. the address of the property, selling price, date of purchase, etc.) and any special conditions must be included in the contract, but its general conditions won't usually need to be amended (unless there's a major problem, such as planning permission not having been obtained). If you're buying a new property from a builder, there are also standard contracts that can be used and there may be separate contracts for the purchase of the site and for the construction of the building. Note that from the moment the signed contracts are exchanged, the sale becomes irrevocable.

Deposits: When you sign the contract for a new or resale property or a plot of land, you must pay a deposit. If you're buying a resale or a new finished property (i.e. not off plan) you usually pay a deposit of 10 per cent when signing the contract (the actual amount may be negotiable), with the balance being paid on completion when the deed of sale is signed.

Conditional Clauses: Most contracts, whether for new or resale properties, contain a number of conditional clauses that must be met to ensure the validity of the contract. Conditions usually apply to events beyond the control of either the vendor or buyer, although almost anything the buyer agrees with the vendor can be included in a contract. If any of the conditions aren't met, the contract can be suspended or declared null and void, and the deposit returned. However, if you fail to go through with a purchase and aren't covered by a clause in the contract, you'll forfeit your deposit and could be compelled to go through with the purchase. Note that if you're buying anything from the vendor such as carpets, curtains or furniture, that are included in the purchase price, you should have them listed and attached as an addendum to the contract. Any fixtures and fittings present in a property when you view it (and agree to buy it) should still be there when you take possession, unless otherwise stated in the contract (see also **Completion** on page 183). In most cases, however, the contract will be conditional only upon the buyer obtaining the necessary mortgage and (if applicable) planning permission being obtained.

Inheritance & Capital Gains Tax: Before registering the title deed, carefully consider the tax and inheritance consequences for those in whose name the deed will be registered. Property can be registered in a single name; both names of a couple or joint buyers' names; the name or names of children, giving the parents sole use during their lifetime; or in the name of an Irish or foreign company (see below). However you decide to buy a property, it should be done at the time of purchase as it will be more expensive (or even impossible) to change it later. Discuss the matter with your solicitor before signing a contract. See also **Capital Gains Tax** on page 125 and **Capital Acquisition Tax** on page 126.

Buying through a company: It's no longer possible to avoid Irish capital gains and inheritance tax by registering a property in the name of an offshore company, as land is regarded as a 'qualified asset', which is always taxable. If a property is owned by a company in a country which has a double-taxation treaty with Ireland, you'll pay the full amount of capital gains tax due in Ireland (see page 125). If the rate of CGT in your country of residence is higher than in Ireland, you'll pay the difference in that country; if it's lower, you *won't* receive a refund! Buying an Irish property through an Irish company has advantages and disadvantages. You can save a considerable amount in stamp duty (see page 158), but you may also have to pay CGT or income tax on the increased value of your shares and, if the company has been running for some time and has a complicated financial history, you may have difficulty finding a buyer who's willing to take it over. Before buying property through any sort of company, it's essential to obtain expert legal advice.

See also **Avoiding Problems** on page 144 and **Conveyancing** on page 179.

COMPLETION

Completion (or closing) is the name given to the signing of the final deed of sale, the date of which is usually five to eight weeks after signing the purchase contract, as stated in that contract (although it may be 'moveable'). The exact date will be set by the buyer's solicitor once his client's mortgage has been approved. Before closing, the buyer's solicitor will carry out the final searches on title, including:

- A land registry or registry of deeds search to ascertain whether there are any restrictions on title such as outstanding mortgages or rights of residence. In the case of registered land, there are some burdens which aren't subject to registration such as outstanding estate duty, succession duty, rent charges, land improvement charges, annuities, rights of the public and short-term tenancies. The vendor is usually required to swear an affidavit that none of these burdens affect the property.

- A company search (with the Companies Registration office) in the case of company purchases.

- A judgement search (at the Central Office of the High Court) to reveal any record of litigation (*lis pendens*) affecting the property and any debts owed by the vendor which don't affect the property directly, but indicate the possibility of the debt having been converted into a 'judgement mortgage' registered against the property.

- A bankruptcy search (if the vendor is bankrupt, the property will be held by an Official Assignee who cannot transfer good title).

• A sheriff and revenue sheriff search (in the case of leasehold property only) to disclose any debts owed by the vendor.

Completion involves the signing of the deed of purchase (the vendor must sign it prior to completion, the buyer within one month of completion), transferring legal ownership of the property and the payment of the balance of the purchase price (less the deposit and, if applicable, the amount of a mortgage), plus other payments such as the solicitor's fees, taxes and duties.

Final Checks: Property is sold subject to the condition that it's accepted in the state it's in at the time of completion; you should therefore be aware of anything that occurs between signing the purchase contract and completion. Before signing the deed of sale it's important to check that the property hasn't fallen down or been damaged in any way, e.g. by a storm or vandals (or the previous owner!). If you have employed a solicitor or are buying through an agent, he should accompany you on this visit. You should also do a final inventory immediately prior to completion (the previous owner should have already vacated the property) to ensure that the vendor hasn't absconded with anything that was included in the price. You should have an inventory of the fixtures and fittings and anything that was included in the contract or purchased separately, e.g. carpets, light fittings or curtains, and check that they're present and in good order. This is particularly important if furniture and furnishings (and major appliances) were included in the price. You should also ensure that expensive items (such as kitchen appliances) haven't been substituted by inferior (possibly second-hand) items. Any fixtures and fittings (and garden plants and shrubs) present in a property when you viewed it should still be there when you take possession, unless otherwise stated in the contract.

If you find anything is missing or damaged or isn't in working order, you should make a note and insist on immediate restitution such as an appropriate reduction in the amount to be paid. In such cases it's normal for your solicitor to delay the signing of the deed until the matter is settled, although an appropriate amount could be withheld from the vendor's proceeds to pay for repairs or replacements. You should refuse to go through with the purchase if you aren't completely satisfied, as it will be difficult or impossible to obtain redress later. If it isn't possible to complete the sale, you should consult your solicitor concerning your rights and the return of your deposit and any other funds already paid.

Power of Attorney: Either the vendor or the buyer may give a third party (e.g. a solicitor) power of attorney to sign the contract or deed for them. This is quite common among foreign buyers and sellers and can be arranged by your solicitor (for a fee of around IR£200). If a couple buy a property in both their names, the wife can give the husband power of attorney (or vice versa). Note, however, that a power of attorney can be a dangerous thing to give someone and in most cases it's unnecessary. If you do need to give power of attorney, you should make sure you give it to someone not only who you can trust, but who knows you well, otherwise you could find yourself bound into an agreement of which you don't approve.

Payment: The balance of the price after the deposit and any mortgages are subtracted must be paid by banker's draft or bank transfer. For most people the most convenient way is by banker's draft, which also means that you'll have the payment in your possession (a bank cannot lose it!) and the solicitor can confirm it immediately. It also allows you to withhold payment if there's a last minute problem that cannot be resolved. Non-resident buyers no longer need a certificate from an Irish bank stating that the amount to be paid has been exchanged or converted from a foreign currency, although it must be reported to the Bank of Ireland in accordance with legislation relating to money laundering (see page 91). Non-residents may also be required to confirm their tax situation (i.e. whether or not they're liable for income tax in Ireland). Note that even if the vendor and buyer are of the same foreign nationality, the final payment must be made in Irish pounds. After you've paid the money, the solicitor should give you a receipt and an unsigned copy of the purchase deed showing that you're the new owner of the property. You will also receive the keys!

Registration: After stamping by the Revenue Commissioners (if stamp duty is payable), the title deed is lodged for registration with either the land registry or the registry of deeds and returned to the buyer or, if the property is mortgaged, to his lender who retains it for the duration of the mortgage. When the mortgage has been paid off, the lending institution issues a 'vacate' (a sort of receipt) confirming that the loan has been repaid and transferring title to the owner.

RENOVATION & RESTORATION

Some old country or village homes are in need of restoration, renovation or modernisation. Before buying a property requiring restoration or modernisation you should consider the alternatives. An extra few thousand punts spent on a purchase may represent much better value for money than spending the money on building work. It's often cheaper to buy a restored or partly restored property, rather than a ruin in need of total restoration, unless you're going to do most of the work yourself. If you aren't into do-it-yourself in a big way, you may be better off buying a new or recently built property, as the cost of restoration can be double or even treble the price of the original property. If you're planning to buy a property that needs restoration or renovation and aren't planning to do the work yourself, make sure you obtain an *accurate* estimate of the costs *before* signing a contract.

Bear in mind that if you buy and restore a property with the intention of selling it for a profit, you must take into account not only the initial price and the restoration costs, but also the fees and taxes included in the purchase, plus capital gains tax if it's a second home. It's often difficult to sell an old renovated property at a higher than average market price, irrespective of its added value. If you're buying for investment, you may be better off buying a new home, as the price of most restored properties doesn't reflect the cost and amount of work that went into them (and many people who have restored a 'ruin' would never do it again and advise others against it).

Inspections and surveys: It's vital to check a property for any obvious faults, particularly an old property. Most importantly, a building must have sound walls, without which it may be cheaper to erect a new building! Almost any other problem can be fixed or overcome (at a price). A sound roof that doesn't leak is desirable, as ensuring that a building is waterproof is the number one priority if funds are scarce. Don't believe a vendor or agent who tells you that a roof or anything else can be repaired or patched up, but obtain expert advice from a local builder. Sound roof timbers are also important as they can be expensive to replace. Old buildings often need a damp-proof course, timber treatment, new windows and doors, a new roof or extensive repairs, a modern kitchen and bathroom, re-wiring and central heating.

Electricity and mains water should preferably already be connected as they can be expensive to extend to a property in a remote area. If a house doesn't have electricity or mains water, it's important to check the cost of extending these services to it. If you're seeking a waterside property, you should check the likelihood of floods and, if fairly frequent, you should ensure that a building has been designed with floods in mind, e.g. with electrical installations above flood level and solid tiled floors.

It may well be worthwhile having a full structural survey carried out (see page 178), as major problems can even be found in relatively new properties and spending a few hundred punts on a survey could save you thousands in repairs.

Planning Permission: If modernisation of an old building involves making external alterations, such as building an extension or installing larger windows or new doorways, you may need planning permission from your local planning authority. If you plan to do major restoration or building work, you should ensure that a conditional clause is included in the contract stating that the purchase is dependent on obtaining planning permission. You should allow at least two months for planning permission to be obtained and a further month for any objections to be raised. (Compared, for example, with just four weeks in the UK and Germany.) Never start any building work before you have official permission.

DIY or Builders? One of the first decisions you need to make regarding restoration or modernisation is whether to do all or most of the work yourself or have it done by professional builders or local artisans. Note that when restoring a period property it's imperative to have a sensitive approach to restoration. You shouldn't tackle jobs yourself or with friends unless you're sure you're doing them right. In general you should aim to retain as many of a property's original features as possible and stick to local building materials, reflecting the style of the property. When renovations and 'improvements' have been botched, there's often little that can be done except to start again from scratch. It's important not to over-modernise an old property, so that its natural rustic charm and attraction is lost. Note that even if you intend to do most of the work yourself, you'll still need to hire artisans for certain jobs.

Finding a Builder: When looking for a builder it's advisable to obtain recommendations from local people you can trust, e.g. an estate agent, solicitor, neighbours or friends. Note, however, that estate agents or other professionals aren't always the best people to ask as they may receive commissions. Always obtain references from previous customers. It may be better to use a local building consortium or contractor rather than a number of independent tradesmen, particularly if you won't be around to supervise them (although it will cost you a bit more). On the other hand, if you supervise it yourself using local hand-picked craftsmen you can save money and learn a great deal into the bargain.

Supervision: If you aren't on the spot and able to supervise work, you should hire a 'clerk of works' such as an architect to oversee a large job, otherwise it could drag on for months or be left half-finished. This will add around 10 per cent to the total bill, but it's usually worth every penny. Be extremely careful who you employ if you have work done in your absence and ensure that your instructions are accurate in every detail. Always make certain that you (and your builder) understand exactly what has been agreed and if necessary get it in writing (with drawings). It isn't unusual for foreign owners to receive huge bills for work done in their absence which shouldn't have been done at all!

Quotations: Before buying a home in Ireland requiring restoration or modernisation it's essential to obtain an accurate estimate of the work and costs involved. You should obtain written estimates from at least two builders before employing anyone. Note that for quotations to be accurate you must detail exactly the work required: e.g. for electrical work this would include the number of lights, points and switches, and the quality of materials to be used. If you have only a vague idea of what you want, you'll receive a vague and unreliable quotation. Make sure that a quotation includes everything you want done and that you fully understand it (if you don't, get it looked at by someone who does). You should fix a date for the start and completion of work and, if you can get a builder to agree to it, include a penalty for failing to finish on time. After signing a contract it's usual to pay a deposit, the amount of which depends on the size and cost of a job.

Cost: The cost of restoration depends on the work involved, the quality of materials used and the region. As a rough guide you should expect the cost of totally renovating an old 'habitable' building to be at least equal to its purchase price and possibly much more. How much you spend on restoring a property will depend on your purpose and the depth of your pockets. If you're restoring a property as an investment, don't be tempted to spend more than what you can ever hope to recoup when you sell it. On the other hand, if you're restoring a property as a holiday or permanent home, there's no limit to what you can do and how much money you can spend. Always keep an eye on your budget (which will inevitably be plus or minus 25 per cent – usually plus!) and don't be in too much of a hurry. Some people take many years to restore a holiday home, particularly when they're doing most of the work themselves. It isn't unknown for buyers to embark on a grandiose renovation scheme, only to run out of money before it's completed and be forced to sell at a huge loss.

Note that if you make major improvements to a property, you should be sure to obtain evidence of your expenditure (i.e. quotations, invoices and receipts) so that you can offset some or all of the costs against tax. See also **Buying a Resale Home** on page 169, **Inspections & Surveys** on page 178, **Water** on page 196 and **Heating** on page 195.

MOVING HOUSE

After finding a home in Ireland it usually only takes a few weeks to have your belongings shipped from within continental Europe. From anywhere else it varies considerably, e.g. around four weeks from the east coast of America, six weeks from the US west coast and the Far East, and around eight weeks from Australasia. Customs clearance is no longer necessary when shipping your household effects between European Union (EU) countries. However, when shipping your effects from a non-EU country to Ireland, you should enquire about customs formalities in advance. If you fail to follow the correct procedure you can encounter problems and delays, and may even be erroneously charged duty or fined (see **Customs** on page 209). Shipping companies usually take care of the paperwork and ensure that the correct documents are provided and properly completed.

It's advisable to use a major shipping company with a good reputation. For international moves it's best to use a company that's a member of the International Federation of Furniture Removers (FIDI) or the Overseas Moving Network

International (OMNI), with experience in Ireland. Members of FIDI and OMNI usually subscribe to an advance payment scheme providing a guarantee, whereby if a member fails to fulfil its commitments to a client the job is completed at the agreed cost by another company or your money is refunded. Some shipping companies have subsidiaries or affiliates in Ireland, which may be more convenient if you encounter problems or need to make an insurance claim.

You should obtain at least three written quotations before choosing a shipping company, as rates vary considerably. Shipping companies should send a representative to provide a detailed quotation. Most companies will pack your belongings and provide packing cases and special containers, although this is naturally more expensive than packing them yourself. Ask a company how they pack fragile and valuable items and whether the cost of packing cases, materials and insurance (see below) are included in a quotation. If you're doing your own packing, most shipping companies will provide packing crates and boxes. Shipments are charged by volume, e.g. the square metre in Europe and the square foot in the USA. You should expect to pay from IR£2,500 to IR£5,000 to move the contents of a three to four bedroom house within Western Europe, e.g. from continental Europe to Dublin. If you're flexible about the delivery date, shipping companies will usually quote a lower fee based on a 'part load', where the cost is shared with other deliveries. This can result in savings of 50 per cent or more compared with a 'special' delivery. However, whether you have an individual or shared delivery, always obtain the maximum transit period in writing, otherwise you may have to wait months for delivery!

Be sure to fully insure your belongings during shipping with a well established insurance company. Don't insure with a shipping company that has its own insurance as they will usually fight every penny of a claim. Insurance premiums are usually 1 to 2 per cent of the declared value of your goods, depending on the type of cover chosen. It's prudent to make a photographic or video record of valuables for insurance purposes. Most insurance policies cover for 'all-risks' on a replacement value basis. Note, however, that china, glass and other breakables can usually only be included in an 'all-risks' policy when they're packed by the shipping company. Insurance usually covers total loss or loss of a particular crate only, rather than individual items (unless they were packed by the shipping company). If there are any broken or damaged items, they must be noted and listed before you sign the delivery bill (although it's obviously impractical to check everything on delivery). If you need to make a claim, be sure to read the small print as some companies require clients to make a claim within a few days of delivery, although a week is usual. Send a claim by registered mail. Some insurance companies apply an excess of around 1 per cent of the total shipment value when assessing claims. This means that if your shipment is valued at IR£20,000 and you make a claim for less than IR£200, you won't receive anything.

If you're unable to ship your belongings directly to Ireland, most companies will put them into storage and some offer a limited free storage period prior to shipment, e.g. 14 days. If you need to put your household effects into storage, it's imperative to have them fully insured, as warehouses have been known to burn down! Make a complete list of everything to be moved and give a copy to the shipping company. Don't include anything illegal (e.g. guns, bombs, drugs or pornography) with your belongings as customs checks can be rigorous and penalties severe. Provide the shipping company with *detailed* instructions regarding how to find your Irish address from the nearest main road and a telephone number where you can be contacted.

After considering the shipping costs, you may decide to ship only selected items of furniture and personal effects, and buy new furniture in Ireland. If you're importing household goods from another European country, it's possible to rent a self-drive van or truck. Note, however, that if you rent a vehicle outside Ireland you'll usually need to return it to the country where it was hired. If you plan to transport your belongings to Ireland personally, check the customs requirements in the countries you will pass through. Most people find it isn't wise to do their own move unless it's a simple job, e.g. a few items of furniture and personal effects only. It's no fun heaving beds and wardrobes up stairs and squeezing them into impossible spaces! If you're taking pets with you, you may need to ask your vet to tranquillise them, as many pets are frightened (even more than people) by the chaos and stress of moving house. They may also need several weeks or even months to become accustomed to their new surroundings.

Bear in mind when moving home that everything that can go wrong often does, so allow plenty of time and try not to arrange your move to your new home on the same day as the previous owner is moving out. That's just asking for Murphy to intervene! Last but not least, if your Irish home has poor or impossible access for a large truck, you must inform the shipping company (the ground must also be firm enough to support a heavy vehicle). Note also that if large items of furniture need to be taken in through an upstairs window, you may need to pay extra. See also **Customs** on page 209 and the **Checklist** on page **Error! Bookmark not defined.**.

HOME SECURITY

When moving into a new home it's often wise to replace the locks (or lock barrels) as soon as possible, as you have no idea how many keys are in circulation for the existing locks. This is true even for new homes, as builders often give keys to sub-contractors. In any case it's advisable to change the external lock barrels regularly, particularly if you let a home. If they aren't already fitted, it's advisable to fit high security locks (e.g. five-lever mortise deadlocks). Patio doors should be fitted with key operated locks and a stop should be fitted in the top of the door frame to prevent the doors from being lifted out. All ground floor windows should be fitted with key operated locks or bolts. Extra keys for high security locks cannot usually be cut at a local hardware store and if they are already fitted you will need to obtain details from the previous owner or your landlord. In areas with a higher risk of theft (e.g. central Dublin) your insurance company may insist on extra security measures.

You may wish to have a security system fitted, which is usually the best way to deter thieves and may also reduce your household insurance (see page 70). It should be fitted to Irish Standard 199 (1987) and include all external doors and windows, and internal infra-red security beams. It may also include a coded entry keypad (which can be frequently changed and is useful for clients if you let) and 24-hour monitoring (with some systems it's even possible to monitor properties remotely from another country). With a monitored system, when a sensor (e.g. smoke or forced entry) detects an emergency or a panic button is pushed, a signal is sent automatically to a 24-hour monitoring station. The person on duty will telephone to check whether it's a genuine alarm and, if he cannot contact anyone, someone will be sent to investigate. Some developments and estates have security gates and are patrolled by security guards.

You can deter thieves by ensuring that your house is well lit at night and not conspicuously unoccupied. External security 'motion detector' lights (that switch on automatically when someone approaches), random timed switches for internal lights, radios and TVs; dummy security cameras; and tapes that play barking dogs (etc.) triggered by a light or heat detector may all help deter burglars. You may wish to fit grilles to your windows, the advantage of which is that they allow you to leave windows open without inviting criminals in (unless they're *very* slim). Note, however, that security grilles must be heavy duty as the bars on cheap grilles can be prised apart. You can also fit UPVC (toughened clear plastic) security windows and doors, which can survive an attack with a sledge-hammer without damage, and external steel security blinds (which can be electrically operated), although these are expensive. A dog can be useful to deter intruders, although it should be kept inside where it cannot be given poisoned food. Regardless of whether or not you actually have a dog, a warning sign showing the image of a fierce dog may act as a deterrent. Bear in mind that prevention is better than cure, as stolen property is rarely recovered.

If you leave your home unoccupied for any length of time, cancel deliveries of milk and newspapers, advise your local police (*garda*) station, and leave them a contact name and number in case anything should happen while you're away. Ask neighbours to park their car in the drive and to pop in from time to time. If they're very friendly, they may even be persuaded to cut the lawn for you! If you have a holiday home in Ireland, it isn't wise to leave anything of real value (monetary or sentimental) there and to have comprehensive insurance for your belongings (see page 70). One 'foolproof' way to protect a home when you're away is to employ a house-sitter to look after it. This can be done for short periods or for six months (e.g. during the winter) or longer if you have a holiday home in Ireland. It isn't usually necessary to pay someone to house-sit for a period of six months or more, when you can usually find someone to do it in return for free accommodation. However, you must take care whom you engage and obtain references.

An important aspect of home security is ensuring you have early warning of a fire, which is easily accomplished by installing smoke detectors. Battery-operated smoke detectors can be purchased for around IR£7 and should conform to Irish Standard 409 (1988). They should be tested periodically to ensure that they're working property and the batteries should be replaced twice a year. Fire extinguishers and fire blankets are also recommended. A 2.5kg dry powder or multi-purpose chemical extinguisher (which should conform to Irish Standard 290 of 1986) is ideal for the average house. Fire blankets should comply with Irish Standard 415 (1988). You can also fit an electric gas-detector that activates an alarm when a gas leak is detected.

When closing a property for an extended period, e.g. over the winter, you should ensure that everything is switched off and that it's secure. If you vacate your home for an extended period, you may also be obliged to notify a caretaker, landlord or your insurance company and leave a key with a caretaker or landlord in case of emergencies. If you have a robbery, you should report it immediately to your local police station, where you must make a statement. You will receive a copy, which will be required by your insurance company if you make a claim.

ELECTRICITY

Ireland's national power company, the Electricity Supply Board (ESB), is one of the largest companies in Ireland. Within the last decade it has developed from a giant monopoly utility that was prohibited from making a profit into a competitive, profitable enterprise. The recent EU directive on electricity means that almost a quarter of the Irish domestic electricity supply market will be open to competition by the year 2000. Electricity demand is increasing by some 7 per cent annually and in 1996 almost 35,000 new customers were connected – the highest number since the late 1950s. Mains electricity is available in virtually all parts of the country. There are no nuclear power stations in Ireland, where most electricity is generated by conventional coal, gas and oil burning stations. Ireland's seven hydroelectric stations and five peat stations produce around 5 and 15 per cent of the national supply respectively. ESB is committed to a billion pound capital investment in a five year 'Network Renewal Programme'.

Registration: Immediately after buying or renting a property (unless utilities are included in the rent), you must register with the ESB. This usually entails a visit to one of the company's 80 regional offices or 'shops'. If you're a resident owner you need only verify that you have purchased a property for the supply to be re-registered in your name. If you're a non-resident owner or are renting a property, you'll be given three options: you can to pay a deposit, set up a direct debit with your bank or appoint a guarantor who's an existing ESB customer.

Wiring Standards: Most modern properties (e.g. less than 20 years old) in Ireland have good electrical installations. However, if you buy a resale property to which the electricity supply has been disconnected for over six months, you'll be required to obtain a certificate from a qualified electrician stating that the electricity installation meets the required safety standards (this may also be required by your mortgage lender). In any case you should ensure that the electricity installation is in good condition before buying a house (e.g. through a survey), as rewiring can be expensive.

Connection Costs: If you buy a new property, you'll be liable for connection charges. If the property is within a large development, electricity connection will usually have been made and meters installed by the builder, but in individual properties you may need to arrange connection with the ESB. Either way you'll have to pay a standard connection charge of IR£650 plus VAT at 12.5 per cent. If a property is over a certain distance from the medium voltage network (50 metres in urban areas and 500 metres in rural areas) an additional charge will be made depending on the extent of the work required. In some cases there's an extra charge even if a property is within the specified distance, e.g. if there's an obstacle in between or where a circuitous route must be taken for aesthetic reasons. Note that the ESB requires a completion certificate from a qualified electrician before connecting new houses. All electrical work must be registered with the Register of Electrical Contractors of Ireland (☎ 01-454 5820) and be carried out in accordance with the National Wiring Rules for Electrical Installations.

Meters: In an old apartment block there may be a common meter, with the bill being shared among the apartment owners according to the size of their apartments. In modern developments each apartment usually has its own meter. It's obviously better to have your own meter, particularly if you own a holiday home that's occupied for a few months of the year only. Meters may be installed in a basement in a special room or be housed in a meter 'cupboard' in a stair well or outside a group of properties, e.g. in an apartment or townhouse development. You should have free access to your meter.

Plugs, Fuses & Bulbs

Depending on the country you have come from, you may need new plugs or a lot of adapters. Plug adapters for most foreign electrical apparatus can be purchased in Ireland, although it's wise to bring some with you, plus extension cords and multi-plug extensions that can be fitted with Irish plugs. Most modern properties will have at least two sockets in each room, although there may be a shortage of electric points in older Irish homes. Most Irish plugs have three flat pins as in the UK, apart from shaving sockets, which are of the standard international two-pin kind. A transformer is needed to convert American appliances (unless they're dual-voltage) and some items, like clocks, won't work even with a transformer. Cordless telephones may not work either and even TVs that do work are of limited use because of the different broadcasting standards in Ireland. As in the rest of Europe, most videos are in PAL format, so American video recorders won't be of any use either.

Small low-wattage electrical appliances such as table lamps, small TVs and computers, don't require an earth. However, plugs with an earth must always be used for high-wattage appliances such as fires, kettles, washing machines and refrigerators. These plugs must always be used with earthed sockets. Electrical appliances that are earthed have a three-core wire and must never be used with a two-pin plug without an earth socket. Always make sure that a plug is correctly and securely wired as bad wiring can be fatal.

In modern properties, fuses are of the earth-trip type. When there's a short circuit or the system has been overloaded, a circuit breaker is tripped and the power supply is cut. If your electricity fails, you should suspect a fuse of tripping, particularly if you have just switched on an electrical appliance. Before reconnecting the power, switch off any high-power appliances such as a stove, oven, washing machine or dishwasher. Make sure you know where the trip switches are located and keep a torch handy so that you can find them in the dark (see **Power Supply** below).

Electric light bulbs in Ireland are generally of the bayonet kind, but screw fitting ('Edison') bulbs are also widely available. Bulbs for non-standard electrical appliances (i.e. appliances that aren't made for the Irish market) such as refrigerators and sewing machines may not be available in Ireland, so you should bring some spares with you.

Power Supply

The standard domestic electrical supply in Ireland is 230 volts AC with a frequency of 50 hertz (cycles). Most shaving sockets also support 100 volts. Power cuts are rare in Ireland. Nevertheless, if you use a computer it's advisable to fit an uninterrupted power supply (UPS) with a battery backup, which not only allows you time to shut down your computer and save your work after a power failure (the battery will continue to supply power for around 15 to 20 minutes), but also protects it from power surges. If the power keeps tripping off or fuses blow when you attempt to use a number of high-power appliances simultaneously, e.g. an electric kettle and a heater, it could mean that the wiring to the property is inadequate. You should never simply put in heavier fuses but get an electrician to check the wiring and if necessary 'uprate' it to your requirements.

Converters & Transformers

Assuming that you have a 230 volt power supply, if you have electrical equipment rated at 110 volts AC (for example, from the USA) you'll require a converter or a step-down transformer to convert it to 110 volts. However, some electrical appliances are fitted with a 110/220 volt switch. Check whether there's one (it may be inside the casing) and make sure that it's switched to 220 volts *before* connecting to the power supply. Converters can be used for heating appliances, but transformers are required for motorised appliances. Add the wattage of all the devices you intend to connect to a transformer and make sure that its power rating *exceeds* this sum.

Generally all small, high-wattage, electrical appliances, such as kettles, toasters, heaters and irons need large transformers. Motors in large appliances, such as cookers, refrigerators, washing machines, driers and dishwashers, will need replacing or fitting with a large transformer. In most cases it's simpler to buy new appliances in Ireland, which are of good quality and reasonably priced, and sell them when you leave if you cannot take them with you. Note also that the dimensions of cookers, microwave ovens, refrigerators, washing machines, driers and dishwashers purchased abroad may differ from those in Ireland (and therefore they may not fit into a standard Irish kitchen).

An additional problem with some electrical equipment is the frequency rating, which in some countries, e.g. the USA, is designed to run at 60Hz (Hertz) and not Europe's 50Hz. Electrical equipment *without* a motor is generally unaffected by the drop in frequency to 50Hz (except TVs). Equipment with a motor may run with a 20 per cent drop in speed; however, automatic washing machines, cookers, electric clocks, record players and tape recorders must be converted from the US 60Hz cycle to Ireland's 50Hz cycle. To find out, look at the label on the back of the equipment. If it says 50/60Hz it should be all right; if the label says 60Hz you can try it, but first ensure that the voltage is correct as outlined above. Bear in mind that the transformers and motors of electrical devices designed to run at 60Hz will run hotter at 50Hz, so make sure that apparatus has sufficient space around it to allow for cooling.

Tariffs

Electricity is charged by the 'unit' in Ireland. One unit is equivalent to a kilowatt/hour (kWh) of electricity. One kWh is roughly enough to run a fridge for 24 hours, a TV for 12 hours, an iron for two hours, a vacuum cleaner for an hour, a dishwasher for half an hour or an instant shower for five minutes. There's a bi-monthly standing charge of IR£4.24 for normal consumption plus 7.97p per kWh (unit). To save on electricity costs, you can switch to the 'NightSaver' tariff and run high-consumption appliances overnight, e.g. water heater, dishwasher and washing machine (which can be operated by timers). A family that uses a lot of water will find it pays to have a large water heater (e.g. 150 litres) and heat water overnight. If you use electricity for your heating, you can install night storage heaters that run on the night tariff. When you use electricity at night for storage heaters only, you pay an extra IR£0.81 standing charge but only 3.17p per unit for night usage. If you run other appliances during the night, you can pay a standing charge of IR£11.15 so that all night use is charged at 3.17p per unit. Night rate is between 2300 and 0800 in winter and between midnight and 0900 in summer. VAT at 12.5 per cent is levied on all charges.

Electricity Bills

Electricity bills are sent out every two months, usually after meters have been read. If the ESB is unable to read your meter, you'll be charged for an estimated consumption. If the estimate is seriously inaccurate, you can submit a corrected reading (make sure you know how to read your electricity meter) and you'll be sent a revised bill. Normally only one estimated reading per year is permitted. Once you have received an accurate bill, you have 14 days in which to pay. If you fail to do so, your supply can be cut off without warning, although in practice no action is usually taken for up to six months. If your electricity supply is cut off, you must pay to have it reconnected. The ESB has four regional headquarters (Dublin, northern, mid-western and southern) – your electricity bill indicates which one serves your area. A free booklet entitled *Getting the most from Electricity* is available from the ESB.

It's advisable to pay all your utility bills by direct debit from an Irish bank account. If you own a holiday home in Ireland, you can have your bills sent to an address abroad. Bills should then be paid automatically on presentation to your bank, although some banks cannot be relied on 100 per cent. Both the electricity company and your bank should notify you when they have sent or paid a bill. Alternatively you can pay bills at any of the authorised banks or at one of the ESB's own 'shops'.

GAS

Most people in Ireland use gas for hot water and central heating (see below) and many for cooking as well. Mains gas is available in virtually all areas of Ireland and is supplied by *Bord Gáis*, the national supply company. When moving into a property with mains gas, you must contact your local *Bord Gáis* office (there's one in all main towns in Ireland) to register the account in your name. Connection to a new property should take around a week, but re-connection to a property that was previously supplied with gas can be done in a day. As with electricity, you're billed every two months and bills include VAT at 12.5 per cent. Like all utility bills, gas bills can be paid by direct debit from an Irish bank account. In fact, if you're a non-resident property owner or are renting a property and want to obtain a gas supply, you'll have to set up a direct debit or pay a deposit of IR£150 (IR£40 if you'll be using gas for a cooker and fire only) or ask someone who has been a customer of *Bord Gáis* for at least 14 months to act as 'guarantor' and sign the form for you.

Tariffs: Mains gas is charged at a standard rate of 1.75p per kWh. There's also a 'supply charge' of IR£22 per bi-monthly bill. If you're buying a new property connection is free, providing it's within 15 metres of a gas main. If it's further there's a connection charge of IR£3.50 per foot. The approximate costs of using gas in an average home is IR£1 a day for central heating, 75p per week for cooking and 6p per hour for a gas fire. It generally works out cheaper to heat your water using a gas boiler than to use an electric immersion heater.

In most areas of Ireland, gas bottles can be delivered by Calor Gas, who supply more than one in four homes. A few developments, such as the Eagle Valley housing estate in Enniskerry and apartment projects in Letterkenny and Wexford, are entirely Calor run. If you want to use bottled gas, you must first have your property inspected and decide whether to use bottles or have a tank installed. A 1,250 litre tank costs around IR£185 to install and IR£60 per year to rent thereafter. The gas itself currently costs IR£1.06 per gallon. Bottles are available in various sizes; a standard 'yellow' bottle (11kg) costs IR£12 for a refill and a 34kg bottle IR£31 (there are also 47kg bottles). You must pay a non-returnable deposit (IR£5 for a yellow bottle). You should keep a spare bottle handy and make sure you know how to change them (get the previous owner or a neighbour to show you).

A bottle used just for cooking will last an average family around six to eight weeks. Bottles can be connected into 'banks' and a four-bottle bank is enough to run a complete central heating system. Calor Gas also install boilers (their 'Combi' boiler provides central heating and instant hot water). If you opt for a 'condensing boiler', you may be able to reduce your annual fuel bills by up to 30 per cent. You must have your gas appliances serviced and inspected at least every five years. If you have a contract with Calor Gas, they will do this for you or it will be done by your local authorised distributor. Calor's headquarters are in Dublin and they also have depots in Cork, Claremorris (Co. Mayo), New Ross (Co. Wexford) and Sligo.

HEATING

Heating is essential in winter (and sometimes in summer!) in Ireland. Central heating systems may be powered by gas, electricity, oil or solid fuel (usually wood or peat).

Gas: Gas central heating is by far the most common in Ireland. But even if you have no mains gas, it's possible to install a central heating system operating from a gas tank or bottles (see above). Stand-alone gas heaters using standard gas bottles cost around IR£90 and are an economical way of providing heating in all but the depths of winter. Note that gas heaters must be used only in rooms with adequate ventilation and it can be dangerous to have too large a difference between indoor and outdoor temperatures.

Electricity: Electric central heating is rare in Ireland as it's relatively expensive and requires good insulation. Stand-alone electric heaters are also expensive to run and are best suited to holiday homes. However, a system of night-storage heaters operating on the night tariff (see page 193) can be economical. If you rely on electricity for all your power and use the night tariff, you should expect to pay around IR£37 per month.

Oil: It's quite expensive to install an oil tank (around IR£165 for a 1,000 litre tank), but the running costs are similar to gas with 1,000 litres of oil (or kerosene – which has lower emissions) costing around IR£200. The tank will need refilling around twice a year depending on the amount you use (further details can be obtained from the South of Ireland Petroleum Company on 021-314221).

Solid Fuel: Many people still have open fires in Ireland, particularly in rural areas, where many houses have open wood or peat-burning fires and stoves that are often combined with a central heating system.

Note that whatever form of heating you use, it's important to have good insulation, without which up to 60 per cent of the heat generated can be lost through the walls and roof.

WATER & WASTE

The Irish Department of the Environment announced an IR£185M water and sewerage investment programme in February 1998, including IR£28M for a rural water programme. The programme is 65 per cent financed by the EU Cohesion Fund, whose only other beneficiaries this side of the Millennium are Greece, Portugal and Spain. A total of 61 major schemes were scheduled to be started in 1998, by far the largest of which is the Dublin Bay Project, which aims to put an end to the dumping of the capital's sewage into the Irish Sea by the year 2000. Major new water supply and treatment works are to be installed in several parts of Ireland including Wexford, Limerick, Mitchelstown (near Cork) and Tuam (near Galway).

Check the Supply: In general the Irish public water supply is good and tap water can safely be drunk in most areas. The peaty nature of Irish soil causes occasional colouring of the water as well as slight alkalinity, but water everywhere is pleasantly 'soft' (which no doubt accounts for those rosy Irish complexions!). Nevertheless, many rural areas have group water supply schemes or small private supplies (i.e. wells), and in some cases the water isn't purified or disinfected in any way, therefore there's a risk of contamination from sources such as septic tanks or animal slurry pits. One of the most important tasks before renting or buying a home in Ireland is therefore to check the reliability of the local water supply (over a number of years). Ask your prospective neighbours and other local residents for information. It's essential to have the water supply checked and if necessary you should install your own water purification system. Domestic water in Ireland is free, so you won't need to worry about paying bills (or being cut off for failing to do so).

Hot Water: Water heating in apartments may be provided by a central heating source for the whole building or apartments may have their own water heaters. If you install your own water heater, it should have a capacity of at least 75 litres. If you need to install a water heater (or fit a larger one), you should consider the merits of both electric and gas heaters. An electric water boiler with a capacity of 75 litres (sufficient for two people) costs between IR£100 and IR£200 and usually takes between 60 and 90 minutes to heat water to 40°C in winter. A gas flow-through water heater is more expensive to purchase and install than an electric water boiler, but you get unlimited hot water immediately whenever you want it. Make sure that a gas heater has a capacity of 10 to 16 litres per minute if you want it for a shower. A gas heater costs between IR£75 to IR£200 (although there's little difference in quality between the cheaper and more expensive heaters), plus installation costs. Note that a gas water heater with a permanent flame may use up to 50 per cent more gas than one without. A resident family with a constant consumption is better off with an electric heater operating on the night tariff (see page 193), while non-residents using a property for short periods will find a self-igniting gas heater more economical.

Connection Costs: The connection of water supplies to new properties is a local matter in Ireland and is controlled by the county or urban district council (or in some cases the borough corporation). Connection charges vary considerably from county to county and can be as low as IR£80 or as high as IR£550 (e.g. in County Meath), and may be even higher if major works are necessary, e.g. roads need to be dug up. The good news is that as there are no standing charges or consumption charges for domestic water anywhere in Ireland, so if you move into a property that already has a water supply you won't have to pay a penny. However, if you run a business from home (or, for example, offer bed and breakfast), you may be liable for commercial water rates.

Sewage: There's no direct charge for sewage services in Ireland. Most urban properties are connected to the mains sewage system, while most rural properties have septic tanks, that are emptied regularly by the local council.

REFUSE COLLECTION

Like water connection, refuse collection is managed locally and charges vary from county to county. In some places (principally Dublin, Limerick and Waterford) there's no charge at all, while in others charges range from as little as IR£30 per year (in Kilkenny and New Ross, for example) to IR£100 or more (e.g. in Cork and Kerry). In many areas the service has been privatised and costs are falling as a result. In some remote parts no refuse collection service is provided and residents must make their own arrangements (often with a local farmer) to dispose of household waste.

PROPERTY INCOME

Many people planning to buy a holiday home in Ireland are interested in owning a property that will provide them with an income, e.g. from letting, to cover the running costs and help with mortgage payments. Note, however, that you're highly unlikely to meet all your mortgage payments and running costs from rental income. Buyers who over-stretch their financial resources often find themselves on the rental treadmill, constantly struggling to raise sufficient income to cover their running costs and mortgage payments. Note that it's difficult to make a living providing holiday accommodation in most areas as the season is too short and there's simply too much competition (the market is saturated in many regions). On the other hand, letting a home for just a few weeks in the summer can recoup your running costs and pay for your holidays.

If you're planning on holiday lets, don't overestimate the length of the season, which can be as little as eight weeks, i.e. the summer holiday period. The letting season is longest in the main cities, particularly Dublin (where properties have year-round letting potential). Note that buying property in Ireland (and in most other countries) isn't a good investment compared with the return on income that can be achieved by investing elsewhere. Most experts recommend that you don't purchase a home in Ireland if you need to rely heavily on rental income to pay for it.

Regulations & Restrictions: If you let a property in Ireland other than for holidays, you must register it with the local authority within a month of the first letting. You will need to apply in writing on a form provided free by the local authority, giving the address of the property, a description, your name and address (or that of your agent), the tenant's name, the amount of rent, and how and when it's to be paid. There's an initial registration fee of around IR£40 and an annual fee of IR£40 for each property for as long as it's let. A rent book isn't necessary for holiday letting, nor does the property need to comply with the Housing (Standards for Rented Houses) Regulations 1993. If you use a letting agency, the agency should apply for the necessary permits and pay income tax on your behalf.

Location: If income from your Irish home is a priority, you should buy a property with this in mind. To maximise rental income, a property should be located as close as possible to main attractions and/or a beach, be suitably furnished and professionally managed.

Rents: Rental rates vary considerably depending on the season, the region, and the size and quality of a property. A small, one or two bedroom apartment (e.g. 50 to 75m²) which rents for IR£200 a month in a rural area (outside the main tourist season) could fetch between IR£450 and IR£800 per month in Dublin. A five bedroom suburban house could rent for anything between IR£2,000 and IR£5,000 a month depending on the location. Rents for short-term lets are usually higher pro rata than for longer lets, particularly in popular holiday areas where many properties are let as self-catering holiday accommodation. However, many agents let self-catering properties in holiday areas at a considerable reduction during the 'low season', which may extend from October to April. The high season generally includes the months of July and August only. The mid-season usually comprises May, June and September, when rents are around 25 per cent lower than the high season; the rest of the year is the low season with rates 50 per cent or more below the high season. Some owners divide the rental year into as many as four seasons, e.g. November to March, April and October, June and September, and July/August. Only a few owners charge the same rate all year round. Note that rental rates usually include linen, but gas and electricity are usually charged extra.

Furnishings & Keys: If you let a property, don't fill it with expensive furnishings or valuable personal belongings. Although theft is rare, items will certainly get damaged or broken over time. When furnishing a property that you plan to let, you should choose hard-wearing, dark coloured carpets which won't show the stains, and buy durable furniture and furnishings. Small two bedroom properties usually have a settee in the living room which converts into a double bed. Properties should be well-equipped with cooking utensils, crockery and cutlery, and it's also usual to provide bed linen and towels. You may also need a cot or high chair for young children. Depending on the price and quality of a property, your guests may also expect central heating, a washing machine, dishwasher, microwave, TV and covered parking in urban areas. Some owners provide bicycles, games and books, etc. It isn't usual to have a telephone in rental homes, although you could install a pay-phone or one that will receive incoming calls only.

You will need several sets of keys, which will inevitably get lost at some time. If you employ a management company, their address should be on the key fob and not the address of the house. If you let a home yourself, you can use a 'key-finder' service, whereby lost keys can be returned to the key-finder company by anyone finding them. You should ensure that you get 'lost' keys returned or you may need to change the lock barrels (in any case it's advisable to change them annually if you let a home). You don't need to provide clients with keys to all the external doors, only the front door (the others can be left in your home). If you arrange your own lets, you can post keys to clients in your home country; otherwise they can be collected from a caretaker in Ireland. It's also possible to install a security key-pad entry system and change the code after each let.

Letting Agents: If you're letting a second home, the most important decision is whether to let it yourself or use a letting agent (or agents). If you don't have much spare time, you're better off using an agent, who will take care of everything and save you the time and expense of advertising and finding clients. An agent will charge commission of 10 to 25 per cent of the gross rental income, although some of this can be recouped through higher rents. The largest holiday letting agent in Ireland is in fact the Irish Tourist Board, which publishes an annual Self-Catering Accommodation Guide listing some 3,000 ITB approved properties throughout the country. If you want your property listed in the Guide, you must contact the regional tourist office where the property is located. Inspections are carried out in February and March for the following year's brochure, so you'll need to plan well ahead. A booklet listing the requirements for inclusion is available from the ITB for IR£6. You then have two options: you can either have your own name and address listed so that all enquiries come directly to you or the property can be included on the Tourist Board's computerised booking system, whereby the ITB handles all bookings for you and take a commission of 10 per cent (client's pay a booking fee of IR£3 plus a deposit equal to one-third of the rental fee).

If you're using any other agent, you should ask the following questions: What sort of people do they let to? Where do they advertise? Do they have contracts with holiday and travel companies? Are you expected to contribute towards marketing costs? Are you free to let the property yourself and use it when you wish? The larger companies market homes via newspapers, magazines, overseas agents and colour brochures, and have representatives in a number of countries.

Note that when letting an apartment short term, you must check that it's permitted under the terms of the lease and you may also be required to notify your insurance company.

Doing Your Own Letting: Some owners prefer to let a property to family, friends, colleagues and acquaintances, which gives them more control (and hopefully the property will also be better looked after). In fact, the best way to get a high volume of lets is usually to do it yourself, although many owners use a letting agency in addition to doing their own marketing in their home country. If you wish to let a property yourself, there's a wide range of Irish and foreign newspapers and magazines in which you can advertise, e.g. *Dalton's Weekly* and newspapers such as *The Sunday Times* and *Sunday Telegraph* in Britain. Many of the English-language newspapers and magazines listed in **Appendix A** also include advertisements from property owners. You will need to experiment to find the best publications and days of the week or months to advertise.

You can also advertise among friends and colleagues, in company and club magazines (which may even be free), and on notice boards in companies, stores and public places. The more marketing you do, the more income you're likely to earn. It also pays to work with other local people in the same business and to send surplus guests to competitors (they will usually reciprocate). It isn't necessary to just advertise locally or stick to your home country and you can extend your marketing abroad (or advertise on the Internet). It's usually necessary to have a telephone answering machine and it's advantageous to have a fax machine and be on the Internet (for e-mail enquiries).

To get an idea of the rent you should charge, simply ring a few letting agents and ask them what it would cost to rent a property such as yours at the time of year you plan to let it. They are likely to quote the highest rent you can charge. You should also check the advertisements in newspapers and magazines. Set a realistic rent, as there's a lot of competition. Add a returnable deposit (e.g. IR£100) as security against loss (of keys, etc.) or breakages. A booking deposit should be refundable only up to six weeks before the letting period. It's normal to have a minimum two-week rental in July and August. You will need a simple agreement form which includes the dates of arrival and departure and approximate times. Note that if you plan to let to non-English speaking clients, you may need to have the letting agreement translated into foreign languages.

If you plan to let a home yourself, you'll need to decide how to handle enquiries about flights and car rentals. It's easier to let clients do it themselves, but you should be able to offer advice and put them in touch with airlines, ferry companies, travel agents and car rental companies (see page 53). You will also need to decide whether you want to let to smokers and accept pets and young children (some people don't let to families with children under five years of age because of the risk of bed-wetting). It's usually best to provide linen (some agents provide a linen hire service), which is expected in Ireland, and to include electricity in the rental fee.

It's advisable to produce a colour brochure containing external/internal pictures (or a single-colour brochure with full-colour photographs affixed to it, although this doesn't look so professional), important details, the exact location, local attractions, details of how to get there (with a map), and the name, address and telephone number of your local caretaker or letting agent. You should enclose a stamped addressed envelope when sending out leaflets. It's necessary to make a home look as attractive as possible in a brochure without distorting or misrepresenting the facts. Advertise honestly and don't over-sell your property.

Local Information: You should also provide an information pack (in your home) for clients explaining how things work (such as heating and appliances); security measures; what not to do; where to shop; recommended restaurants; local emergency numbers and health services such as doctors, hospitals and dentists; and assistance such as a general repairman, plumber and electrician. If you allow young children and pets, you should make a point of emphasising any dangers, such as falling into the pool. It's also beneficial to have a visitor's book where your clients can write their comments and recommendations. If you want to impress your guests you may wish to arrange for fresh flowers, fruit, a good bottle of wine and a grocery pack to greet them on their arrival. It's little touches like this that ensure repeat business and recommendations. If you go 'the extra mile' it will pay off and you may even find after the first year or two that you rarely need to advertise. Many people return to the same property each year and you should do an annual mail-shot to previous clients and send them some brochures. Word-of-mouth advertising is the cheapest and always the best.

Caretaker: If you own a second home in Ireland, you'll find it beneficial or even essential to employ a local caretaker, irrespective of whether you let it. You may also need to employ a gardener. You can have your caretaker prepare the house for your family and guests as well as looking after it when it isn't in use. If you have a holiday home in Ireland it's wise to have your caretaker check it periodically (e.g. weekly) and to give him authority to effect minor repairs. If you let a property yourself, your caretaker can arrange for (or do) cleaning, linen changes, maintenance and repairs, gardening and bill paying. If you employ a caretaker or housekeeper, you should expect to pay at least the minimum Irish hourly wage.

Increasing Rental Income: It's possible to increase rental income outside the high season by offering special interest or package holidays, which could be organised in conjunction with other local businesses in order to broaden the appeal and cater for larger parties. These may include activity holidays such as golf, fishing, cycling or hiking; cookery or gastronomy; cultural or historical tours; and courses in arts and crafts such as painting, sculpture, photography and writing. You don't need to be an expert or conduct courses yourself, but can employ someone to do it for you. It's also worth finding out when the local festivals take place so that you can offer accommodation to coincide with them.

Long-term Lets: As used here, 'long-term' refers to lets of between one and six months, usually outside the high season. Make sure that you use the correct contract. Although the law is on your side, you should be aware that if a tenant with a short-term rental contract refuses to leave, it may take months to have him evicted. Note also that if you receive rent and accept a lessee without protest, you're deemed under Irish law to have entered into a landlord-tenant relationship, even if there's no written contract. Most people who let all year round have low, medium and high season rates. Rates are naturally much lower for winter lets, although less so in urban areas (see above). The tenant usually pays for electricity and heating. Note that central heating is essential if you want to let long term.

Most Irish auctioneers also act as long-term letting agents and produce their own lists of accommodation, which are usually updated frequently (sometimes twice a week). Agents may be quite selective in taking on new properties, but they will generally accept more than they refuse. Take care when selecting an agent. Always ask him to substantiate rental income claims and occupancy rates by showing you examples of actual income received from other properties. Ask for the names of satisfied customers and check with them. Also make sure that your income is deposited in an interest-bearing escrow account and paid regularly, or even better choose an agent with a bonding scheme who pays you the rent *before* the arrival of guests (some do). It's absolutely essential to employ a reliable and honest (preferably long-established) company. Note that anyone can set up a holiday letting agency and there are a number of 'cowboy' operators.

If you're letting a property long term (in this case one year or longer), you may wish to use a property management service, which is offered by most estate agents. This can include finding suitable tenants and checking their references (bank credit, etc.); drawing up a lease and producing an inventory; transferring accounts for gas, electricity, cable TV, etc. into the tenant's name; setting up standing orders for rental payments; inspecting the property periodically (e.g. every three months); and reporting to the landlord. Charges for property management vary but are usually either a proportion or a percentage of the annual letting fee (e.g. 5 weeks rent or 10 per cent).

Closing a property for the winter: Before closing a property for the winter, you should turn off the water at the mains (required by insurance companies) and drain all pipes, remove all fuses (except the one for a security alarm if you have one), empty the food cupboards and the refrigerator/freezer, disconnect gas cylinders and empty dustbins. You should also leave interior doors and a few small windows (with grilles or secure shutters) open to provide some ventilation. Lock all exterior doors and shutters and secure anything valuable against theft or leave it with a neighbour or friend. Check whether any essential work needs to be done before you leave and if necessary arrange for it to be done in your absence. Most importantly leave a set of keys with a neighbour or have a caretaker check your home periodically.

See also **Renting** on page 151 and **Income Tax for Property Owners** on page 121.

SELLING A HOME

Although this book is primarily concerned with buying a home in Ireland, you may wish to sell your home at some time in the future. Before offering your Irish home for sale it's wise to investigate the state of the property market. For example, unless you're forced to sell, it definitely isn't adviseable during a property slump when prices are depressed. It may be better to let your home long term and wait until the market has recovered. It's also unwise to sell in the early years after purchase, when you'll probably make a loss unless it was an absolute bargain.

Having decided to sell, your first decision will be whether to sell it yourself (or try) or use the services of a real estate agent. Although the majority of properties in Ireland are sold through estate agents, a significant number of people sell their own homes (or attempt to). If you need to sell a property before buying a new one, this must be included as a conditional clause (see page 182) in the contract for a new home. Your next decision will be whether to sell at auction or by private treaty. Generally only the more expensive properties are sold at auction, although if you think there will be considerable demand for your property there's no reason why you shouldn't consider selling it at auction. You should of course advise your solicitor of your intention to sell and give him the title deeds. If there's still a mortgage outstanding on the property, you'll have to sign an authorisation for your solicitor to obtain the deeds from your lending institution so that he can prepare the sales contract. This can take up to two weeks.

Price: It's important to bear in mind that (like everything) property has a market price and the best way of ensuring a fast sale (or any sale) is to ask a realistic price. Although Ireland is very much a seller's market at the moment, it is of course easier to sell a cheaper property (say one priced below IR£75,000) than an expensive one. However, there's also a strong and constant demand for exceptional homes priced from around IR£300,000 to IR£1M, particularly those that are particularly attractive and in a popular area or a superb location.

If your home's fairly standard for the area, you can find out its value by comparing the prices of other homes on the market or those that have recently been sold. Most agents will provide a free appraisal of a home's value in the expectation that you'll sell it through them. However, don't believe everything they tell you, as they may over-price it simply to encourage you. You can also hire a professional valuer (e.g. a surveyor) to determine the market value. Note that you should be prepared to drop the price slightly (e.g. 5 or 10 per cent) and should set it accordingly, but you shouldn't grossly over-price a home as it will deter buyers. Don't reject an offer out of hand unless it's ridiculously low, as you may be able to get a prospective buyer to raise his offer. When selling a second home in Ireland, you may wish to include the furnishings and major appliances in the sale. You should add an appropriate amount to the price to cover the value of the furnishings or use them as an inducement to a prospective buyer at a later stage.

Presentation: The secret to selling a home quickly lies in its presentation (assuming that it's competitively priced). First impressions (both exterior and interior) are vital when marketing a property and it's important to present it in its best light to make it as attractive as possible to potential buyers. It may pay to invest in new interior decoration, new carpets, exterior paint and landscaping. A few plants and flowers can also do wonders. Note that when decorating a home for resale, it's important to be conservative and not to do anything radical (such as install a red or black bathroom suite or paint the walls purple). White is a good neutral colour for walls, woodwork and porcelain.

It may also pay you to do some modernisation such as installing a new kitchen or bathroom, as these are of vital importance (particularly kitchens) when selling a home. Note, however, that although modernisation may be necessary to sell an old home, you shouldn't overdo it as it's easy to spend more than you could ever hope to recoup on the sale price. If you're using an agent, you can ask him what you should do (or need to do) to help sell your home. If a home is in poor repair, this must be reflected in the asking price and if major work is needed which you cannot afford, you should obtain a quotation (or two) and offer to knock this off the price. Note that while you have a duty under Irish law to inform a prospective buyer of any legal issues affecting the title of the property, you aren't obliged to disclose any defects which aren't readily apparent. It's up to the buyer to discover them – caveat emptor!

Selling Your Home Yourself: While certainly not for everyone, selling your own home is a viable option for many people and is particularly recommended when selling an attractive home at a *realistic* price in a favourable market. The principal advantage is of course that you save yourself an estate agent's fee of 2 or 2.5 per cent. You can use this saving to offer the property at a more appealing price, which could be an important factor if you're after a fast sale. How you market your home will depend on the kind of property, the price and the country or area from where you expect your buyer to come. For example, if your property isn't of a kind and style or in an area that's desirable to local people, it's usually a waste of time advertising it in the local Irish press.

Marketing: Marketing is the key to selling your home. The first step is to have a professional looking 'For Sale' sign made (showing your telephone number) and erect it in the garden or place it in a window. Do some research into the best newspapers and magazines for advertising your property (see **Appendix A**), and place an advertisement in those that look most promising. You could also have a leaflet printed (with pictures) extolling the virtues of your property and drop it into local letter boxes or have it distributed with a local newspaper (many people buy a new home in the immediate vicinity of their present home). You may also need a 'fact sheet' printed (if your home's vital statistics aren't included in the leaflet mentioned above) and could offer a finder's fee, e.g. IR£500, to anyone who finds you a buyer. Don't omit to market your home around local companies, schools and organisations, particularly if they have many itinerant employees. Finally, it may help to provide information about local financing sources for potential buyers. With a bit of effort and practice you may even make a better job of marketing your home than an estate agent! Unless you're in a hurry to sell, set yourself a realistic time limit for success, after which you can try an agent. When selling a home yourself, you'll need to provide a contract or engage a solicitor to do this for you.

Using An Agent: Most owners prefer to use the services of an agent or agents, either in Ireland or in their home country, when selling a second home in Ireland. If you purchased the property through an agent, it's often advisable to use the same agent when selling, as he will already be familiar with it and may still have the details on file. You should take particular care when selecting an agent, as they vary considerably in their enthusiasm and standard of service (the best way to investigate agents is by posing as a buyer). Note that many agents cover a relatively small area, so you should take care to choose one who regularly sells properties in your area and price range. If you own a property in an area popular with foreign buyers, it may be worthwhile using an overseas agent or advertising in foreign newspapers and magazines, such as the English-language publications listed in **Appendix A**.

Agents' Contracts: Before he can offer a property for sale, an Irish agent requires a signed authorisation from the owner in the form of an exclusive or non-exclusive contract. An exclusive contract (known as 'sole agency') gives a single agent the right to sell a property, while a non-exclusive contract allows you to deal with any number of agents and to negotiate directly with private individuals. In Ireland the normal procedure is for the property to be placed with a maximum of two agents. You may think it's to your advantage to place it with as many agents as possible, but in practice, if they know they're one of several, they will put little effort into finding you a buyer. In most cases two agents will happily communicate with each other to ensure that they aren't duplicating their efforts. Some agents, however, will insist on a sole agency contract. Note that if you sign an exclusive contract, you must pay the agent's commission even if you sell your home yourself! Don't forget to ask an agent how your property will be marketed and to check regularly that he's actively seeking a buyer. Agents' contracts are usually for three months, but can be extended.

Agents' Fees: When selling a property in Ireland, the agent's commission is usually paid by the vendor and included in the purchase price. Fees vary between around 2 and 2.5 per cent, depending on the price of a property, and may be lower with an exclusive contract than with a non-exclusive contract. Shop around for the best deal as there's fierce competition among agents to sell good properties. Check the contract and make sure that you understand what you're signing. Contracts state the level of the agent's commission and what it includes. Generally you shouldn't pay any additional fees unless you require additional services (e.g. advertising, which is usually extra) and you should never pay the agent's commission before a sale is completed and you have been paid.

Capital Gains Tax: Note that anyone selling a second home in Ireland must pay capital gains tax (see page 125). When a non-resident sells a property in Ireland for over IR£150,000, 15 per cent of the price must be retained by the buyer (the solicitor will ensure that this is done) and be paid to the Revenue Commissioners as a deposit against tax due. Note that if you're resident in Ireland and are selling your principal home and buying another in Ireland, you must sell your existing home before buying a new one in order to benefit from the CGT concession for residents. One way round this if you need to buy a new home before you've sold your current one, is to buy it on a private contract and not register it until after you've sold your present home (obtain legal advice).

Warning: As when buying a home in Ireland, you must be *very* careful who you deal with when selling a home. Make sure that you're paid with a certified banker's draft before signing over your property to a buyer as, once the deed of purchase has been signed, the property belongs to the buyer, whether you have been paid or not. Be extremely careful if you plan to use an intermediary, as it isn't uncommon for a 'middle man' to disappear with the proceeds! Never agree to accept part of the sale price 'under the table', as if the buyer refuses to pay the extra money, there's nothing you can do about it (at least legally). Sellers occasionally end up with no property *and* no money! All sales should be conducted through a solicitor. See also **Estate Agents** on page 176.

5.

ARRIVAL & SETTLING IN

On arrival in Ireland, your first task will be to negotiate immigration and customs. Fortunately this presents few problems for most people, particularly European Union (EU) nationals since the establishment of 'open' EU borders on 1st January 1993. Note, however, that non-EU nationals coming to Ireland for any purpose other than as visitors may require a visa (see page 19).

In addition to information about immigration and customs, this chapter contains checklists of tasks to be completed before or soon after arrival in Ireland and when moving house, plus suggestions for finding local help and information.

IMMIGRATION

Ireland is one of the least bureaucratic countries in Europe when it comes to the red tape of immigration. There's little of the 'fill-it-out-in-triplicate' system found in countries such as France, Italy and Spain. In fact Irish immigration laws have traditionally been so lax (more people have always wanted to leave Ireland than go there!) that many African and East European émigrés, attracted by Ireland's new-found prosperity and generous welfare handouts, are knocking at her door and requesting asylum. Compared with a mere 39 applications for asylum in 1992, there were expected to be some 6,000 in 1998. The largest and most visible group are Romanians, and other substantial contingents come from Algeria, Nigeria, Somalia and Zaire. Nine out of ten of these asylum seekers are illegal immigrants, but are automatically eligible for a range of benefits until their status is decided (which can take up to three years).

For those who prefer to enter the country legally, there are of course certain formalities which must be observed. If you arrive in Ireland from the UK, there are usually no immigration checks or passport controls at the port of entry into Ireland. The Irish Republic and Great Britain are part of a 'Common Travel Area', which means that foreigners travelling to Ireland via the UK must meet British immigration requirements and will then be free to enter Ireland. If you're a British citizen arriving in Ireland from Britain, you don't require a passport, although it's advisable to take some form of identity with you in case you're required to complete any formalities (e.g. when hiring a car). All other nationals require a valid passport (or national identity card) and in some cases a visa. However, citizens of many non-EU countries including Australia, Canada, New Zealand, South Africa and the USA don't require visas (see page 19). If you're taking your car with you, ensure that you have its registration document, insurance certificate valid for Ireland and driving licence, and that the car has a nationality sticker on the back.

If you're a non-EU national and arrive in Ireland by air or sea from outside the EU, you must go through immigration for non-EU citizens. Non-EU citizens are required to complete immigration registration cards, which are provided on aircraft and ferries (e.g. from France). If you need a visa to enter Ireland and attempt to enter without one, you'll be refused entry. Some people may wish to get a stamp in their passport as confirmation of their date of entry. If you're a non-EU national coming to Ireland to work, study or live, you may be asked to show documentary evidence. Immigration officials may also ask non-EU visitors to produce a return ticket, proof of accommodation, a health insurance certificate and evidence of sufficient financial resources, e.g. cash, travellers cheques and credit cards. The onus is on visitors to show that they're genuine and that they don't intend to breach Irish immigration laws. Immigration officials aren't required to prove that you'll breach those laws and can refuse you entry on the grounds of suspicion only.

CUSTOMS

The Single European Act, which came into effect on 1st January 1993, created a single trading market and changed the rules regarding customs for EU nationals. The shipment of personal (household) effects to Ireland from another EU country is no longer subject to customs formalities. If you use a shipping company to transport your belongings to Ireland, they will usually provide all the necessary forms and take care of the paperwork. Always keep a copy of all forms and communications with customs officials (both in Ireland and in your previous country of residence). Note that if the paperwork isn't in order, your belongings may end up incarcerated in an Irish customs storage depot for a number of months. If you personally import your belongings, you may need to employ a customs agent at the point of entry to clear them. You should have an official record of the export of valuables from any country, in case you wish to re-import them later.

Permanent Residence

If you're transferring you residence to Ireland, you're entitled, under certain conditions, to import property (including vehicles) for your and your family's use free of import charges (i.e. customs duty and VAT) and vehicle registration tax VRT). This excludes property that's intended for commercial use, with the exception of the 'tools of the trade' of people such as artists, doctors, solicitors and barristers. However, other self-employed people transferring their business activities to Ireland may be eligible for relief from import duty (you should make enquiries with Irish Customs and Excise).

EU Citizens: If you're importing personal effects from another EU country, there are no customs formalities. Note, however, that in order to obtain relief on any belongings, you must originally have paid duty and VAT on them in your home country or have owned them for at least six months prior to importation. You may import your belongings up to one year before or after you take up residence and there are no restrictions on disposing of them after you move. A detailed inventory is advisable (although it's unlikely that anyone will check it) and the shipping company should have a photocopy of the owner's passport legalised by an Irish consulate.

Vehicles: If you're importing a vehicle, you must present form C&E 1077 as well as the appropriate VRT form, which must be completed at the vehicle registration office of the county where you plan to live not later than the next working day following the vehicle's arrival in Ireland. You will also need to produce appropriate documentation such as the vehicle registration document and insurance certificate. In order to qualify for relief, you must be able to show that you have owned and used the vehicle outside Ireland for at least six months before the date of your transfer of residence. In addition you may not dispose of, hire or lend the vehicle to anyone during the 12 months following its registration in Ireland.

Non-EU Citizens: Non-EU nationals planning to take up permanent residence in Ireland are permitted to import furniture and belongings free of duty or taxes. You must have owned them for at least six months and had your usual place of residence outside the EU for a continuous period of at least 12 months prior to your move (relief may also be granted if you can prove that it was your intention to reside outside the EU continuously for 12 months). Note that 'normal residence' is considered to be the place where you live for at least 185 days in each year. You will therefore need to produce documentary evidence such as relevant sales invoices or receipts, proof of residence abroad and transfer of residence to Ireland, evidence of disposal of your home in your previous country of residence and of employment in Ireland (if applicable).

You must declare all property at the place of importation and complete forms C&E 1076 and VRT 4 (for cars) or VRT 5 (for motor cycles) as appropriate. Form C&E 1076 should include an inventory of all items imported, except used clothes, toiletries and accessories. If all your belongings aren't being imported at once, you'll need to present a copy of the inventory each time you import something. The form must also contain three declarations: your own (that you have complied with the conditions for obtaining relief from import duty); your import agent's (e.g. shipping company or customs' clearance agent); and that of the transport company responsible for delivering the goods to your home. Another form, C&E 136 or CU 56, is required for any articles of gold or silver plate which you may be bringing with you.

You may import personal effects (excluding vehicles) not more than six months in advance or one year after your arrival, and you may not sell or otherwise dispose of them during your first year of residence.

Secondary Residence

The same criteria regarding customs duty relief on the importation of household effects (i.e. furniture, furnishings and equipment) apply to a secondary residence. However, non-EU citizens are additionally required to have owned or rented that secondary residence for not less than two years and to undertake not to let it to any third parties. In practice, this means that non-EU citizens will be unlikely to be able to furnish a second home in Ireland with duty-free imported goods and may as well buy new furnishings locally.

Visitors

Certain goods may be temporarily imported into Ireland without payment of customs duty or VAT. The maximum time they can remain in the country is two years. This applies to the import of private cars, camping vehicles (including trailers or caravans), motorcycles, aircraft and personal effects. Certain other items may qualify for partial relief from customs duty. Goods may be imported without formality, providing that their nature and quantity doesn't imply any commercial aim and that they're re-exported when you leave Ireland. If you cross into Ireland by road from Northern Ireland you may drive slowly through the border post without stopping (unless asked to do so). However, any goods (see below) and pets (see page 78) that you're carrying mustn't be subject to any prohibitions or restrictions. Customs officials can still stop anyone for a spot check, e.g. for drugs or illegal immigrants. If you arrive at a seaport by private boat there are no particular customs' formalities, although you must show the boat's registration papers and VAT receipts on request.

Prohibited & Restricted Goods

There are of course restrictions on the quantities of certain goods you're permitted to import into Ireland and certain others may require a licence or permit or be prohibited.

Alcohol and Tobacco: You may import a limited amount of alcoholic and tobacco products without paying import duty providing that you have paid the relevant tax in another EU country, i.e. they aren't duty-free. The limits are 110 litres of beer, 90 litres of wine, 20 litres of fortified wine (e.g. port or sherry), 10 litres of spirits, 800 cigarettes, 400 cigarillos, 200 cigars and 1kg of tobacco. If you want to exceed these limits, you'll need evidence that it's all for your own use!

Perfume: Perfume and certain kinds of gifts and new goods are also subject to restrictions, which vary according to whether you're resident in the EU and whether the goods were purchased in an EU country.

Vehicles: New or unregistered vehicles (including boats and aircraft) brought into Ireland on a permanent basis must be presented immediately to a vehicle registration office (there's one in most main towns) where they will be assessed for Vehicle Registration Tax (VRT). If you don't qualify for exemption (see above), you'll be taxed according to a vehicle's market value: at a rate of 29.25 per cent for cars up to 2,500cc, at 23.2 per cent for cars over 2,500cc and at 13.3 per cent for small vans (including certain types of 'jeep' and motor caravan). The rate for motor cycles is IR£2 per cc up to 350cc and IR£1 per cc thereafter (less a deduction for age in the case of used machines). The rate for most other vehicles (i.e. trucks, tractors, etc.) is a fixed rate of IR£40.

Currency: There are no restrictions on the import or export of Irish or foreign bank notes or securities, although if you enter or leave Ireland with a large amount of currency (see page 91), you must make a declaration to Irish customs.

Certain goods are subject to special regulations in Ireland and in some cases their import and export is prohibited or restricted. This applies in particular to firearms and ammunition, certain plants and foodstuffs, dangerous drugs and pornography. If you're unsure whether any goods you're importing fall into these categories, you should check with Irish customs.

Firearms: If you're planning to import sporting guns into Ireland, you must obtain a certificate from an Irish consulate abroad, which is issued on production of a valid firearms licence. The consular certificate must be presented to the customs authorities on entry into Ireland and can be used to exchange a foreign firearms licence for an Irish licence when taking up residence.

Plants: To import certain kinds of plants into Ireland, you must obtain a licence or a 'plant passport'. There are no prohibited plants within the EU, although some require a passport. Plants from outside the EU may need a licence from the Department of Agriculture. Note also that you may not be allowed to import hay or straw, so these shouldn't be used to pack personal effects. To find out whether a licence is required contact the Plant Health Section of the DoA on 01-607 2089. Licences are issued free of charge.

Food: Certain kinds of food may not be taken into the Republic, e.g. pet food must be tinned and pre-cooked and have been manufactured in the EU (even then only a limited amount may be imported).

Illegal drugs: Visitors arriving in Ireland from 'exotic' regions, e.g. Africa, South America, and the Middle and Far East, may find themselves under close scrutiny from customs and security officials looking for illegal drugs.

Value Added Tax (VAT)

VAT is levied on goods imported from outside the EU, in addition to any customs and excise duties which may be payable. In general goods are liable to VAT at the same rate as applies to the sale of similar goods within Ireland (e.g. vehicles are subject to VAT at 21 per cent). VAT is also payable on import duty and on the transportation, handling and insurance costs of goods as they're conveyed to their final destination (i.e. your home). VAT is usually due at the same time as customs duty, but payment may be deferred, subject to the approval of the Revenue Commissioners. The criteria for relief from VAT aren't quite the same as those for relief from import duty. For example, relief from VAT cannot be obtained for personal effects imported for a secondary residence, nor for tobacco and alcoholic products, perfumes or toilet water.

If you require general information about Irish customs regulations or have specific questions, contact Customs Procedures (☎ 01-679 2777). Copies of the forms mentioned above can be obtained from any customs and excise or vehicle registration office. Information about duty-free allowances can be found on page 77 and **Pets** on page 78.

RESIDENCE PERMITS

Non-UK nationals must report to the police within three months and obtain a residence permit from the Department of Justice, Equality and Law Reform (see page 19). Unless you're retired or otherwise financially independent, the duration of the residence permit will be governed by the length of your employment or course (in the case of students) up to a maximum of five years. If you're employed in Ireland, the permit must be completed by your employer, who must also submit a letter detailing the nature and period of your employment. If you're a student, retired or financially independent, you'll be required to show that you have private health insurance. In addition, anyone applying for a residence permit may be required to undergo a medical examination. If you intend to stay for less than a year but more than three months, you'll be issued with a temporary residence permit.

FINDING HELP

One of the major problems facing new arrivals in Ireland is how and where to obtain help with day to day problems such as finding accommodation, schooling, insurance and so on. In addition to the comprehensive information provided in this book, you'll also need detailed *local* information. How successful you are at finding local help depends on your employer, the town or area where you live (e.g. residents of large towns and cities are far better served than those living in rural areas), your nationality and your English (or Irish) language proficiency. An additional problem is that much of the available information isn't intended for foreigners and their particular needs. You may find that your friends and colleagues can help by offering advice based on

W & G FOYLE LTD

113-119 CHARING
CROSS ROAD
LONDON
WC2H OEB

20-04-01 14:45 SALE   11 6788 TRAVEL

PRODUCT	QTY	£
9789999012133	1	14.99
9780873648158	1	12.99
9780873641012	1	14.99
9781901130102	1	9.95
TOTAL	4	52.92
MASTER CARD		52.92
AMOUNT DUE		52.92

THANK YOU FOR YOUR CUSTOM
PLEASE CALL AGAIN SOON...

their own experiences and mistakes. But take care! Although they mean well, you're likely to receive as much misleading and conflicting information as accurate (it may not necessarily be wrong, but often won't apply to your particular situation).

Your local city or county hall may be a good source of information, but you may well be sent on a wild goose chase from department to department. Apart from assisting with routine everyday matters, the town hall can be helpful when applying for an Irish driving licence and other official documents. One of the best places to obtain expert and impartial advice is at a Citizen's Information Centre (CIC), which provide free, confidential information on virtually any subject. There are CICs in most Irish towns, but opening times vary (many are open only in the morning). A wealth of valuable information is available in the major cities and towns, where foreigners are served by embassies and consulates. These will usually provide their nationals with local information including details of solicitors, doctors, schools, and social and expatriate organisations. Contacts can also be made through many expatriate magazines and newspapers (see **Appendix A**).

CHECKLISTS

The checklists on the following pages include tasks which you need (or may need) to complete before and after arrival in Ireland, and when moving your home permanently to Ireland.

Before Arrival

- Check that your family's passports are valid.

- Obtain a visa, if necessary, for all your family members (see page 19). Obviously this *must* be done before arrival in Ireland.

- Arrange health and travel insurance for yourself and your family (see pages 65 and 73). This is essential if you aren't already covered by an international health insurance policy and won't be covered by Irish social security.

- If you don't already have one, it's advisable to obtain an international credit or charge card.

- Obtain an international driving licence if necessary (see page 50).

- Open a bank account in Ireland (see page 95) and transfer funds. You can open an account with many Irish banks while abroad, although it's best done in person in Ireland.

- It pays to obtain some Irish punts before arrival, as this will save you having to queue to change money at the port of airport (and you'll probably get a better exchange rate abroad).

- If you plan to become a permanent resident, you may also need to do the following:

  - Arrange schooling for your children.

  - Organise the shipment of your personal and household effects.

- Obtain as many credit references as possible, for example from banks, mortgage companies, credit card companies, credit agencies, companies with which you have had accounts, and from professionals such as solicitors and accountants. These will help you when opening bank accounts, setting up a business in Ireland and obtaining credit.

If you're planning to become a permanent resident in Ireland, don't forget to take all your family's official documents with you. These may include birth certificates; driving licences; marriage certificate, divorce papers or death certificate (if a widow or widower); educational diplomas and professional certificates; employment references and curricula vitae; school records and student ID cards; medical and dental records; bank account and credit card details; insurance policies (plus records of no-claims bonuses); and receipts for any valuables. You will also need the documents necessary to obtain a residence permit plus certified copies, and numerous passport-size photographs (students should take at least a dozen).

After Arrival

The following checklist contains a summary of the tasks to be completed *after* arrival in Ireland (if not done before):

● On arrival at an Irish airport or port, have your visa cancelled and your passport stamped, as applicable.

● If you aren't taking a car with you, you may wish to rent (see page 53) or buy one locally.

● Open a cheque account (see page 95) at a local bank and give the details to your employer (if applicable) and any companies that you plan to pay by direct debit or standing order (such as utility and property management companies).

● Arrange whatever insurance is necessary, such as health, car, household and third-party liability.

● Contact offices and organisations to obtain local information (see page 212).

● Make courtesy calls on your neighbours and local shops (etc.) within a few weeks of your arrival. This is particularly important in small villages and rural areas if you want to be accepted and integrate into the local community.

● If you plan to become a permanent resident in Ireland, you'll need to do the following within a few weeks of arrival (if not done before):

- Apply for a residence permit at the Department of Justice, Equality and Law Reform within 90 days of your arrival.
- Register with the Aliens Registration Office in Dublin.
- If necessary, apply for an Irish driving licence (see page 50).
- Find a local doctor and dentist.
- Arrange schooling for your children.

Moving House

When moving permanently to Ireland there are many things to be considered and a 'million' people to be informed. Even if you plan to spend only a few months a year in Ireland, it may still be necessary to inform a number of people and companies in your home country. The checklists below are designed to make the task easier and help prevent an ulcer or a nervous breakdown (providing of course, you don't leave everything to the last minute). See also **Moving House** on page 187.

- If you live in rented accommodation, you'll need to give your landlord notice (check your contract).

- Arrange to store or dispose of everything you aren't taking with you (e.g. car and furniture). If you're selling a home or business, you should obtain expert legal advice as you may be able to save tax by establishing a trust or other legal vehicle. Note that if you own more than one property, you may need to pay capital gains tax on any profits from the sale of second and subsequent homes.

- Arrange shipment of your furniture and belongings by booking a shipping company well in advance (see page 187). Major international shipping companies usually provide a wealth of information and can advise on a wide range of matters concerning an international relocation. (There are also specialist companies, such as RSI in Dublin, that offer a complete relocation service.) Find out the exact procedure for shipping your belongings to Ireland from your local Irish embassy or consulate.

- If you have a car that you're exporting to Ireland, you'll need to complete the relevant paperwork in your home country and re-register it in Ireland after your arrival. Contact your local Irish embassy or consulate for information.

- Check whether you need a 'green card', an international driving licence or a translation of your foreign driving licence(s) for Ireland. Note that some foreigners are required to take a driving test before they can buy and register a car in Ireland.

- Check whether you're entitled to a rebate on your road tax, car and other insurance. Obtain a letter from your motor insurance company stating your no-claims bonus.

- Arrange inoculations and shipment for any pets that you're taking with you (see page 78).

- You may qualify for a rebate on your tax and social security contributions. If you're leaving a country permanently and have been a member of a company or state pension scheme, you may be entitled to a refund or you may be able to transfer to another pension scheme or continue payments to qualify for a full (or larger) pension when you retire. Contact your company personnel office, local tax office or pension company for information.

- It's advisable to arrange health, dental and optical check-ups for your family before leaving your home country. Obtain a copy of all health records and a statement from your private health insurance company stating your present level of cover

.Terminate any outstanding loan, lease or hire purchase contracts and pay all bills (allow plenty of time as some companies are slow to respond).

- Return any library books or anything borrowed.
- Inform the following:

  - Your employers (e.g. give notice or arrange leave of absence) or clients if you're self-employed.
  - Your local town hall or council. You may be entitled to a refund on your local property or utilities taxes.
  - If it was necessary to register with the police in your home country (or present country of residence), you should inform them that you're moving abroad.
  - Your electricity, gas, water and telephone companies. Contact companies well in advance, particularly if you need to get a deposit refunded.
  - Your insurance companies (for example health, car, home contents and private pension); banks, post office (if you have a post office account), stockbroker and other financial institutions; credit card, charge card and hire purchase companies; solicitor and accountant; and local businesses where you have accounts.
  - Your family doctor, dentist and other health practitioners. Health records should be transferred to your new doctor and dentist in Ireland, if applicable. You may also need to do this for your pets.
  - Your children's schools. Try to give a term's notice and obtain a copy of any relevant school reports or records from your children's current schools.
  - All regular correspondents, social and sports clubs, professional and trade journals, and friends and relatives. Give them your new address and telephone number and arrange to have your mail redirected by the post office or a friend. Give close friends, relatives and business associates a telephone number where you can be contacted in Ireland or have calls redirected from your current number.
  - If you have a driving licence or car, you'll need to give the local vehicle registration office your new address in Ireland and, in some countries, return your car's registration plates.

- If you'll be living in Ireland for an extended period (but not permanently), you may wish to give someone 'power of attorney' over your financial affairs in your home country so that they can act for you in your absence. This can be for a fixed period or open-ended and can be for a specific purpose only. Note, however, that you should always take expert legal advice before doing this!

- Finally, allow plenty of time to get to the airport or port, register your luggage, and clear security and immigration.

As they say in Ireland, "May the ground rise up to meet you"!

Bon Voyage!

APPENDICES

APPENDIX A: USEFUL ADDRESSES

Embassies & Consulates

Foreign embassies and consulates in Ireland are located in Dublin and Cork, and are listed under 'Embassies and Consular Missions' in telephone books. Note that business hours vary considerably and all embassies close on their national holidays and on Ireland's public holidays. Always telephone to check the business hours before visiting. Embassies and consulates in Dublin are listed below:

Argentina: 15 Ailesbury Drive, Dublin 4 (☎ 01-269 1546).

Australia: Fitzwilton House, Wilton Terrace, Dublin 2 (☎ 01-676 1517).

Austria: 15 Ailesbury Court, 93 Ailesbury Road, Dublin 4 (☎ 01-269 4577).

Belgium: Shrewsbury House, Shrewsbury Road, Dublin 4 (☎ 01-269 2082).

Brazil: Europe House, Harcourt Street, Dublin 4 (☎ 01-475 6000).

Bulgaria: 22 Burlington Road, Dublin 4 (☎ 01-660 3293).

Canada: 65 St. Stephen's Green, Dublin 2 (☎ 01-478 1988).

China: 40 Ailesbury Road, Dublin 4 (☎ 01-269 1707).

Czech Republic: 57 Northumberland Road, Dublin 4 (☎ 01-668 1135).

Denmark: 121 St. Stephen's Green, Dublin 2 (☎ 01-475 6404).

Egypt: 12 Clyde Road, Ballsbridge, Dublin 4 (☎ 01-660 6566).

Finland: Stokes Place, St. Stephen's Green, Dublin 2 (☎ 01-478 1344).

France: 36 Ailesbury Road, Dublin 4 (☎ 01-260 1666).

Germany: 31 Trimleston Avenue, Booterstown (☎ 01-269 3011).

Greece: 1 Upper Pembroke Street, Dublin 2 (☎ 01-676 7254).

Hungary: 2 Fitzwilliam Place, Dublin 4 (☎ 01-661 2902).

India: 6 Lesson Park, Dublin 6 (☎ 01-497 0843).

Iran: 72 Mount Merrion Avenue, Blackrock (☎ 01- 288 0252).

Israel: 122 Pembroke Road, Dublin 4 (☎ 01-668 0303).

Italy: 63 Northumberland Road, Dublin 4 (☎ 01-660 1744).

Japan: Merrion Centre, Nutley Lane, Dublin 4 (☎ 01-269 4244).

Korea: 20 Clyde Road, Dublin 4 (☎ 01-660 8800).

Mexico: 43 Ailesbury Road, Dublin 4 (☎ 01-260 0699).

Morocco: 53 Raglan Road, Ballsbridge, Dublin 4 (☎ 01-660 9449).

Netherlands: 160 Merrion Road, Dublin 4 (☎ 01-269 3444).

Nigeria: 56 Leeson Park, Dublin 6 (☎ 01-660 4366).

Norway: 34 Molesworth Street, Dublin 2 (☎ 01-662 1800).

Poland: 5 Ailesbury Road, Dublin 4 (☎ 01-283 0855).

Portugal: Knocksinna House, Foxrock, Dublin 18 (☎ 01-289 4416).

Romania: 60 Merrion Road, Dublin 4 (☎ 01-668 1336).

Russia: 186 Orwell Road, Dublin 14 (☎ 01-492 3525).

South Africa: Earlsfort Centre, Dublin 2 (☎ 01-661 5553).

Spain: 17a Merlyn Park, Dublin 4 (☎ 01-269 1640).

Sweden: Sun Alliance House, Dawson Street, Dublin 2 (☎ 01-671 5822).

Switzerland: 6 Ailesbury Road, Dublin 4 (☎ 01-269 2515).

Turkey: 11 Clyde Road, Ballsbridge, Dublin 4 (☎ 01-668 5240).

United Kingdom: 29 Merrion Road, Dublin 4 (☎ 01-205 3700).

USA: 42 Elgin Road, Dublin 4 (☎ 01-668 8777).

Government

Central Statistics Office, Skehard Road, Cork (☎ 021-359 000).

Collector General (Taxes), Sarsfield House, Limerick (☎ 01-677 4211).

Customs Procedures, A Branch, Castle House, South Great St George's Street, Dublin 2 (☎ 01-679 2777).

Department of Agriculture and Food, Agriculture House, Kildare Street, Dublin 2 (☎ 01-607 2000).

Department of Enterprise and Employment, Adelaide Road, Dublin 2 (☎ 01-661 4444).

Department of Foreign Affairs, 72/76 St Stephen's Green, Dublin 2 (☎ 01-478 0822).

Department of Health and Children, Hawkins House, Hawkins Street, Dublin 2 (☎ 01-671 4711).

Department of Justice, Equality and Law Reform, 72/76 St Stephen's Green, Dublin 2 (☎ 01-602 8202).

Department of Social, Community and Family Affairs, Store Street, Dublin 1 (☎ 01-874 8444).

Garda Síochána **(Police)**, Phoenix Park, Dublin 8 (☎ 01-677 1156).

National Social Service Board, Hume House, Ballsbridge, Dublin 4 (☎ 01-605 9000).

Revenue Commissioners, Central Information Office, Dublin (☎ 01-878 000).

Business

Chambers of Commerce of Ireland, 22 Merrion Square, Dublin 2 (☎ 01-661 2888).

Companies Office, Parnell House, 14 Parnell Square, Dublin 1 (☎ 01-804 5200).

Forbairt, Wilton Park House, Wilton Place, Dublin 2 (☎ 01-660 2244).

Shannon Development, Shannon, Co. Clare (☎ 061-361 555).

Small Firms Association, Confederation House, 84/86 Lower Baggot Street, Dublin 2 (☎ 01-660 1011).

The Small Business and Services Division of the Department of Enterprise, Trade and Employment (☎ 01-661 4444).

Training & Employment Authority (*FÁS*), 27/33 Upper Baggot Street, Dublin 4 (☎ 01-607 0500).

VAT Enquiries, Findlater House, Cathal Brugha Street, Dublin 1 (☎ 01-874 6821).

Property

Calor Gas, Long Mile Road, Dublin 12 (☎ 01-450 5000).

Construction Industry Federation, Construction House, Canal Road, Dublin 6 (☎ 01-497 7487).

Electricity Supply Board, Fleet Street, Dublin 2 (☎ 01-677 2961).

Gas Board (*Bord Gáis*), D'Olier Street, Dublin 2 (☎ 01-602 1212).

Irish Brokers Association, 87 Merrion Square, Dublin 2 (☎ 01-661 3067).

Irish Home Builders Association, Construction House, Canal Road, Dublin 6 (☎ 01-497 7487).

Land Registry, Nassau Building, Setanta Centre, Nassau Street, Dublin 2 (☎ 01-873 2233).

Register of Electrical Contractors of Ireland, Parnell Avenue, Harold's Cross, Dublin 12 (☎ 01-454 5820).

Royal Institute of Architects of Ireland, 8 Merrion Square, Dublin 2 (☎ 01-676 1703).

Society of Chartered Surveyors, 5 Wilton Place, Dublin 2 (☎ 01-676 5500).

Telecom Ireland (*Telecom Éireann*), St Stephen's Green, Dublin 2 (☎ 01-671 4444).

Timeshare Council of in Ireland, PO Box 78, Waterford.

Publications

Examiner/Evening Echo, PO Box 21, Academy St, Cork (☎ 021-272 722).

Home Buyers Guide, MAP Publications, 3 Lower Abbey Street, Dublin 1 (☎ 01-878 6622). Available free from estate agents, architects, property developers, the Irish Home Builders Association, and central and local authorities (or it can be purchased at Eason bookshops or on subscription).

The Irish Times, 10–16 D'Olier St, Dublin 2 (☎ 01-679 2022).

Image, Image Publications Ltd, 22 Crofton Road, Dun Laoghaire (☎ 01-280 8415).

International Property Magazine, 2a Station Road, Gidea Park, Romford, Essex RM2 6DA, UK. Monthly magazine.

Irish Independent/Evening Herald, 90 Middle Abbey St, Dublin 1 (☎ 01-705 5333).

Phoenix Magazine, 44 Baggot Street, Dublin 2 (☎ 01-661 1062).

The Star, Star House, 62A Terenure Road North, Dublin 6 (☎ 01-490 1228).

World of Property, Outbound Publishing, 1 Commercial Road, Eastbourne, East Sussex BN21 3XQ, UK (☎ 01323-412001). Quarterly magazine.

Miscellaneous

BUPA Ireland, Mill Island, Fermoy, Co. Cork (☎ 025-42121).

Car Rental Council of Ireland, 5 Upper Pembroke Street, Dublin 2 (☎ 01-676 1690).

Disability Federation of Ireland, 2 Sandyford Office Park, Dublin 18 (☎ 01-295 9344).

Dublin Bus (*Bus Átha Cliath*), 59 Upper O'Connell Street, Dublin 1 (☎ 01-873 4222).

Garda Síochána **(Police)**, Phoenix Park, Dublin 8 (☎ 01-677 1156).

Incorporated Law Society of Ireland, Blackhall Place, Dublin 7 (☎ 01-671 0711).

Irish Co-operative Society Ltd. (ICOS), Plunkett House, 84 Merrion Square, Dublin 2 (☎ 01-676 4783/6).

Irish League of Credit Unions, 33/41 Lower Mount Street, Dublin 2 (☎ 01-614 6700).

Irish Rail (*Iarnród Éireann*), Connolly Station, Dublin 1 (☎ 01-836 3333).

Irish Tourist Board (*Bord Failte Éireann*), Baggot Street, Dublin 2 (☎ 01-602 4000).

Law Society of Ireland, Blackhall Place, Dublin 7 (☎ 01-671 0711).

The Pensions Board, Holbrook House, Holles Street, Dublin 2 (☎ 01-676 2622).

Radio and Television Ireland (*Radio Telefís Éireann*), Dublin 4 (☎ 01-208 3111).

Voluntary Health Insurance Board (VHI), VHI House, Lower Abbey Street, Dublin 1 (☎ 01-872 4499).

APPENDIX B: FURTHER READING

The books listed below are just a small selection of the many books written for those planning to buy a home or work in Ireland. Some titles may be out of print, but you may still be able to find a copy in a bookshop or library. Books prefixed with an asterisk (*) are recommended by the author.

Tourist Guides & Travel Literature

Around Ireland with a Fridge, Tony Hawkes (Ebury)
***Baedeker's Ireland** (Baedeker)
Berlitz Pocket Guides: Ireland (Macmillan)
Discover Ireland, Martin Gostelow (Berlitz)
***Dublin: The Miniguide**, Dan Richardson (Rough Guides)
***Fodor's Exploring Ireland** (Fodor)
***Fodor's Ireland (Fodor's Gold Guides)** (Fodor)
***Frommer's Guide to Ireland from $50 a Day** (Pocket books)
***Frommer's Ireland** (Frommer)
***Ireland**, Catharine Day (Cadogan Books)
Ireland, a Bicycle and a Tin Whistle, David A. Wilson (Blackstaff)
Ireland: A Cultural Encyclopaedia (Thames and Hudson)
***Ireland: A Travel Survival Kit**, Tom Smallman (Vacation Work)
***Ireland: The Rough Guide**, Sean Doran (The Rough Guides)
***Let's Go: Britain & Ireland** (Pan)
***Lonely Planet: Ireland**, Tom Smallman & Sean Sheehan (Lonely Planet)
***Michelin Green Guide to Ireland** (Michelin)
***Round Ireland in Low Gear**, Eric Newby (Picador)
***The Time Out Guide to Dublin** (Time Out)

Architecture & Gardens

150 Years of Architecture in Ireland, John Graby (Eblana Editions)
20th Century Architecture in Ireland, Annette Becker & Wilfred Wang (Prestel)
Buildings of Irish Towns, Patrick & Maura Shaffrey (O'Brien Press)
***Daily Telegraph Gardener's Guide to Britain and Ireland** (Dorling Kindersly)
***A Field Guide to the Buildings of Ireland**, Sean Rothery (Lilliput)
A Guide to Irish Houses, Mark Bence-Jones (Constable)
***In the Houses of Ireland**, Marianne Heron & Walter Pfeiffer (Thames & Hudson)
Irish Castles and Castellated Houses, Harold G. Leask (Dundalgan)
Irish Cottages, Joe Reynolds (Real Ireland Design)
***Irish Country Houses**, Terence Reeves-Smith (Appletree)
Irish Countryside Buildings, Patrick & Maura Shaffrey (O'Brien Press)
Irish Gardens, Terence Reeves-Smith (Appletree)

*In an Irish House, David Davidson & Molly Keane (Weidenfeld & Nicolson)
Irish Houses (Gill & Macmillan)
Irish Houses and Gardens, Sean O'Reilly (Aurum Press)
New Irish Architecture, John Oregan (Gandon)
Vanishing Country Houses of Ireland, Knight of Glin (Irish Georgian Society)

Accommodation

*Bed and Breakfast in Ireland, Elsie Dillard (Appletree)
Bed & Breakfast: Great Britain and Ireland (RAC Guides)
Bridgestone 100 Best Places to Stay in Ireland, Mckenna (Estragon)
*The Good Hotel Guide: Great Britain & Ireland, Hilary Rubinstein & Caroline Raphael (Ebury)
Ireland Self Catering Guide (Jarrold)
*The Irish Bed and Breakfast Book, Frank & Fran Sullivan (Pelican)
*Karen Brown's Charming Inns and B&Bs: Ireland, June Brown & Barbara Tapp (Fodor)
*Les Routiers Guide to Great Britain and Ireland (Les Routiers)
*Michelin Red Hotel and Restaurant Guide: Great Britain and Ireland (Michelin)
Special Places to Stay in Ireland, Simon Greenwood (Alastair Sawday)
Stilwell's Ireland: Bed and Breakfast, Tim Stilwell (Stilwell)

Miscellaneous

Enterprise Ireland: A Directory of Sources of Assistance for Entrepreneurs and Small Business Owners (Oak Tree Press)
Home Away from Home: The Yanks in Ireland, Mary Pat Kelly (Stackpole)
*Irish Traditional Cooking, Darina Allen (K. Cathie)
Laying Down the Law, Olive Brennan (Oak Tree Press)
*Moving to Ireland: Abhail go hEirinn, Eileen McKay (Brent Irish Advisory Service)
Moving to Ireland: A Guide to Living and Investing, Brendan Connolly & Peter Steadman (Windrow & Greene)
*Real Irish Cookerey, Mary Caherty (Hale)
*Starting a Business in Ireland, Brian O'Kane (Oak Tree Press)
*Taste of Ireland: In Food and Pictures, Theodora Fitzgibbon (Weidenfeld)
*Wining and Dining at Home in Ireland, Sandy O'Byrne & Jacinta Delahaye (A&A Farmer)
*Working and Living in Ireland, Eugenie Houston (Oak Tree Press)
Your Guide to Irish Law, Mary Faulkner, Gerry Kelly & Padraig Turley (Gill Macmillan)

APPENDIX C: MAP OF PROVINCES & COUNTIES

The map of Ireland opposite shows the four provinces (or regions) and 26 counties of Ireland, which are listed below. Note that most of the province of Ulster, with the exception of the counties of Cavan, Donegal and Monaghan, is part of the United Kingdom. The counties of Antrim, Armagh, Down, Fermanagh, Londonderry and Tyrone, which aren't shown on the map opposite, form the region know today as Northern Ireland, which remained part of the United Kingdom when the Republic of Ireland was established in 1921. A map of Ireland showing the main towns and geographical features is shown on page 6.

Connacht

Galway
Leitrim
Mayo
Roscommon
Sligo

Munster

Clare
Cork
Kerry
Limerick
Tipperary
Waterford

Leinster

Carlow
Dublin
Kildare
Kilkenny
Laois
Longford
Louth
Meath
Offaly
Westmeath
Wexford
Wicklow

Ulster

Cavan
Donegal
Monaghan

APPENDIX D: GLOSSARY

Acceptance: Agreeing to accept an *offer* on a property, which constitutes a contract.

Acceptance Fee: See *Mortgage Application Fee*.

Administration Fee: See *Vacate*.

Advance: The *mortgage* loan.

Amortisation: The gradual process of systematically reducing debt in equal payments (as in a *mortgage*) comprising both *principal* and interest, until the debt is paid in full.

Annual Percentage Rate (APR): Everything financed in a loan package (interest, loan fees and other charges), expressed as a percentage of the loan amount.

Annuity Mortgage: A *mortgage* loan in which both the *capital* and the interest are repaid over a fixed or variable *term*. Also called a Repayment Mortgage.

Arrangement Fee: See *Mortgage Application Fee*.

Auctioneer: A person licensed to represent buyers and sellers in property transactions. Also called an estate agent.

Broker: A more or less independent agency through which you can seek the most appropriate or economical financial service or product (e.g. insurance, *mortgage*).

Building(s) insurance: An insurance policy that protects homeowners from damage to their home. Required by lenders (*premiums* are usually included in monthly *mortgage* payments).

Buy-Back: An agreement between a seller and a purchaser that the seller will repurchase a *security* within a specified time at a predetermined price.

Cap: The maximum rate by which a *variable rate mortgage* can change,

either annually or over the *term* of the mortgage.

Clearing Fee: A charge arising from the clearing of a cheque paid to a lending institution on *redemption* of a *mortgage*.

Closing: The final procedure in a property transaction when documents are executed and recorded, funds are disbursed and the *title* transferred from the *vendor* to the buyer. Also called *completion* or settlement.

Closing Costs: Costs the buyer must pay at the time of closing in addition to the *deposit*, including solicitor's fees, *mortgage indemnity fee* and *buildings insurance*.

Closing Statement: A statement prepared by a solicitor detailing the closing costs for both the seller and the buyer.

Collateral: The *title deeds* of a property pledged as *security* against the repayment of a loan.

Common Elements: The parts of a property (e.g. apartment or flat) that aren't individually owned and in which all owners have an indivisible interest.

Completion: The final legal transfer of ownership of a property. See also *closing*.

Contents Insurance: An insurance policy protecting a homeowner from loss or damage to personal property (possibly outside as well as in a home).

Conveyance: The act of transferring the *title* of a property and also the document (such as a *deed*) used to transfer ownership. Also called conveyancing.

Conveyancer: Solicitor who undertakes *conveyance*.

County Development Plan: A plan drawn up by a county council for the use of land over a period of five years. See also *Zoning*.

Deed: A written legal document that conveys *title* to property.

Deed of Assignment: A *deed* used to transfer *leasehold unregistered land.*

Deed of Conveyance: A *deed* used to transfer *freehold unregistered land.*

Deed of Mortgage: A *deed* used to transfer *title* in a property to the *mortgagee.*

Deed of Transfer: A *deed* used to transfer *registered land.*

Deed Restrictions: A clause in a deed that restricts the use of land.

Deferred Start Mortgage: A type of *mortgage* whereby no repayments are made for the first one to three months of the *term*. Only available with *repayment mortgages.*

Deposit: The amount that needs to be paid in cash in order to obtain a *mortgage*, e.g. if you have an 80 per cent mortgage, you must make a 20 per cent deposit.

Disbursements: Fees such as *stamp duty*, *land registry* and *search* fees which are incurred by the *conveyancer.*

Earnest Money: Funds paid with an offer to show good faith to complete a purchase. Earnest money is placed by a broker in an *escrow* account until *closing*, when it becomes part of the *deposit* or *closing costs.*

Easement: The interest, privilege or right that a party has in the land of another party, e.g. rights of way.

Encumbrance: Any right or interest in a property that affects its value such as outstanding loans, unpaid taxes, *easements* and *deed* restrictions.

Endowment Mortgage: A type of *mortgage* loan in which repayments are combined with savings through a life assurance policy. By the end of the mortgage *term*, the value of the endowment policy should have grown sufficiently to repay the mortgage and

(hopefully) will leave the *mortgagor* with a surplus.

Equity: The value an owner has in a property after the deductions of any outstanding *liens* such as a *mortgage*, e.g. if a property is valued at IR£100,000 and the amount outstanding on a mortgage is IR£50,000, the owner has IR£50,000 equity.

Equity Loan: A second *mortgage* where the owner borrows against his *equity* in a property.

Escrow: A procedure in which documents of cash and property are put in the care of a third party, other than the buyer or seller, pending completion of agreed conditions and terms in sales contracts. An escrow company performs escrow services.

Estate Agent: See *Auctioneer.*

Fixed Rate Mortgage: A *mortgage* with a fixed *interest rate*, usually over a period of up to five years.

Flexible Month Mortgage: A type of *mortgage* whereby no repayments are made in one or two months of a year.

Foreclosure: Legal proceedings instigated by a lender to deprive a person of ownership rights when *mortgage* payments haven't been maintained. Also called repossession.

Freehold: The highest interest in a property that can be held by an individual. In theory the owner is free to do with the property what he wishes, although in practice various restrictions (e.g. *planning permission*) are placed on this right.

Freeholder: One who owns *freehold.*

FSBO: An abbreviation for 'For Sale By Owner', when a home is being sold without the assistance of an *estate agent.*

Funding Fee: A fee incurred by the *mortgagor* when switching from a *fixed rate* to a *variable rate mortgage* before the end of the fixed rate period.

Ground Rent: An annual fee payable by the *leaseholder* to the *freeholder*.

Interest Rate: A percentage that when multiplied by the *principal* determines the amount of money that the *principal* earns over a period of time (usually one year).

Joint Tenancy: Property ownership by two (e.g. a married couple) or more persons with an undivided interest and the right of survivorship, where if one owner dies the property automatically passes to the joint owner(s).

Land Registry: A public record of property and its ownership.

Lease: Permission to own or rent property for a limited period.

Leasehold: Ownership of property but not the land on which it stands. Leasehold ownership is restricted to a number of years and creates a landlord-tenant relationship between the *lessor* (*freeholder*) and the *lessee*.

Leaseholder: One who owns a *leasehold* property.

Lessee: Person to who a *lease* is granted.

Lessor: Person who grants a *lease*.

Lien: A charge against property making it *security* for a debt such as a *mortgage*.

Management Company: An organisation which a buyer must usually join when buying a property such as a flat or apartment with *common elements*.

Market Value: The current value of a property compared with similar properties, generally accepted to be the highest price a buyer will pay and the lowest price a vendor will accept.

Mortgage: A written instrument that creates a *lien* against a property as *security* against the repayment of a loan.

Mortgage Application Fee: A fee charged by the lender for evaluating, preparing and submitting a proposed *mortgage* loan. Also called an acceptance or arrangement fee.

Mortgage Indemnity Fee: A charge paid by the borrower (usually as part of the *closing costs*) to obtain financing particularly when borrowing more than a certain percentage of the purchase price. Also called a Mortgage Indemnity Bond.

Mortgage Protection Plan: Insurance against *foreclosure* in the event of job loss, major accident, illness or death.

Mortgagee: One who holds a *lien* or *title* to a property as *security* for a debt, i.e. the lender.

Mortgagor: One who pledges property as *security* for a loan, i.e. the borrower.

Offer: A bid to buy a property at a specified price.

Pension Mortgage: A type of *mortgage* loan in which the repayments cover only the interest on the loan, while separate payments are made into a personal pension plan. They are usually available only to those who are self-employed or whose employer doesn't offer an occupational pension scheme.

Planning Permission: Permission granted by a local planning authority to erect or alter a building.

Power of Attorney: Authority to act on behalf of another.

Premium: Payment in respect of a *mortgage* or insurance policy.

Principal: The amount of money borrowed to buy a property and the amount still owed. Also one who owns or will use a property.

Principal and Interest Payment: A periodic (usually monthly) *mortgage* repayment that includes interest charges plus an amount applied to the *amortisation* of the *principal* balance.

Private Treaty Sale: A method of selling a property by agreement between the vendor and the purchaser, either directly or through an *estate agent*.

Provisional Loan Approval: A service offered by lenders whereby they provide provisional approval of a loan (for a maximum sum) thus establishing a buyer's price range, strengthening his buying position and shortening the loan approval period.

Redemption: Full repayment of a *mortgage* loan.

Redemption Fee: A fee incurred by the *mortgagor* when redeeming a loan (or part of it) before the end of the *term*.

Refinance: To replace an old loan with a new one, either to reduce the *interest rate*, secure better terms or increase the amount borrowed.

Register of Deeds: A public record of *unregistered land*.

Registration Fee: A fee payable by a purchaser to have *title deeds* registered in the *Land Registry* or the *Register of Deeds*.

Registered Land: Land which is recorded in the *Land Registry*.

Repayment Mortgage: See *Annuity Mortgage*.

Repossession: See *Foreclosure*.

Searches: Enquiries made by or on behalf of a purchaser to ensure proper *title* to a property.

Security: Assets such as house *deeds* pledged in support of a loan.

Settlement: See *Closing*.

Sole Agency: An agreement giving an *estate agent* the exclusive right to sell a property and to collect a commission if the property is sold by anyone (including the owner) during the term of the agreement.

Stamp Duty: A tax payable on the purchase of property.

Survey (or **Structural Survey**): A thorough examination of the condition of a property before purchase, performed by a professional surveyor. You can make a purchase contingent on a satisfactory survey.

Term: The life-span of a *mortgage*, which can be either fixed (e.g. 15 or 25 years) or variable according to the rate of repayment.

Tenancy in Common: A form of ownership in which two or more persons buy a property jointly, but with no right of survivorship. Owners are free to will their share to anyone they choose, which is the main difference between this and *joint tenancy*. Often used by friends or relatives buying together.

Title: The right of possession and evidence of ownership.

Title Search: A professional scrutiny of public records to establish the chain of ownership of a property and record any outstanding *liens*, *mortgage*, *encumbrances* or other factors that may restrict clear *title*.

Unregistered Land: Land which isn't recorded in the *Land Registry*.

Vacate: An official receipt by the *mortgagee* acknowledging that a *mortgage* has been paid off and effecting the transfer of *title* from the mortgagee to the *mortgagor*.

Valuation: The professional examination of a property to determine its *market value*.

Variable Rate Mortgage: A *mortgage* loan whose *interest rate* changes in accordance with prevailing *interest rates*.

Vendor: Person selling a property.

Zoning: The procedure that classifies land and property according to usage, e.g. residential, commercial or industrial, in accordance with a *county development plan*.

APPENDIX E: SERVICE DIRECTORY

This **Service Directory** is to help you find local businesses and services in Ireland and the UK, serving residents and visitors in Ireland. Note that when calling Ireland from abroad, you must dial the international access number (e.g. 00 from the UK) followed by 353 (the country code for Ireland), the area code, minus the leading zero (e.g. 1 for Dublin), and the subscriber's number. Please mention *Buying a Home in Ireland* when contacting companies.

AGENTS (PROPERTY)

Emerald Isle Properties, Suite 401, 302 Regent Street, London W1R 6HH, UK (☎ +44-0181-289 9697).

Green Valley Properties, Caherhurley, Bodyke, Co. Clare (☎/fax 061-921498). Contact: Steve Symes. County Clare's leading rural property specialist; cottages, smallholdings and farmhouses. Some within reach of a Steiner school. List available.

Joe C. Keating & Sons Ltd., Caherciveen, Co. Kerry (☎ 0667-2033, fax 0667-2197).

John Earley Estate Agents Ltd., Goff Street, Roscommon (☎ 0903-26579/26796, fax 0903-25405).

Joseph G. Brady Financial Services, Carrick-on-Shannon, Co. Leitrim (☎ 078-20193, fax 078-20411).

Keane Mahony Smith, 44 South Mall, Cork (☎ 021-270311, fax 021-271296).

Leyden Auctioneers & Valuers, Old Mill Road, Ennis, Co. Clare (☎ 065-28286, fax 065-29794).

Manuel Di Lucia, Corbally, Kilkee, Co. Clare (☎ 065-56211).

Martin Finn & Co., D'alton Street, Claremorris, Co. Mayo (☎ 094-62316, fax 094-62216).

McCarrick & Sons, Tubbercurry, Co. Sligo (☎ 071-85050, fax 071-85922).

Michael A. O'Leary & Associates Ltd, The Bullring, Wexford (☎ 053-24611).

M. B. Mulcahy Associates, 208 Merton High Street, South Wimbledon, London SW19 1AX, UK (☎ +44-0181-543 2212, fax +44-0181-296 0883).

O'Mahony Farrelly, Wolfe Tone Square, Bantry, Co. Cork (☎ 027-51553, fax 027-50603).

Youhgal Auctioneers, 117 North Main Street, Youghal, Co. Cork (☎ 026-13198, fax 024-91355).

BUILDING SERVICES

Leeside Homes, Unit 18, Kilbarry Enterprise Centre, Dublin Hill, Cork (☎ 021-393990).

O'Flynn Construction Co. Ltd., Melbourne House, Model Farm Road, Cork (☎ 021-343111, fax 021-343053).

John F. Supple Ltd, Ardrostig, Bishopstown, Cork (☎ 021-343340).

FINANCIAL SERVICES

Crowleys – DFK, 16/17 College Green, Dublin 2 (☎ 01-679 0800, fax 01-679 0805). Contact: John Twomey. **See advertisement on page 103.**

Farrell Grant Sparks, Molyneux House, Bride Street, Dublin 8 (☎ 01-418 2000, fax 01-418 2044). Contact: Louise Caffrey. **See advertisement on page 108.**

Joseph G. Brady Financial Services, Carrick-on-Shannon, Co. Leitrim (☎ 078-20193, fax 078-20411).

INSURANCE

VHI, VHI House, Lower Abbey Street, Dublin 1 (☎ 01-872 4499). **See advertisement on page 66.**

National Insurance Ltd., 47A Upper Dorset Street, Dublin 1 (☎ 01-874 5392, fax 01-874 5395).

LEGAL SERVICES

Clifford Sullivan & Co., 31 Westland Square, Dublin 2 (☎ 01-670 4022, fax 01-670 4989, e-mail cliffsull@law.securemail.ie). **See advertisement on page 180.**

Denis O'Sullivan & Co. Solicitors, St Patrick's Buildings, 64 Patrick Street, Cork (☎ 021-271985, fax 021-272558).

John Hussey & Company Solicitors, 3 O'Rahilly Row, Fermoy, Co. Cork (☎ 025-33756).

O'Mahony Farrelly, Wolfe Tone Square, Bantry, Co. Cork (☎ 027-51553, fax 027-50603).

PROPERTY EXHIBITIONS

World of Property, Outbound Publishing, 1 Commercial Road, Eastbourne, East Sussex BN21 3XQ, UK (☎ 01323-412001).

PROPERTY SERVICES

O'Mahony Farrelly, Wolfe Tone Square, Bantry, Co. Cork (☎ 027-51553, fax 027-50603).

RELOCATION

Relocation Services International Ltd, Clareville, Streamstown, Malahide, Co. Dublin (☎/fax 01-845 4046).

OTHER SURVIVAL BOOKS

There are other 'Buying a Home' books in this series including *Buying a Home Abroad* plus buying a home in Florida, France, Italy, Portugal and Spain. We also publish a best-selling series of *Living and Working* books for America, Australia, Britain, France, New Zealand, Spain and Switzerland, which represent the most comprehensive and up-to-date source of practical information available about everyday life in these countries.

Survival Books are available from good bookshops throughout the world or direct from Survival Books. **Order your copies today by phone, fax, mail or e-mail from:** Survival Books, PO Box 146, Wetherby, West Yorks. LS23 6XZ, United Kingdom (tel/fax: 01937-843523, E-mail: survivalbooks@computronx.com Internet: computronx.com/survivalbooks. If you aren't entirely satisfied simply return them within 14 days for a full and unconditional refund.

INDEX

BUYING A HOME IN . . .

Survival Book's 'Buying a Home' series of books are essential reading for anyone planning to purchase a home abroad and are designed to guide you through the jungle and make it a pleasant and rewarding experience. Most importantly, they are packed with valuable information to help you avoid the sort of disasters that can turn your dream home into a nightmare! Topics covered include:

- Homework & Avoiding Problems
- Choosing the Region
- Finding the Right Home & Location
- Real Estate Agents
- Finance, Mortgages & Taxes

- Home Security
- Utilities, Heating & Air-Conditioning
- Mving House & Settling In
- Renting & Letting
- Permits & Visas

- Retirement, Working & Starting a Business
- Travelling & Communications
- Health & Insurance
- Renting a Car & Driving
- And Much, Much More!

Survival Books are the most comprehensive and up-to-date source of practical information available about buying a home abroad. Whether you're seeking a mansion, villa, farmhouse, townhouse or apartment, a holiday or permanent home, these books will help make your dreams come true. Buy them today and save yourself time, trouble <u>and</u> money?

ORDER FORM

Please rush me the following Survival Books:

Qty	Title	Price*			Total
		UK	Europe	World	
	Buying a Home Abroad	£11.45	£12.95	£14.95	
	Buying a Home in Florida	£11.45	£12.95	£14.95	
	Buying a Home in France	£11.45	£12.95	£14.95	
	Buying a Home in Ireland	£11.45	£12.95	£14.95	
	Buying a Home in Italy	£11.45	£12.95	£14.95	
	Buying a Home in Portugal	£11.45	£12.95	£14.95	
	Buying a Home in Spain	£11.45	£12.95	£14.95	
	Living and Working in America	£14.95	£16.95	£20.45	
	Living and Working in Australia	£14.95	£16.95	£20.45	
	Living and Working in Britain	£14.95	£16.95	£20.45	
	Living and Working in France	£14.95	£16.95	£20.45	
	Living and Working in NZ	£14.95	£16.95	£20.45	
	Living and Working in Spain	£14.95	£16.95	£20.45	
	Living and Working in Switzerland	£14.95	£16.95	£20.45	
	The Alien's Guide to France (spring 1999)	£5.95	£6.95	£8.45	
				TOTAL	

Cheque enclosed/Please charge my Access/Delta/Mastercard/Switch/Visa* card,

Expiry date _____ No. __ __ __ __   __ __ __ __   __ __ __ __   __ __ __ __

Issue number (Switch only) _____   Signature: _____

* Delete as applicable (price for Europe/World includes airmail postage)

NAME: _____

ADDRESS: _____

_____

_____

Send to: Survival Books, PO Box 146, Wetherby, West Yorks. LS23 6XZ, United Kingdom **or tel/fax/e-mail credit card orders to 44-1937-843523.**